THE PANAMA PAPERS

'The biggest leak in t[...] [...]nowden

'This is the inside sto[...] [...]tions and organised crime groups have used the secret world of offshore jurisdictions to engage in systematic cheating and thieving. It's an almost perfect tale for the 21st century – the failure of democracy, the triumph of commercial power and greed, greed, greed.'

Nick Davies, special correspondent, *Guardian*

'The fascinating struggle of David against Goliath . . . A brilliantly written book.'

Frankfurter Rundschau

'The authors expose a shockingly corrupt system . . . [an] important indictment of the shadow economy that flourishes even as the legitimate economy suffers.'

Kirkus

THE PANAMA PAPERS

Breaking the Story of How the Rich & Powerful Hide Their Money

BASTIAN OBERMAYER AND FREDERIK OBERMAIER

ONEWORLD

A Oneworld Book

Published in North America, Great Britain and
Australia by Oneworld Publications Ltd, 2016
Reprinted 2017 (four times), 2018, 2020, 2022

This revised edition published by Oneworld Publications Ltd, 2017

First published in the German language as "Panama Papers.
Die Geschichte einer weltweiten Enthüllung"

ISBN 978-1-78607-070-8
ISBN 978-1-78607-149-1 (eBook)

Typeset by Hewer Text UK Ltd, Edinburgh
Printed and bound in Great Britain by Clays Ltd, Elcograf S.p.A.

Oneworld Publications Ltd
10 Bloomsbury Street
London WC1B 3SR
England

Stay up to date with the latest books,
special offers, and exclusive content from
Oneworld with our newsletter

Sign up on our website
oneworld-publications.com

MIX
Paper from
responsible sources
FSC
www.fsc.org   FSC® C018072

CONTENTS

FOREWORD

There are moments in history when a big truth is suddenly revealed. In 2010 leaked US diplomatic cables showed the White House's private thinking about its friends and enemies. Three years later a contractor working for the National Security Agency exposed how the US and the UK are secretly spying on their own citizens.

His name was Edward Snowden. We learned that spooks from Britain's listening station GCHQ could – if they wanted – bug your iPhone. Or remotely activate your laptop web camera. Snowden's revelations caused outrage and started a global conversation about the boundaries of privacy in a digital age. Except in Britain, land of James Bond, where many met his revelations with a complacent shrug.

In April 2016 something else hidden in plain sight was exposed. Namely that the secret offshore industry – centred in tax havens like the British Virgin Islands – was not, as had been previously thought, a minor part of our economic system. Rather it *was* the system. Those who dutifully paid their taxes were, in fact, dupes. The rich, it turned out, had exited from the messy business of tax long ago.

The journalists who unearthed this bitter truth were Bastian Obermayer and Frederik Obermaier of Germany's *Süddeutsche Zeitung*. (They are not related but their German and international colleagues fondly nickname them the 'Brothers Obermay/ier'.)

The paper, based in Munich, has an excellent track record of working on difficult and important investigations.

Reporters often get offered information, stuff. Generally, it turns out to be disappointing. As Obermayer recounts, in early 2015, late one evening, he received an anonymous message. It said: 'Hello. This is John doe. Interested in data?' Obermayer replied: 'We're very interested, of course.'

The data turned out to be bigger than anyone might have imagined. The source – his or her identity remains unknown – had got hold of the entire internal database of a major Panamanian law firm. The firm's name was Mossack Fonseca. It specialized in setting up anonymous offshore shell companies.

The motivation here was simple. Like Snowden, the source wanted to expose criminal wrongdoing among the firm's shadowy clients. The leak was an act of bravery. It eventually amounted to 11.5 million documents, delivered in real-time instalments. It was the biggest leak ever, and far larger than the top-secret Snowden Files or US State Department cables.

It included the records of 214,000 offshore companies, names of real or 'beneficial' owners, and passport scans. There were bank statements. And email chains. Often these were between Mossack Fonseca's head office in Panama and 'intermediaries', typically other lawyers, accountants and banks. And from the firm's branches in UK crown dependencies like Jersey or the Isle of Man.

What followed was a thrilling and secret year-long journalistic collaboration across more than eighty countries. The *Süddeutsche Zeitung* shared its material with the International Consortium of Investigative Journalists, the ICIJ, which is based in Washington DC. The ICIJ in turn gave access to the data to 100 media organizations across the planet. In Britain that was my newspaper, the *Guardian*, and the BBC.

The journalists gave the leaked files a name. They were the Panama Papers. The name was a conscious echo of the Pentagon

Papers: volumes of secret documents leaked in 1971 by Daniel Ellsberg that lifted the lid on the US war in Vietnam.

I found myself back in the *Guardian*'s investigations 'bunker'. Actually, it had a bucolic view of Regent's Canal in London: houseboats, joggers, coots. In 2013 I'd been part of a small group that had studied the Snowden Files here. This project was different. Via a secure platform, called the iHub, journalists were encouraged not to compete with each other but to share information actively and to swap leads and tips. We did, in a flurry of encrypted emails.

For some time the global media industry has been in a state of gloom. Newsrooms are downsizing; the ad market has collapsed. Suddenly, though, this counter-intuitive model of cooperation looked like the way to go at a time when media organizations were broke. Paradoxically, it felt to us like a golden age for investigative journalism. The leaks kept coming. And grew bigger: in this case, an astonishing 2.6 terabytes.

But would anyone care? By 2016 almost 400 journalists were working secretly on the story, with an agreed publication date of 3 April. Clandestine group meetings had taken place in Washington, Munich and London. There were two concerns. One, that the leak might itself leak – that someone would accidentally bust the embargo. The other was that the public would respond to the Panama Papers with an indifferent yawn.

We needn't have worried. In Iceland the prime minister resigned. In Argentina there were demonstrations. In Azerbaijan a small war was initiated – so some believed – to distract from revelations featuring the president and his daughters. In China censors blocked the words 'Panama Papers' and jammed the website of the *Guardian*. In Russia aides to Vladimir Putin fumed about a Western 'spy' conspiracy.

In Britain, meanwhile, David Cameron experienced the worst week of his premiership. The Panama Papers revealed that the offshore fund run by Cameron's late father Ian had paid no British tax. For three decades. The fund, Blairmore Holdings Inc, had gone to absurd lengths to pretend it was based in the Bahamas. It hired a small army of Bahamas residents to sign paperwork, including a part-time bishop.

Downing Street refused to answer questions about Cameron's tax affairs, saying they were a 'private matter'. Eventually Cameron came clean: he'd owned shares in Dad's tax haven fund. He sold them for £31,500 just before becoming prime minister in 2010. Cameron was reluctant to acknowledge what was obvious: that his family's fortune – legally of course – came from privileged offshore wealth.

Brexit did for Cameron three months later. Viewed in retrospect, the Panama Papers was the beginning of his end. Cameron's spin doctor Craig Oliver later admitted that his boss had almost resigned over Blairmore. 'There is a real danger of this going out of control,' Oliver wrote in his post-Brexit memoir, adding: 'There's no doubt about it – we *are* on the run on the PM's father's offshore company.'

It's too early to say whether the Panama Papers will usher in a new era of transparency. There were a few encouraging signs. The G20 promised to act. Before his government imploded, Cameron and George Osborne published their tax returns. So did Jeremy Corbyn – a start. But as former US president Barack Obama noted, tax avoidance is a huge global problem. It's made worse, Obama said correctly, by the fact that using offshore structures is perfectly legal.

Still, the last year has seen a victory for those of us, the little people, who do pay our taxes. From now on, the super-rich and other characters who use exotic offshore structures will be a nervous bunch. How long, they must be wondering, before the next leak?

Luke Harding
London, January 2017

PROLOGUE

Bastian Obermayer

'Ping.'

My wife, our children and I have been at my parents' for three days, and for the past two days everyone's been ill. Everyone except me. It's ten o'clock in the evening, and having stroked the last patient and handed out the last cup of tea, I sit down at the dining table, open my laptop and put down my smartphone next to it.

Then there's a 'ping'. A new message.

[john doe]:Hello.
This is John doe.
Interested in data? I'm happy to share.*

'John Doe' has been in use in Great Britain for centuries and is also common in Canada and the United States. People whose true identity must be protected in court are called 'John Doe', as are unidentified corpses. 'John Doe' has also long been used as a name for bands, TV series and various products.

---

* In order to protect our source, parts of the indented, sans serif exchanges that would endanger our informant have been abbreviated in this book or else reproduced with minor alterations that do not distort their meaning.

So 'John Doe' is a cover, another term for 'Joe Bloggs'. But this 'Joe Bloggs' is obviously offering secret data.

Investigative journalists are genetically programmed to prick up their ears at this kind of offer. Secret data is always good news. At the *Süddeutsche Zeitung* we've published lots of articles based on leaked data in the past three years. Offshore Secrets was about tax secrecy in the Caribbean, the HSBC Files tackled secret Swiss bank accounts and the Luxembourg Tax Files revealed Luxembourg's dodgy tax schemes. The mechanism is always the same – a large volume of secret data flows out and ends up in the hands of journalists. If the volume of secrets is large enough, it is, statistically speaking, almost bound to contain some good stories.

Also, journalists often spend weeks, sometimes even months, chasing a specific source. So if a potential source comes to you, you need to react fast. Or at the very least you need to react: there's almost nothing more annoying than finding a story in the *Spiegel* or the *Zeit* that you were offered first.

[Obermayer]: Hello. We're very interested, of course.

You can immediately tell the worst sources – bad sources, or at any rate crazy or confused ones – from their emails. Crazy people do sometimes have good stories, but it's the exception rather than the rule.

The advantage with data is that it's not self-important or verbose. It doesn't have a mission and it isn't looking to deceive you. It's simply there, and you can check it. Every good dataset can be collated with reality and that's exactly what you must do as a journalist before you start to write. At some stage you also have to consider very carefully which part of the data you're going to exploit.

And for several reasons, legal as well as journalistic, we cannot post thousands of documents online, like the coordinators of the whistle-blowing website WikiLeaks. In Germany we have quite harsh laws on leaked information. We have to review and check every single page, and we would have to black out a lot...

[Obermayer]: How would we get the data?
[john doe]: I would like to assist but there are a couple of conditions. You need to understand how dangerous and sensitive some of this information is. My life is in danger, if my identity is revealed. I've spent the past several weeks considering how to handle this. We will only chat over encrypted channels. No meeting, ever. The choice of stories is obviously up to you.

I can live with those conditions. Journalists obviously prefer to get to know their source to be able to gauge what they're like and understand their motives, but for the informants it's often better to remain in the shadows. Whistle-blowers aren't particularly well protected, even in Germany, and each person who knows an informant's identity is a potential risk – even, or perhaps especially, if that person is a journalist.

However, the source communicates clearly and concisely, and I can do the same. This someone has obviously got something they want to get rid of, and they want to give it to me.

[Obermayer]: So how to proceed?

I send the person my contact details for further encrypted communications. In the subsequent exchanges we agree on how the transfer will take place, and I'm told that I can expect to receive a first sample soon via an encrypted channel.

The source doesn't ask for money – a good sign. A few months earlier someone had got in touch with me claiming to have records of secret foreign bank accounts belonging to a German political party and supposedly containing $26 million. Our conversation went back and forth for a week, poor-quality photos of bank documents were sent, absurd telephone calls ensued and then, over the phone, the person suddenly demanded cash.

The fact is that the *Süddeutsche Zeitung* never pays for information, not only because we don't have the money, but primarily on principle. This also reduces people's temptation to fob us off with fake documents. We just have to be able to stomach reading stories we were forced to pass up in other newspapers. However, the story of the secret party account appeared neither in the *Spiegel* nor in *Stern*: if they were ever offered the documents, our colleagues must also have judged them to be fakes.

'Ping.'

The sample has arrived: a big bunch of documents, most of them PDFs. I open the files on my computer and analyse them, one by one. There are companies' articles of incorporation, contracts and extracts from databases. It takes me a while to grasp the links between them, but after a quick Internet search I understand the context. The location is Argentina. A public prosecutor, José María Campagnoli, suspects that shady business people have helped the Kirchners – i.e. the then president Cristina Kirchner and her late husband Néstor – to smuggle around $65 million out of the country. This theft was allegedly conducted via a labyrinthine system of 123 shell companies, all of them set up, predominantly in the US tax haven of Nevada, by a Panamanian law firm called Mossack Fonseca. Nevertheless, none of the accusations have as yet been proved and Cristina Kirchner disputes the accuracy of the allegations.

What makes the case topical is that there is a litigation case pending in the United States. Directed by its founder Paul Singer, the investment fund NML had bought millions of dollars' worth of Argentinian government debt – and then the country went bankrupt. Most creditors agreed to debt relief, but not NML. The fund is filing lawsuits around the world for the seizure of Argentinian state assets. It has even had an Argentinian warship impounded off the coast of Africa. Warships are valuable and can be sold off.

The goal of the current lawsuit in Nevada, USA, is to force the disclosure of this network of shell companies. NML wants Mossack Fonseca to surrender all documents pertaining to the 123 shell companies. I have some of those files in front of me on my screen right now, documents that NML has been chasing in vain for years. One thing jumps out at me: the payments run into millions of dollars.

The papers show the transfer of $6 million into a Deutsche Bank account in Hamburg. The accompanying contract raises further questions: it's a commission on a gambling deal.

Two other files name the real owners of two of the firms whose documents NML is seeking to obtain. Access to these two files would constitute a huge leap forward in their case.

The interesting thing is that all the documents appear to originate from the same law firm. I'm familiar with Mossack Fonseca, but only ever as an impenetrable wall, a black hole. Every time our research has led us to this law firm, it has spelled the end of the investigation. Mossack Fonseca is one of the largest providers of anonymous shell companies and is not exactly famed for being fussy about its clientele; quite the opposite, in fact.

In plain English: while many of its clients are doing nothing illegal, some of the world's biggest scumbags have used Mossack Fonseca's anonymous offshore companies to disguise their business dealings. During the Offshore Secrets and HSBC Files investigations we came across convicted drug kingpins and suspected traders of blood diamonds who had used companies established by Mossack Fonseca for camouflage purposes. Search the Internet for Mossack Fonseca's clients and you will also find accomplices of Gaddafi, Assad and Mugabe allegedly working hand in glove with the Panamanian law firm.

Please note that I say *allegedly*, as Mossack Fonseca denies any association with these people and its client list is confidential. So far, at least.

[Obermayer]: The material seems to be good.
Can I see more?

But 'John Doe' doesn't answer. Has he or she had second thoughts? Or are they merely considering their next move?

[Obermayer]: Is all about the argentine case?

When I still haven't received an answer twenty minutes later, I close my laptop, put my smartphone away and go to bed.

The next morning (with the sickbay still as full as ever) there's an answer. And a lot more besides.

[john doe]: I am sending a few more documents. Some have to do with Russia. Another part of a PDF is specially intended for you Germans. Look for Hans Joachim. . . There's a lot more from where that came from.

I'm desperate to look through the documents straight away, but – and this is very tough – I first have to go to the pharmacy and shop for bread, fruit and tea. I'm the only one in a fit state to leave the house. The positive effect of this epidemic is that no one wants me to take them to the woods, play football or go for a walk. By late afternoon every bed in the house has a sleeping patient in it and I can return to my computer.

The new documents also seem to come exclusively from the files of the Panamanian law firm Mossack Fonseca. The company clearly has a serious problem.

A leak.

First I study a document many hundreds of pages long that whoever-it-is has named 'Records'. Several hundred pages of bank transfers, but one sticks out: on 19 November 2013 a sum of almost $500 million in gold was paid into the account of a man called Hans-Joachim K. at Société Générale Bahamas.[1]

$500 million. Half a billion. A vast sum of money.

I've never heard of Hans-Joachim K., but a Google search reveals him to be a little-known Siemens manager in Germany who used to be CEO in Colombia and Mexico. This might be a lead. For many years Siemens ran slush funds in South America to reward people who helped its business to flourish. I find dozens of articles, including some in the international press.

One thing baffles me, though. This jaw-dropping sum was transferred into the Siemens man's account in autumn 2013, yet the company's Latin American slush funds had been uncovered way back in 2007/8. There were lawsuits, some of which continue to this day.

This is strange, to put it mildly. You don't just suddenly come by $500 million, so where's this money from? A bookkeeping error?

Before I can become absorbed in further details, I hear the kids calling me. They want more salted snacks and toast. I give in and snap the laptop shut. That $500 million isn't going anywhere.

I spend the afternoon reading stories, making tea and filling hot water bottles. It's late in the evening before I get a chance to take a good look at the new material. At first glance it seems to be predominantly about shell companies, most of which appear to be linked to the same secret owner, a certain Sergei Roldugin. Many of the documents are contracts involving sums running into many millions. $8 million here, $30 million there; $200 million, then $850 million; all share deals or loans. Yet the name Roldugin doesn't ring any bells.

So I do a search, and what I find sets my spine tingling. Sergei Roldugin is 'Vladimir Putin's best friend', or at least that's how *Newsweek* describes him. There is good evidence for this: Roldugin is godfather to Maria, the Russian president's eldest daughter.

The godfather's offshore dealings would be interesting enough on their own, but then I read something that completely bemuses me. Sergei Roldugin, a man who handles zillions of US dollars according to the documents, is neither an investor nor an oligarch: he's an artist, a famous cellist and the former director of the St Petersburg Conservatory. I find an interview Roldugin gave to the *New York Times* in September 2014, in which he explicitly states that he is not a businessman and doesn't have millions.

If the documents are authentic, about which I now have little doubt, either he lied – or it isn't his money. Whose is it then? Is Roldugin merely a straw man? And if so, for whom?

For Vladimir Putin?

If it is Putin's money lying in these companies, even a fraction of it, the story would make headlines around the world.

Whoever leaked these papers to me also spotted Roldugin's name, and he or she is worried. Probably with good reason.

[Obermayer]: Who are you?
[john doe]: I'm no one. Just a concerned citizen.

This is a clear reference to the whistle-blower Edward Snowden, who called himself 'Citizen Four' when he made contact with the journalist and filmmaker Laura Poitras. Snowden has been trapped in Moscow since fleeing from Hong Kong.

[Obermayer]: Why are you doing this?
[john doe]: I want you to report on the material and to make these crimes public. This story could rival the Snowden documents in importance but you're publishing in German. You need to partner with the *New York Times* or a similar caliber English paper.

The *Süddeutsche Zeitung* isn't what you'd call a natural partner for the *New York Times*, but we have already worked with the *Guardian*, the *Washington Post* and the BBC on investigations such as Offshore

Secrets and the Luxembourg Tax Files. I explain this to 'John Doe' and he or she seems satisfied.

> [john doe]: We should discuss what is the best way for me to send you a large amount of material. Any ideas?

Honestly? I have no idea. I've never had an anonymous source asking to hand over material to me by the gigabyte. I can also hear my son crying upstairs.

> [Obermayer]: I will have to think about it. How much data are we talking about?
> [john doe]: More than anything you have ever seen.

It turns out not only to be more than anything I've ever seen; it's bigger than any leak that *any* journalist has ever seen. It will also mark the beginning of the largest international investigative journalism project of all time. Ultimately, around 400 journalists from over eighty countries will be investigating stories originating from this data. Stories that report on the secret offshore companies of dozens of heads of state and dictators; stories explaining how billions are earned from arms, drug and blood-diamond trafficking and other illegal business; and stories that bring home to readers the scale of tax evasion by the wealthy and super-rich of this world.

And all those stories begin with Mossack Fonseca on that first night.

1

START

The Russian president's best friend. Businessmen close to the Argentinian president and her late husband and predecessor as head of state. A mysterious German with $500 million? There are worse starting points for an investigation.

Within days of our first contact, it is clear from a discussion with my head of department Hans Leyendecker that this topic will be handled by the same team that has already led a number of similar investigations, meaning the two of us: the 'Brothers Obermay/ier' as some of our colleagues have called us ever since our editor-in-chief Kurt Kister coined the phrase at a conference.

Otherwise, we try to keep the circle of those in the know as tight as possible for now. Who knows if the files are genuine, if they're verifiable and whether they'll ever produce a good story?

Our plan is to analyse the data closely and then consider how and when we publish our findings. So we read up on Putin's business interests (by this time we've seen his best friend's name linked to three offshore companies), gather material about the NML hedge fund's lawsuits against Argentina and carry out research into our mysterious ex-Siemens executive and the $500 million in gold. The only problem is that we keep getting distracted by new firms and possible new stories. That's because the material has been growing constantly since the night of my first contact with

'John Doe', and we repeatedly find new names worth investigating: South American government ministers, German aristocrats, US bankers. Very soon we have over 50 gigabytes of data and several thousand digital folders stored on various USB sticks. Each folder bears a number associated with a particular offshore company. These folders obviously contain files that Mossack Fonseca drew up for the respective firm: certificates, passport copies, lists of shareholders and trustees, invoices, emails. A clear, practical system – for them, and for us.

There are thousands of shell companies. Thousands of people who obviously have a compelling reason for camouflaging their business dealings. Thousands of potential articles. The unique selling point of offshore companies is that they provide anonymity. A nondescript name is presented to the outside world and no one knows who is really behind it.

There are of course many reasons for using an offshore company and of course owning one is not in itself a criminal offence. But the fact is that people often have recourse to an anonymous offshore company because they want to hide something – from the taxman, their ex-wife, their former business partner or the prying eyes of the public. That 'something' might be property, bank accounts, paintings, investments, shares or other kinds of securities.

Experience shows that it is usually individuals whose business depends on anonymity who favour the anonymity that shell companies provide. These include gunrunners, people traffickers, drug smugglers and other criminals, as well as investors who do not wish to reveal their true identities and their true intentions, senior politicians who'd like to spirit their wealth abroad (perhaps because they have accumulated it dishonestly) and companies looking to funnel bribes. The list could go on and on.

We are now sitting studying secret data that could potentially bring hundreds of these cases to light, sifting through computer folders no journalist has ever had access to before. We could easily spend weeks floating around in it, not only because we're always looking for the next big story to break, but also because there's no such thing as a trivial detail: with every company we examine and every email conversation we read, we learn more about how the Mossack Fonseca law firm operates. There is an incredibly strong temptation to drill down into these secret dealings and thus into the entire mechanism, from the initiation of business to the opening of the account and on to its closure. It's almost an addiction, and if we didn't both have families we would probably spend every evening on our laptops, clicking and clicking away. Yet even while keeping halfway regular working hours, it takes us only a few weeks to grasp the basic business model.

This is usually how it works. Contact is made with Mossfon (the common abbreviation for Mossack Fonseca) via an intermediary – for example a bank, a lawyer or an asset manager. These are Mossack Fonseca's actual 'clients': they order the product, they handle communications and they pay the bills. The product is mainly an off-the-peg offshore company. Mossfon offers firms in some twenty jurisdictions, most frequently in the British Virgin Islands and Panama, but also in the Bahamas, Bermuda, Samoa, Uruguay, Hong Kong, the US tax havens of Nevada, Wyoming and Delaware and, more recently, Florida and the Netherlands. The newest name is that of the emirate of Ras Al-Khaimah in the United Arab Emirates. The companies are sold from nearly fifty offices worldwide or from Mossfon's headquarters in the centre of Panama City, on the top floors of a squat building whose glass façade reflects the emblem of the city, the Revolution Tower.

Mossack Fonseca isn't the only provider of shell companies headquartered in Panama. Other major players are also based there (although there are hardly any official figures regarding this secretive industry), for instance the law firm Morgan y Morgan, probably Mossfon's great competitor. It is no coincidence that offshore providers have clustered together in this small Latin American state of all places, squeezed between Costa Rica and Colombia at the point where the Americas meet.

[ ]

Panama has always been an extremely dependent country. Having long been a poor province of Colombia, the country gained its independence in 1903 partly because American bankers and industrialists managed to persuade the then US president Theodore Roosevelt to support Panamanian separatists. US lobbies hoped to make money from the Panama Canal, which was under construction at the time. Roosevelt sent troops to occupy parts of the newly independent state and make it clear to Colombia that it could kiss goodbye to its former province. A nation was created by the grace of the United States and the US flag did indeed fly over the Panama Canal Zone, where big business was to be done. Thousands of American soldiers protected the sovereignty that the Panamanian government granted to the USA in 1903 and which was only returned to Panama in 1999.

The lucrative business with shell companies is based on a law that came into force on 26 February 1927. This law – Law 32 – guarantees the secrecy of estates, money transfers and, most importantly, company owners, and offers so-called 'sociedades anónimas' exemption from taxation. This name sounds more mysterious than it actually is, because an 'anonymous society' is actually nothing more than a public limited company. The secrecy afforded by Law 32 has changed very little to this day, with the exception of the odd – largely cosmetic – reform driven by efforts to have Panama deleted from a number of black and grey lists of countries that abet money laundering and tax evasion. The favourable environment for the offshore industry has remained more or less unaffected over the years, and the state also benefits, for example from corporation tax from law firms, their employees' income tax payments, and fees for setting up companies.

Another reason this business is so attractive is because it is as simple as it is lucrative. A standard shell company costs the seller next to nothing and the formalities are quickly dispatched. The buyer has his company in a click of the fingers for only a few hundred US dollars, and can dispose of it again quickly and easily once it has served its purpose. Also, no one will ever find out to whom it belonged, which is ideal for dodgy dealings.

Ideal for Siemens too, we discover. While reading up on Putin, we simultaneously sniff out the trail of Hans-Joachim K., the German with the curious $500 million in an account in the Bahamas. First, we do some research without the data, simply because we don't have the right software with which to conduct a systematic search of the 50 gigabytes of information. We find K.'s name in an indictment against a past Siemens board. It becomes clear from reading this that K. had for many years run slush funds containing money siphoned off from official Siemens channels so as to be more quickly and easily available, for instance to pay so-called advisers. Hans-Joachim K. names one of these bribery firms, supposedly called Casa Grande. We come across its full name in the transcript of a police interrogation: Casa Grande Development. This is also the title under which it was entered into Panama's public database of companies, with Mossack Fonseca listed as its 'registered agent'. Yet the database gives no indication of any connection to Siemens or even K. himself. The company's directors are given as three women who have almost certainly never done a day's work for Siemens in their entire lives: Francis Perez, Diva de Donada and Leticia Montoya.[1]

This is the mechanism for offshore companies: the firms that sell them – offshore providers like Mossack Fonseca – make sure that there's a protective screen around the real owners. In this case Mossack Fonseca appoints three directors. We would call Francis

Perez, Diva de Donada and Leticia Montoya 'straw men' – if they weren't women, that is. They work for Mossack Fonseca. Their job is to sign the documents placed before them. They sign if the real 'beneficial' owner wishes to open an account in the name of his or her shell company (as in the case of Casa Grande Development for Siemens) or if the real owner would like to buy something in the company's name – a flat, a house or a yacht, say. However, they also sign contracts, loans for millions of dollars and other papers. This means that these directors – known in the jargon as 'nominees' or 'nominee directors' – act as the company's official representatives, and the real owner hides behind this façade.[2]

The real owners (or, if they are more cautious, their lawyers) are generally given a power of attorney by the nominee directors to access the bank account or the safe. In most cases, however, no one but the bank, the nominee directors and Mossack Fonseca knows about this power of attorney. It is this secret yet (when seen in isolation) completely legal arrangement that confirms the company's true purpose – to stay shut away from the prying eyes of inquisitive public prosecutors, tax officials and fraud investigators.

[ ]

In one of the Excel files that we find in the data we come across Casa Grande Development's folder number, and we actually have this folder. This is a complete stroke of luck: the Excel file lists over 200,000 active and expunged Mossack Fonseca companies, but we currently only have the documents of a few thousand.

In the folder we find a power of attorney for one of Hans-Joachim K.'s former colleagues at Siemens. This ex-colleague is named as the real owner of the company, but neither he, K. nor Siemens was ever mentioned when Casa Grande Development was handing out millions from the slush funds, entering into contracts or conducting business. The nominee directors signed, and from the outside it was impossible to tell who was really controlling matters. The company was an ideal vehicle for kick-starting the business of Siemens's South American division anonymously and circumventing both the law and internal oversight.

Even if someone had discovered who owned Casa Grande Development's shares, they would not have been able to prove any link to Siemens. That is because only so-called bearer shares were issued at first. There is usually no record of who owns these shares. It's very simple: the person who holds all of a company's bearer shares – physically, that is, as pieces of paper – owns the company. This is an open invitation to indulge in the kind of dealings where you don't want to leave any traces behind. Money on the table, bearer shares the other way, transaction complete; the company has a new owner.

If there is a need for even more stringent anonymity, then Mossack Fonseca can provide not only nominee directors but also 'nominee shareholders'. These are individuals or shell companies that hold shares virtually, on trust. Should Mossack Fonseca be forced to name one or more of a company's shareholders, for example during an investigation, this does not mean that they are the ultimate owners, not in the slightest. The real owners can hide behind this second protective screen.

The company has become a completely impenetrable entity. Tax investigators and the police, creditors and defrauded business partners, even spouses and children have no way of proving that the company with the peculiar made-up name belongs to any tangible human being. From the outside at least, it is a black box.

Not from the inside, though. Inside, in the computer folders we mine day after day (and often night after night), lie thousands of internal email exchanges between Mossack Fonseca employees. These messages are a seam of gold running through this mountain of data, repeatedly turning up vital nuggets of information about the true owners.

Unfortunately, this is not much help in Hans-Joachim K.'s case. We still have no idea of how, and if, he came by the $500 million. So far, we know only that he left Siemens in 2009 at the latest.

We'll have frequent cause to return to this case, though. Every time new data arrives we look for new Siemens shell companies and for K. It's like an incurable fever – we just have to solve this puzzle.

2

VLADIMIR PUTIN'S
MYSTERIOUS FRIEND

There's a lot of money at stake. That is about the only thing we realize immediately as we battle our way through the folders of the three offshore companies featuring Sergei Roldugin's name. The folders contain hundreds of documents, many with page after page of descriptions of share deals it would take us weeks to understand. Yet even in our ignorance we are capable of picking out the sums, and they take our breath away. Here a loan for a few hundred million US dollars, there another one for many billions of rubles. Millions of dollars in 'advisory fees' flow from shell company to shell company, and the documents suggest that share packages worth millions change hands twice within twenty-four hours.

We read in the share transaction contracts that some of the deals involve shares in major Russian companies. The fact that these particular companies show up here doesn't necessarily mean anything, but it may do. Virtually every Russian expert critical of Putin assumes that he'll leave office as a multi-billionaire – if, that is, he ever does leave office. But where has he stashed his fortune? There is a theory among experts that he gets companies to allocate him shares – companies such as the ones we have just found.

If Putin did indeed own shares in major Russian companies, would he really want people to know about it? Would he hold them under his own name? Certainly not. So then he would need people he could trust. People like Sergei Roldugin?

We know quite a lot about the two men's relationship, particularly because Roldugin, the virtuoso cellist, is not exactly shy about it. He enjoys talking to journalists and authors about Putin, and of course he gives the president good press. He would be badly advised to do anything else.

The two men have known each other since the 1970s. Roldugin is one of Putin's circle of friends from his time in St Petersburg – people that Putin later made very, very wealthy. It is therefore conceivable that Roldugin does only represent Roldugin here, for he has owned a small stake in a St Petersburg private bank, Rossiya Bank, since the 1990s. Under Putin's protection it has grown into one of the largest and most influential banks in the country. Putin made sure that various state enterprises took their money to Rossiya Bank, which in turn belongs for the most part to other Putin confidants besides Roldugin.

Most of these confidants, by the way, are on the US sanctions list announced after Putin's annexation of the Crimea. Rossiya Bank itself is on the list as the bank of 'Putin's innermost circle', according to the rationale. Managers of precisely this bank administrated several offshore companies ordered from Mossack Fonseca, including two of the three companies for which Sergei Roldugin is named as either a shareholder or the owner. This of course means that Mossack Fonseca is doing business with managers of a company that is subject to US sanctions. This is a gamble with wide-ranging potential consequences. Should the US authorities judge that there has been a breach of sanctions, they could freeze the assets of Mossfon's subsidiary in the USA, and its owners and executives would no longer be able to travel to the United States without fear of arrest. In the worst-case scenario, Mossfon itself might end up on the US sanctions list.

The precise structure of the Roldugin system would appear to be as follows. A Rossiya Bank representative has a sort of power of attorney in most of the companies, and is thus the contact for a Zurich-based law firm. In turn, this law firm is officially responsible for the offshore companies set up by Mossack Fonseca and informs Mossfon of the end clients' wishes. Mossack Fonseca's Geneva subsidiary handles the Zurich law firm. So if Mossack Fonseca in Panama has a question, it turns to its Geneva office, the people in Geneva ask the Zurich lawyers and they get in touch with Rossiya Bank. It's a long process, but it's also a practical one, for should the overall set-up come under scrutiny, Mossack Fonseca could argue that it was merely doing business with a reputable Swiss law firm. What is the world coming to if you can't even trust the Swiss!

From previous years' emails it is clear that Mossack Fonseca was fully aware of Rossiya Bank's involvement at the other end of the chain. The critical question as far as we're concerned is whether Sergei Roldugin and the other men in his network were really acting on their own initiative. He does state in one document that he is the sole and real owner of at least one of these firms, a company by the name of International Media Overseas S.A. based in Panama. This is in papers Roldugin provides when applying for an account with the Zurich branch of a Russian bank in May 2014, only weeks after the US announced its sanctions against Rossiya Bank.

Roldugin declares in the questionnaire that the company's assets run into billions of rubles, the first transfer will be for 5 million Swiss francs and he expects a long-term income of over 1 million Swiss francs per year. This is the self-same Roldugin who announced to the *New York Times* a few months later that he didn't 'have millions' and wasn't a businessman.

Roldugin also explains to the bank where International Media Overseas S.A.'s money comes from, stating that the company owns a 100 per cent stake in a certain Med Media Network Ltd (as indeed it does). Med Media was mentioned in the same *New York Times* interview with Roldugin. According to the newspaper, the company owns a 20 per cent stake in a major Russian media company called Video International. What the *NYT* reporters didn't realize was that there is a link: Roldugin is also one of Video International's owners. On paper, at least.

We decide to examine the ownership of Video International in more detail, but we defer this task for a little while. More accessible, and at the same time more entertaining, is a questionnaire completed to open an account for one of Roldugin's companies with the aforementioned bank in Switzerland. One of the questions is: *Is the owner of the company a politically exposed person (PEP) or a very important person (VIP)?*

Roldugin answers no.

Does the owner have any relationship with a PEP or a VIP?

Roldugin again answers no.

This second answer is a barefaced lie. The best friend of the Russian president, who also happens to be godfather to the president's daughter, cannot seriously deny having 'any relationship' with VIPs or a politically exposed person.

Nowadays, banks systematically enquire about this kind of relationship because the experience of recent decades has shown that most corrupt politicians do not declare their secret bank accounts in their own names but rather in the name of a trusted relative or friend. However, the risk of the bank being regarded as an abetter of thieving heads of state is almost as high, and banks therefore want to find out more about their clients as part of the anti-money laundering drive and the related 'Know Your Customer' policy. Of course, they may ultimately decide to accept a customer who is the best friend of a politician, but they must know what they're doing – in part because they might later be called upon to justify their decision.

[ ]

As we try to follow the Russian trails, the files keep growing, gigabyte after gigabyte. It's not easy to transfer such large volumes of data, and it's even more time-consuming if you also wish to encrypt the information. Then we have the additional problem that our source insists on absolute anonymity, which only complicates matters further.

The solution we find after many weeks of head-scratching is awkward but relatively secure. We cannot describe it for reasons of confidentiality. Slowly but surely, the data makes its way to us. Yet as we torment ourselves with technical issues, a single question keeps worming its way into our minds: why would anyone run the risk of passing on such sensitive data for no benefit?

There's obviously no money, but there's also no fame for someone who chooses to remain anonymous. There is danger, though.

[SZ]: Why are you taking this risk?
[john doe]: I can't explain my rationale without making my identity clear. But generally speaking, I feel that I must do it because I'm able. It's too important. There is just a mind-boggling amount of criminal activity going on here – I struggle to even wrap my head around it.
[SZ]: Aren't you afraid?
[john doe]: Definitely. But I am trying to be careful.

Some days we write to each other virtually non-stop via a variety of anonymous, encrypted chats. It's generally about technical issues. Have we received folder XY? Do we know this or that file format? Otherwise we talk about politics, about Angela Merkel and Greece, about Chávez, Putin, Obama and China, or about our source's fears. Then we return to discussing gigabytes.

What we don't realize in these first few weeks, however, is that it's going to continue like this for months. For months and months.

[ ]

After a preliminary examination we set the Argentinian documents aside. The public prosecutor has identified 123 companies that all seem to have been founded by Mossack Fonseca. That is more than we can handle, certainly now and perhaps ever. However interesting the story might be, we must naturally focus our attention on major German scoops.

At the same time, we don't want the stories to be ignored or lost in countries where they might be of interest.

That is a compelling argument for a large-scale international collaboration of the kind we participated in during Offshore Secrets, the Luxembourg Tax Files and the HSBC Files.

Of course we promised our source that we would try to get the *New York Times* on board, even if we're not likely to be successful at the first attempt.

We call Gerard Ryle, the director of the Washington-based International Consortium for Investigative Journalists, to capture his imagination for our data. The ICIJ is a sort of international club of investigative journalists that you can only join by nomination and invitation. Something like 200 of our colleagues worldwide now belong to this club, and we became members in 2013. To be precise, the ICIJ is an initiative of the Center for Public Integrity (CPI), an American non-profit organization for investigative journalism. The CPI was set up by Charles Lewis, a leading US investigative reporter responsible for countless successes over the past thirty years. Both the CPI and the ICIJ are financed by donations, one of their main donors being the left-leaning billionaire George Soros.

Since it was founded in 1997, the ICIJ has coordinated joint cross-border investigations into global tobacco trafficking, the international trade in body parts and questionable World Bank projects. The idea behind the ICIJ is that journalists achieve more by sharing their material when it is of international relevance. This results in more and better stories, because they are handled by experts in a particular field, often the best investigative reporters in a specific country. Our colleagues from Argentina's *La Nación*, for example, are deeply involved in the case of NML, the hedge fund that is suing the Argentinian state. We have seen online that the newspaper has been writing about this affair for years, whereas we are starting from scratch.

Our telephone conversation with Gerard Ryle goes well. After a quarter of an hour he's determined to make it an ICIJ story, even though we cannot name any names on the phone and can only hint at Mossack Fonseca's implication.

It's important to say that Gerard Ryle has a soft spot for shell companies. When he took up his position as ICIJ director in 2011, he brought with him a hard drive containing the largest leak any journalist had ever been party to until then. He had been handed 260 gigabytes of information from the inner sanctum of two firms called Portcullis TrustNet and Commonwealth Trust Ltd. The core business of these two firms was – exactly like Mossack Fonseca's – to sell shell companies. It is no exaggeration to say that Gerard Ryle produced a worldwide scoop from that data. In April 2013, under the headline 'Offshore Secrets', nearly 100 journalists from some fifty countries revealed how the world's rich and powerful used these offshore companies to cover their tracks and hide their true assets. In Germany we worked on the story for the *Süddeutsche Zeitung* along with our colleagues at the Norddeutscher Rundfunk radio station. The basic model of our data is therefore very similar to that of Offshore Secrets, although we have far less – about 50 gigabytes – when we ring Ryle. However, we have the feeling that our data on individual companies is more comprehensive and, above all, more up to date. During the Offshore Secrets investigations in 2013 we published information gleaned from files dated 2010 or earlier. This time we note with a shudder that we keep finding fresh emails, which means that our source has had access to internal Mossack Fonseca data until very recently. Possibly, indeed probably, the source still has such access.

At the end of our conversation Gerard Ryle promises to fly to Munich in the next few weeks to see the files with his own eyes.

Almost accidentally, during one of our evening browsing sessions, we stumble upon something that we had overlooked until now. There are several documents containing internal memos about many of the brokers, i.e. the banks or asset managers. The general secretiveness of Mossfon staff – abbreviated client names and codenames – suggests that there is something fishy going on,[1] but what we read in these memos is of a quite different tenor. They mention brokers with 'large numbers of clients with undeclared accounts', a law firm with 'a separate department for illegal funds' and that Mossack Fonseca 'offers solutions' for withholding tax on payments of interest in Europe.

Reading this, we know we're on the right track. If we can prove that Mossack Fonseca knowingly helped its clients to evade tax, the law firm will have a real headache. At this juncture we ask ourselves whether Mossack Fonseca has ever been prosecuted for a similar crime, but find no evidence of any lawsuits against the firm.

Around now we become aware of a fact that sucks our attention away from everything else. It concerns the man who made all this secret business possible in the first place and who must have earned an absolute fortune in the process. He is the man who founded Mossack Fonseca, a law firm that has apparently entertained dealings with criminals of all stripes for several decades.

His name is Jürgen Mossack. He's German.

3

THE SHADOW OF THE PAST

Jürgen Mossack makes no secret of his background. Quite the opposite, in fact. Google his name and you soon end up on a website presenting thousands of lawyers and their areas of expertise. Jürgen Mossack's profile says, 'Born in Fürth, Bavaria, Germany.'

Yet Jürgen Mossack is a completely unknown quantity in Germany, and not a single article has appeared about him in the German press, even though he is at the head of a company linked to some particularly shady characters. And he's German.

That fact has pushed this story a little closer to the top of our priorities. Or a lot? It doesn't matter that much. At the very least we now have a hook that will catch people's attention: 'A German has helped some of the worst criminals and dictators of our time to hide their tracks.'

[john doe]: Is Jürgen Mossack actually known in Germany?
[SZ]: No. No one knows him here.
[john doe]: That will change soon. . .

We want to find out more about the man at the centre of our leak, so we start searching, first on the Internet and then in international press databases. We come up with next to nothing. There is the occasional mention of Jürgen Mossack, who is now in his late sixties, but we find no portrait, no in-depth article. The only traces of Mossack online, other than the meagre CV on the lawyers' website, are trivial details such as his membership of the Panama Rotary Club, the International Maritime Association and various professional bodies concerned with tax law and the like. We also come across a few photos of our man at a range of events, for instance at a meeting with the prime minister and the finance minister of the British Virgin Islands, a major tax haven and hence a natural partner for Mossack Fonseca.

Jürgen Mossack appears to have no interest in the wider public, or at least our archives turn up no interviews with him. However, he does give talks and writes articles in the specialized press, fulminating against radical reforms to the offshore industry.

We decide to proceed methodically and obtain a copy of his birth certificate. This provides official confirmation that Jürgen Mossack was indeed born in Germany – on 20 March 1948 in Fürth's municipal clinic at precisely 6.25am. His full name at birth was Jürgen Rolf Dieter Herzog. His mother is recorded as Luise Herzog, a saleswoman, his father as Erhard Peter Mossack, a mechanical engineer.

[ ]

Erhard Mossack would appear to have switched from mechanical engineering to journalism in the postwar years. In 1951 the *Spiegel* mentions a sports reporter by the name of Erhard Mossack, who wrote for Nuremberg's *8-Uhr-Nachrichten* about a mysterious masked freestyle wrestler whom spectators had nicknamed the 'Viennese Strangler'. This particular Erhard Mossack speculated that the 'Viennese Strangler', whose trademark was a chokehold from behind, might actually be the 'Prague Executioner', a Czech man alleged to have sent 'a bunch of Czechs to the German gallows' during the Nazi occupation. The *Spiegel* journalist comes to the conclusion that Mossack's supposition is wrong, however.

It was probably the same Erhard Mossack who emerged as the author of a number of books, one of which was published in 1952 with the belligerent title *The Last Days of Nuremberg*. The book, a work of non-fiction about Nuremberg during the final days of the war before its eventual capture by the Allies, is easily available from antiquarian booksellers. Contrary to what one might expect from the title, the book expresses no particular sympathies, no political revanchism, no glorification of the Nazi era. More entertaining is a short potboiler from 1955 entitled *Smuggled Goods for Tangier*, in which the author, Erhard Mossack, relates working as a journalist with international detectives from Interpol's headquarters in Paris in 1954 to uncover an international car smuggling ring that was operating in Western Europe after the war. The blurb reads: 'Mossack carried out his own investigations in France and Spain, gradually untangling the confusing trail left by the bandits.' Mossack supposedly even drove one of the stolen vehicles, a Mercedes 300, back to Germany.

The author's biography in *Smuggled Goods for Tangier* also contains this Erhard Mossack's date of birth – 16 April 1924, the same as Jürgen Mossack's birth certificate gives for Erhard Mossack – confirming that he is definitely one and the same man. How ironic that some decades later his son should be setting up offshore companies for far worse criminals than smugglers.

In October 1958, three years after his potboiler was published, the register of residents shows that Erhard Mossack has moved to Lutzerath in Rhineland-Palatinate. He signs himself off the register in July 1961, stipulating that he intends to emigrate – 'probably to the USA'. It is therefore clear that Jürgen Mossack spent the first thirteen years of his life in Germany.

This is backed up by an article published at the beginning of January 2012 in a local edition of the *Frankfurter Rundschau*. It is a portrait marking the 2010 appointment of a certain Peter Mossack, an IT manager and founder of the Justus von Liebig Darmstadt chapter of the Lion's Club, a worldwide community organization, as the Republic of Panama's honorary consul to the federal states of Hesse, North Rhine-Westphalia, Rhineland-Palatinate, Saarland and Baden-Württemberg.

[ ]

Mossack and Panama? Exactly. Peter Mossack isn't simply Jürgen Mossack's namesake; he's his younger brother. He tells the *Frankfurter Rundschau* that his family emigrated to Panama when he was about six years old. This tallies with his father's statement in the residents' register. In his interview with the newspaper he adds that he returned to Germany from Panama after his studies, but goes back to visit his brother 'every couple of years or so'. His brother has a law firm in Panama and is 'well-connected'.

Why did the Mossacks leave Germany in the early 1960s? Those who tried their luck in South America after the war were often there to escape deeds they committed under the Third Reich. We make some requests to databases and archives in Germany and the US, and await the results. It sometimes takes weeks or months for the answers to arrive. So far we know only that Erhard Mossack returned to Germany and died in Aichach, near Munich, in 1993.

What is certain is that Erhard Mossack landed in Panama at the beginning of the 1960s with his son Jürgen. We learn from a CV of Jürgen Mossack that we find among our files that he studied at Santa María La Antigua University in Panama City after attending school at the Instituto Pedagógico in Las Cumbres. During his studies he worked part-time at a law firm familiar to us from studying the offshore industry: Arosemena Noriega & Castro. It is there that Mossack is evidently first employed as a paralegal, starting some time in 1970, and later, after his exams in 1973, as a fully fledged lawyer. He then works for two years in London before setting up his own law firm in Panama in 1977 before he has even turned thirty.

Now it's time for serious business. The country is ruled at the time by a military junta led by the corrupt general Omar Torrijos. Such a regime represents no particular impediment to a law firm specializing in company incorporations. We search for Jürgen Mossack in Panama's register of companies and find a large quantity of documents testifying to business dealings immediately after he established his law firm. They describe the law firm as a 'registered agent' and name Jürgen Mossack himself as a director of numerous offshore companies. Even then, this means only one thing: nominee director.

When the dictator Manuel Noriega comes to power in 1983, the affairs of Jürgen Mossack's law firm continue as usual; at least, entries in the public registry show no signs of a decline in the number of newly established companies. Under Noriega – who later turns out to be in the pay of various drug dealers – Panama becomes the preferred banking centre of the Colombian Medellín cartel, precisely because it offers such a favourable environment for opaque business deals.

During this time Jürgen Mossack helps at least one of the major drug lords – Caro Quintero, a Mexican businessman as gruesome as he is shrewd. Quintero orders the execution of the US drug investigator Enrique 'Kiki' Camarena Salazar in February 1985, prompting a furious manhunt by the US authorities. Quintero is arrested in Costa Rica in April 1985. Mere days earlier, a middleman had used Jürgen Mossack's law firm to set up a company into which Caro Quintero's assets could flow unchecked. This was closely followed by a second company, which owns a villa in Costa Rica that is later confiscated and put at the disposal of Costa Rica's National Olympic Committee (NOC), but to all intents and purposes still belongs to Quintero's shell company, for which Jürgen Mossack acts as a nominee director.

When, a few years ago, Costa Rica's NOC officially requests Mossack Fonseca to hand over the villa once and for all, Jürgen Mossack refuses. He explains in writing that even the legendary drug baron Pablo Escobar is 'a baby' compared to Caro Quintero and under no circumstances does he want 'to be among those Quintero visits after he is released'.[1]

Quintero is indeed released in 2013 after nearly thirty years in jail and he has apparently paid no visit to Jürgen Mossack thus far. Quintero is, however, once more one of the world's most wanted criminals.

On 1 March 1986 Jürgen Mossack and the Panama-born lawyer Ramón Fonseca merged their businesses, creating the law firm Mossack Fonseca, which is still headed, thirty years after its birth, by the two men who lent it their names.

[ ]

Finding information about Mossack's partner is a piece of cake; in fact, it's rather harder to sift through the surfeit of details. This is because Ramón Fonseca Mora, to give him his full name, is not only one of Panama's leading politicians but also a famous and prize-winning author. Fonseca is currently an adviser to the Panamanian president Juan Carlos Varela with a seat in the cabinet, as well as being a deputy chairman of the governing party, Panameñista.[2] In short, Ramón Fonseca is a very big fish in this small country.

The Panamanian press has even speculated that President Varela intended to make Fonseca minister for public security but backed down after pressure from the United States. The US government made it clear that it would be less than pleased to see someone whose law firm is suspected of enabling money laundering appointed as a minister, which suggests that the Americans are quite aware of Mossack Fonseca's business dealings.

Ramón Fonseca is obviously the type of politician who loves publicity and the limelight. There are countless photos of him at events, he writes comment pieces for newspapers and he frequently posts on Facebook and Twitter, where he has thousands of followers. At the same time he comes across as someone who will not shy away from a fight, even going so far as to challenge his political opponents to settle a dispute as real men purportedly do – with their fists.

His political influence might have something to do with the fact that Ramón Fonseca is a very wealthy man. His business has grown and grown over the years. 'We've created a monster,' Fonseca said in a TV interview in 2008, probably referring only to the *size* of his company, Mossfon, which even back then had several hundred staff in dozens of offices around the world.[3]

Unlike its German proprietor, this monster has left some traces in the press. Latin American newspapers, in particular, have linked Mossack Fonseca very directly to a considerable number of corruption and money laundering scandals. Most articles refer to the suspicions of the Argentinian public prosecutor about the former Argentinian president Cristina Kirchner (as described in the prologue of this book). Depending on the country and the date of publication, this allegation is accompanied by further reported anomalies. The names of the dictators Bashar al-Assad and Muammar Gaddafi frequently crop up, generally without any detailed description of how they might be connected to Mossack Fonseca, and the law firm vehemently denies any links.

We find the longest, most eye-catching article about Mossfon on the online portal of *Vice* magazine. The publication is best known for entertaining, off-beat stories about the pen friends of serial killers, smoking weed in Palestine or meth consumption in North Korea, but it frequently features well-researched investigative reports. In early December 2014 *Vice* publishes an article about Mossack Fonseca. It is a furious, fact-filled tirade, a settling of scores with the Panamanian law firm, which the author christens 'Evil LLC'.

Mossack Fonseca is understandably unhappy with this kind of attention. An email exchange from 2012 reveals just how rattled they are by the articles online. In it, Mossfon employees hire a firm called Mercatrade to carry out what experts call 'online reputation management': if someone types in 'Mossack Fonseca', they should not be immediately confronted with negative articles on the first few pages of results.

However, for some reason Mercatrade breaks off the business relationship within a few months and terminates the contract.

If you browse Mossack Fonseca's homepage, you will find that Mossfon has had its own compliance department for years. This unit is supposed to ensure that the company genuinely abides by all national and international laws and regulations.

That's the theory, but a spectacular case we manage to reconstruct in detail from the files demonstrates how Mossfon deals with compliance in practice.

[ ]

It is the case of Iceland's prime minister, Sigmundur Davíð Gunnlaugsson. He appears in 2007, together with his later wife, the well-known Icelandic anthropologist Anna Sigurlaug Pálsdóttir, as a shareholder in the shell company Wintris Inc., which is based in the British Virgin Islands. At the end of 2009, just as his political career is gathering pace, Gunnlaugsson 'sells' his 50 per cent stake in the company to his wife (by official contract) for the symbolic price of one dollar. Ever since, Anna Sigurlaug Pálsdóttir has been registered in Mossack Fonseca's files as its sole owner as well as a director and a shareholder. There is even a scanned identity card in the digital folder of the company, which is still active according to the British Virgin Islands' register of companies.[4]

In fact, Sigmundur Davíð Gunnlaugsson only becomes prime minister in May 2013, long after the company was set up in 2007. Yet even at the time he is a politician, and when he becomes chairman of Iceland's Progressive Party, the Oxford graduate is still a shareholder in Wintris.[5]

All of this would already make a pretty good story. The whole of Europe is fighting tax evasion and offshore companies, yet in Iceland the current prime minister has a secret offshore company of his own. 'It just had to be Iceland,' the press might say, for offshore companies played a significant role in the country's sovereign default. Illegal loans were channelled through them and some of those involved received prison sentences.

Our daily newspaper reflexes kick in. We have not yet come to any agreement with Gerard Ryle and the ICIJ. What reason is there for not publishing the story about the Icelandic prime minister right now?

The man is still in office. Will he still be there if we wait for a few months?

For the moment we have an exclusive scoop. Who knows whether someone will tip off another journalist?

On the other hand, this case would of course be an extremely useful way to interest European partners in a joint ICIJ investigation. We would love to be part of an international team investigation – and publishing the best case in advance would ensure that nothing came of that dream.

At the end of the day, it is the state of our knowledge that convinces us to hold the story back. Right now, we have no idea what Sigmundur Davíð Gunnlaugsson did with his shell company. We can see from the data that he opened an account with the major Swiss bank Credit Suisse in London, but we have no bank statements. Breaking the story would definitely put Gunnlaugsson under pressure; after all, we could explain that a European head of government had used a Panamanian provider to obtain an offshore company in the British Virgin Islands that holds an account with a Swiss bank in London. That alone raises some interesting questions. But it would be better if we knew exactly what lies behind this, and for *that* investigation we really could do with having an Icelandic colleague on board.[6]

Can you speak Icelandic? No, neither can we, and that makes it nigh on impossible to do any research in the Icelandic media. Maybe the existence of this company has long been public knowledge?

We decide to give the Gunnlaugsson files a rest and instead call ICIJ Director Gerard Ryle to tell him about the case. Well, as much as we can tell him over the phone in the post-Snowden age – the rest will follow in encrypted form. We notice that Gerard is getting twitchy. An incumbent European prime minister: he likes the sound of that! He also realizes that we're dying to publish it, because he would feel the same way. Everything plays out exactly the way we prayed it would: Gerard puts his foot to the floor. We check our diaries, find three days in mid-March that suit us all, and he books his flight from Washington.

Now, back to Mossack Fonseca's compliance department. The affair with the Icelandic prime minister shows just how seriously Mossfon takes its 'due diligence'. Due diligence means checking if specific people represent a particular risk to a company. We have already mentioned one such risk in relation to Vladimir Putin's friend Sergei Roldugin: if an end client has the status of a 'politically exposed person' it is a good idea to request specific evidence, such as enquiring about the precise source of the money or the company's purpose. The same applies when someone, like Sergei Roldugin, entertains a close relationship with such a PEP.

This would have been the case with Sigmundur Davíð Gunnlaugsson's wife since May 2013 at the latest. Anna Sigurlaug Pálsdóttir has been the sole owner of the shell company Wintris since late 2009, but it is beyond doubt that she has a close relationship with a PEP – her husband.

Mossfon's compliance department does indeed pick this up. Mossfon has access to expensive databases that list thousands of people who are either PEPs or VIPs themselves, or else are in close contact with PEPs or VIPs. These databases are maintained and updated by professional providers such as Reuters. And so Anna Sigurlaug Pálsdóttir catches Mossfon compliance's eye during a routine check. In summer 2013 a Mossfon employee sends an email to the Luxembourg-based company Interconsult, which looks after the company for the prime minister's wife, to tell the firm that its client has PEP status because of her husband and that Mossfon would therefore need more information in order to conduct a broader due diligence test. However, Interconsult does not appear to have supplied this information, for there soon follows a friendly reminder of the first email, then a second, then a third. All of these come to nought: a year on from the first email, nothing seems to have happened.

Do the emails we see contain any threats from Mossfon staff to break off the business relationship? Do they copy in their superiors or even Jürgen Mossack himself?

No. The friendly reminders apparently cease in October 2014, only to resume in mid-2015. And then it happens: in October 2015 the wife of the Icelandic prime minister signs a form designed to clarify the source of the company's money. She puts a cross beside 'Income from inheritance/trust fund' and describes the company as a 'passive non-financial entity'. A Mossfon employee answers, explaining that they are still waiting for other papers 'in this important matter' – for example a photocopy of her passport, proof of the owner's address and a letter of recommendation from a bank or a business partner.

Mossack Fonseca waited patiently for over two years. Not what one would call uncompromising compliance.

It looks as if Mossack Fonseca's compliance department is there to lend the firm a veneer of legitimacy without seriously jeopardizing its business. This is an impression we will get more than once.

For the moment we put the case of the Icelandic prime minister on a pile of stories we want to investigate with local colleagues. This pile already contains the dossiers regarding Putin and the Argentina v NML hedge fund affair. If our data gives rise to an international project, the ICIJ will look for suitable investigative journalists in each country; if the ICIJ doesn't come on board, we'll do it ourselves.

[ ]

Gunnlaugsson isn't the only head of government whose business we investigate at this time. We stumble across a second name as we routinely scour the data, which continues to pour in, for stories that have already spread across the Internet.

Fairly soon we find one of the shell companies mentioned online – the Panamanian firm Nicstate Development S.A. It was apparently controlled by the then Nicaraguan president Arnoldo 'Fat Man' Alemán, whom Transparency International has declared one of the ten most corrupt politicians of all time. In practice, Alemán is alleged to have used Nicstate and other shell companies to funnel almost $100 million of public funds into his own pockets. That is the claim by investigators from the Stolen Asset Recovery Initiative (StAR), a joint project between the World Bank and the UN Office on Drugs and Crime. StAR's mission is to help states to recover embezzled assets. In other words, StAR looks for the money that autocrats and dictators have stolen from their own countries.

However, the Stolen Asset Recovery Initiative is immediately up against it when a country's own judicial system views the situation differently. For instance, Alemán was sent to prison for twenty years for money laundering and corruption in 2003, but the sentence was lifted by the Supreme Court in January 2009. The opposition suspects that this was for reasons of political expediency, as Alemán's successor Daniel Ortega had sealed a pact with the ex-president's party. A major vote took place immediately after the sentence was lifted, indeed on the very same day.

The aforementioned *Vice* article named Alemán as one of the beneficial owners of Nicstate, the company incorporated in Panama, and StAR even explains in detail how the funds were probably channelled. According to investigators, Nicstate was at the centre of a system for shunting money around, orchestrated by Alemán's associates and led by a man called Byron Jerez. The papers in our possession prove the connection: Byron Jerez Solis not only had access to the company, but also to the account Nicstate held with Banco Aliado. The money on this account, which amounted to many millions of US dollars, was later split between several companies or distributed as cheques made out to Maria Fernanda Flores de Alemán, his wife.[7]

The former Nicaraguan president's account was, incidentally, opened and run by Dresdner Bank Lateinamerika, one of Mossack Fonseca's most reliable business partners. An initial check reveals that this German bank set up over 300 companies.

We quickly grow accustomed to finding German banks in the data. For a long time they got away with their offshore business, but now the chickens are coming home to roost.

And sooner than we expect.

4

COMMERZBANK AND ITS LIES

In the early hours of 24 February 2015, police cars carrying public prosecutors and tax investigators pull up outside Commerzbank in Frankfurt. Germany's second largest bank is based in one of the most recognizable tower blocks in Frankfurt's financial district. At night the three towers, illuminated by yellow spotlights, stick up into the sky like fingers. The architectural design is highly symbolic. It says, here lies power. This particular Tuesday morning, however, some bankers have to forget this maxim for a moment as agents from the newly established Organized Crime and Tax Evasion Investigation Unit haul away all kinds of documents related to covert and secret financial investments.

A few days prior to this we receive a phone call from an insider. We try to dig up further background information, and what we discover is electrifying. The bank apparently helped German clients on a routine and systematic basis to evade taxes, and one of its accomplices was the Panamanian law firm Mossack Fonseca.

The raid is based on bank data purchased by the police. People still call them CDs, even though CDs have long been replaced by memory sticks or hard drives. The data shows that the Luxembourg subsidiary of Commerzbank has for many years been setting up shell companies for its German clients. This gets round paying German tax – and the EU Savings Tax Directive, which orders all Luxembourg and Swiss banks to deduct a flat rate of up to 35 per cent withholding tax on all gains on unregistered accounts, if those accounts belong to EU citizens. So Commerzbank established shell companies for its clients in Panama, except that these were *pro forma* account holders. As offshore companies are not EU citizens, the EU Savings Tax Directive did not apply to them, and their revenue was exempt from tax.

That, however, is called tax evasion, which is why the special unit deployed that Tuesday in Frankfurt has the words 'Organized Crime' in its name.

Mossack Fonseca is therefore to all intents and purposes involved in organized crime, as is Commerzbank and numerous other German banks.

As we delve into the case before this raid, we learn that the Luxembourg bank data, which a whistle-blower sold to the German investigators, partially matches our own material: it too comes from Mossack Fonseca. The only difference is that the information the investigators have is far less up to date and above all there is much, much less of it. It only appears to concern a few hundred offshore companies, whereas our data already covers several thousand.

We later discover that the German investigators paid €1 million for these few hundred companies. How much would a few thousand be worth?

The man who got his hands on the Luxembourg bank data is Peter Beckhoff, the head of the Wuppertal Finance Office for Tax Crime and Tax Investigations. It is Beckhoff who reels in one 'tax CD' after another and persuades his minister to loosen the purse strings and take responsibility, all in the knowledge that there is a vast amount of opposition to these actions in political circles. Probably no one has done more for tax justice in Germany than Peter Beckhoff, not least because the news of each new tax CD prompts a flood of voluntary declarations. Motivated by a justifiable fear of potentially finding their names on the next tax CD, and by the hope of getting away with settling their arrears, countless citizens disclosed to the authorities where they had stashed their money. This means many millions of euros for the state coffers.

Tax havens such as Luxembourg fear Peter Beckhoff. An arrest warrant has even been issued for him in Switzerland, where he is suspected of being an 'accomplice to industrial espionage' and of breaching banking secrecy. Beckhoff risks being arrested if he travels there and in 2015 some branches of the media, including the *Süddeutsche Zeitung*, reported that the Swiss secret service supposedly even tried to set an agent on Beckhoff – in Germany, please note.

Lots of journalists will report on the search of the Commerzbank offices, that much is clear. We are scared that other journalists researching the subject of shell companies will happen upon Mossfon and then Jürgen Mossack, and that our competitors will then make something of this German connection. So we decide to do it ourselves.

On 18 February 2015 we write a very long email to Mossack Fonseca containing questions about its role in greasing the wheels of Commerzbank's tax evasion machine. We also retrieve many of the online allegations of links between Mossack Fonseca and dictators such as Gaddafi, Mugabe and Assad – none of whom we have so far found in the data – and anything else we can turn up in the Latin American press. We take even the sketchiest accusations we can find and confront Mossack Fonseca with them to see how it reacts.

[ ]

We get a call from a woman by the name of Ana María Garzón from Burson-Marsteller, a large global crisis management firm with its headquarters in New York. Burson-Marsteller is famous for not shying away from negative campaigning and for playing hardball. The firm allegedly hired out its services to Argentina's junta, the Romanian leader Nicolae Ceaușescu and the Indonesian military regime after a massacre in East Timor, and is said to have tried to play down passive smoking and discredit cancer research on behalf of the US tobacco lobby.[1]

Ana María Garzón praises us for conducting what she terms 'responsible journalism' and for submitting our allegations to Mossack Fonseca first. She responds to our specific questions with a very vague and generalized answer, which doesn't address the points. She writes that it is clear from our questions that we are not interested in a factual report, but are basically being piloted by NML. (A quick reminder: NML is the hedge fund whose founder Paul Singer is hunting down Argentinian public funds and is therefore suing Mossack Fonseca for being an accessory. Singer has been trying for some time to obtain through the courts the very Mossfon documents that we have by this time largely acquired.)

Garzón responds with greater precision to a second email containing more detailed follow-up questions – and dismisses all the allegations. She also explains that Mossack Fonseca has never been charged, complies with all relevant laws, cooperates with the authorities, places great store by due diligence and works exclusively with reputable brokers such as banks or lawyers.

Our request to speak to Jürgen Mossack is declined. On principle. What a shame; we had a few questions to ask and, above all, we'd have liked to know more about the man who has allegedly been helping lawbreakers of all kinds to hide their tracks for decades.

However, for an investigative journalist it is generally a good sign if communications experts refuse to communicate, as it usually means that they have quite a lot to hide. You soon notice if, for a change, that's not the case. A meeting or a lengthy phone call is set up and your interlocutor explains his or her position and side of the story in detail. Just occasionally, there is simply nothing left that strikes you as dubious or worthy of criticism; a host of seemingly good stories die this death. From a purely selfish standpoint, that alone is reason enough always to establish contact: there's nothing more devastating as a reporter than for the explanations to come out after your article has been published. The consequences can range from your paper having to print a right of reply to being sued for libel.

You can tell from Mossack Fonseca's answers that it is eager to come across as an ordinary, respectable firm. You can also tell that it's determined not to divulge any details.

[ ]

One of the demonstrable lies in Mossfon's answer is the claim that Mossack Fonseca never works with end clients, but always with brokers such as lawyers, asset managers and banks.[2] Garzón makes the following analogy: basically, Mossfon is rather like a wholesaler who supplies retailers with products, only the products are companies, and companies are not, *per se*, illicit or bad. To whom the retailers sell on the companies, and what those end clients do with them, is the retailers' responsibility.

It's an interesting analogy, but an incorrect one. We have already seen countless cases, including that of the former Siemens employee Hans-Joachim K., where Mossfon does work directly with end clients. We also see that in many cases Mossfon knows full well who controls the fate of these companies.

We prefer to stick to the image chosen by the former US tax investigator Keith Prager. He says that shell companies are to a wide range of wily criminals what getaway vehicles are to bank robbers – they allow the criminals to escape.

On the day of the raids on Commerzbank the *Süddeutsche Zeitung*'s front-page headline reads: 'New blow for Luxembourg'.

On page two we describe the precise allegations against the bank and its Luxembourg subsidiary, and on page three, where the *SZ* always carries a special report, we publish a full-page article on Mossack Fonseca.

We include hardly any of our data in the piece on Mossack Fonseca, though. For the moment there is very little that we have properly researched and could confidently use. It wouldn't be a good idea to fire off any half-baked stories – and not just with a view to a possible joint international investigation.

Instead, we discuss all the allegations that have been publicly levelled at Mossack Fonseca and combine them with the previously unpublished fact that Jürgen Mossack was born in Germany.

It's a delicate balancing act.

To put the wind up the firm, though, we do write in our article that we possess about 80 gigabytes of internal files that we have barely analysed as yet. We are certain that the article will find its way to Panama, even if it is in German.

In the meantime, we find among our data old emails from our digital contact Ana María Garzón regarding the business relationship between Mossack Fonseca and Burson-Marsteller. In early 2013 she offers to produce a 'crisis handbook' for Mossack Fonseca and we see that it doesn't come cheap. However, it would entitle Mossfon to round-the-clock care in the event of an emergency.[3]

[ ]

Mossack Fonseca isn't the only company that needs help with crisis management; others are too, for example Commerzbank. On the day of the raid and the next day, Germany's second largest bank attempts to feed journalists the following line: certainly it had made some mistakes, but those were the old days; it's long since ceased all dubious dealings. Your attention please, these were 'old cases from ten years back or more', and since 2007 the bank had 'strictly forbidden even the forwarding of requests by clients' for shell companies in Panama.

Old cases? Really?

We check our data again and have no trouble finding one firm after another that Commerzbank ordered from Mossack Fonseca for its German clients between 2005 and 2015.

2006. 2007. 2008. 2009. 2010. 2011. 2012. 2013.[4]

We have emails from financial advisers, certificates of incorporation, powers of attorney from clients, permits to access safes and all the company names, from Badenweiler S.A. to Clandestine Ltd and Pinguin Holding S.A. The owners of these companies, as far as we can see from our checks, are wealthy individuals unknown to the general public.

But there's more. There are even shell companies looked after by Commerzbank that are still open in the spring of 2015.

Old cases?

Commerzbank would have made a far better impression if it had simply stuck to the truth. That's because it appears that the bank identified this line of business as problematic at the latest in 2008 and subsequently scaled it back. We even find emails and memos about conversations in which bank employees tell Mossfon staff that they are no longer allowed to engage in this kind of proceeding. However, the daughter company in Luxembourg, Commerzbank International, didn't really keep to this. The final warnings were sent out to clients with Panamanian companies and an ambiguous tax status only in December 2014. The message was now clear: anyone who didn't want to clean up their act would have to look for another bank.

One can understand why they might have changed tack. After all, the German government had injected €18 billion to prop up Commerzbank during the 2008/9 financial crisis. Its then chair Eric Strutz assured the German parliament that 'Commerzbank

explicitly distances itself from any fiscal crimes and does not tolerate any wrongdoing'. It doesn't look very good to take billions
from the state with one hand and yet help other clients to cheat
the same state with the other.

Along with lawyers, asset managers and accounting firms, banks
are the biggest players in the offshore business. Very few people
contact firms such as Mossfon directly. It is usually their bankers or
lawyers who take care of that part. They grease the wheels of the
offshore machine: they advise, order and manage. Even for blatant
tax evaders.

The data contains countless examples of advisers explicitly
telling Mossack Fonseca, during meetings in random hotel
lobbies or at their offices, for example, that their clients have tax
problems. Naturally, these conversations took place behind closed
doors.

It is mainly large financial institutions that send money around
the globe – the major US banks, but German banks are pretty
good at this business too. Years back, Deutsche Bank was pilloried
in US Senate reports. For a long time the company advertised its
offshore services on one of its websites, describing Mauritius, for
example, as a 'tax-neutral environment'. This hint vanished when
the media got hold of the story.

It is only in the past ten years that the major banks have slowly
and reluctantly begun to row back on this business, as the danger
of being exposed has become too great in comparison with the
relatively modest profits it brings. Anyone who romanticizes this as
an ethical decision almost invariably turns out to be representing
a bank.

Our data sketches out how entangled almost all German banks
were or are in the offshore system.

We search for Deutsche Bank. Thousands of hits.

Dresdner Bank? Same result.

A number of regional banks also get thousands of hits each.[5]

Of course, not every case involves assistance with tax evasion – but as we shall see, a great many do. Even state-owned banks help clients to cheat the state. You have to admire their chutzpah.

HypoVereinsbank is said to have reported itself to the Cologne public prosecutor's office shortly after the raid on Commerzbank. The bank allegedly told the authorities, 'We're coming to you before you come to us', and admitted having conducted the same business as Commerzbank via its former Luxembourg office. This resulted in a deal between HypoVereinsbank and the authorities. In return for cleaning up its serious tax offences the bank would get a reduced fine; it paid the state more than €10 million.[6]

Other banks followed this example, even ones in which the government has a stake such as HSH Nordbank. In its case the deal was €22 million, as our colleague Klaus Ott was able to ascertain.[7]

[ ]

In the background, as the *Süddeutsche Zeitung* reports on these developments in Germany (the raid, Commerzbank's lies and the deals), the data mountain grows. There's the occasional technical glitch and sometimes everything seems to be moving at an unbearably slow pace, but there is more and more information.

We now have 100 gigabytes.

Our head of department Hans Leyendecker has got into the habit of asking us every other day whether the mountain is still growing. He has been infected with our enthusiasm, which has promising implications for us and our project.

Sometime in March, ICIJ Director Gerard Ryle comes to Munich to take a first look at the data. We sit in our offices high up in the SZ Tower and for a whole day we click him through the offshore companies. There's a glint in Ryle's eyes. When we are forced to leave him alone for a few minutes, he does the first thing any investigative journalist would do – he searches for names that appeared in his own investigations. And he finds some.

So Gerard Ryle knows what it feels like to be in our shoes. You sit on a treasure trove, poking around in it at night, early in the morning, at odd times, and every find might turn into a story that shakes the country to its core. But it takes ages for the story to make it into the media: Ryle was leaked the data that formed the basis for Offshore Secrets roughly three years before publication. We really hope that we'll be quicker.

Offshore Secrets brought the business practices of shell companies to the attention of a wider audience. The political fallout was huge. Such was the pressure on tax havens for a while that for the very first time the Austrian and Luxembourg governments publicly questioned their own banking secrecy laws. EU Commissioner Algirdas Šemeta said at the time that Offshore Secrets was a game-changer for future fiscal policy.

The project was a massive success for the ICIJ and suddenly everyone knew about them. It was followed by Offshore Secrets China, the Luxembourg Tax Files and, in February 2015, the HSBC Files, based on the French whistle-blower Hervé Falciani's leak.

After two days in Munich Ryle is certain that our data can spark a new project. We run through possible next steps. How would the material get to Washington where the ICIJ has its headquarters and where its data specialists are? When would be a good time to publish? Which colleagues should we speak to first?

Again and again we come back to the central issues we've been debating for weeks:

Why does the source insist on remaining anonymous?

What is the source's motivation?

And most importantly, can we trust the material?

We don't have any cast-iron answers to these questions. How could we? What we *do* have are hundreds of pages of files that we can check, in some cases because we can verify the documents by asking the authorities. We find dozens of court proceedings against which we can counter-check our papers, we have material from previous investigations and we also compare the leaked information with public databases.

The result is always the same – the information tallies perfectly.

One of the cases we discuss in depth with Gerard Ryle is that of Wintris Inc., the company that used to belong to the incumbent Icelandic prime minister, Sigmundur Gunnlaugsson. The world has almost grown accustomed to hearing about dictators and rulers who park their wealth in shell companies, but a European leader?

What makes the affair even thornier is that we have found out that a rule came into force in Iceland's parliament in March 2009, the *Hagsmunaskráning þingmanna*, which obliges members of parliament to declare all their shares and assets. A parliamentary spokesperson confirms to us that anyone owning over 25 per cent of a company must declare it.

Following the approval of this law, Gunnlaugsson, who has been an MP since April 2009, ought of course to have reported Wintris Inc. It takes us only a few clicks to establish that he obviously didn't do so.[8]

By the following year Gunnlaugsson no longer needed to keep his offshore company a secret, as he had of course sold it to his wife for one dollar in late 2009.

ICIJ Director Ryle is excited, but he still flies back to the United States without having provided us with a firm undertaking that the ICIJ will come on board. He needs a few days to think it over.

5

MOSSACK FONSECA'S ROLE IN THE SYRIAN WAR

It's uncanny.

When we look at our files we keep coming across emails that are only a few days old. It's almost as if we were following events in real time, as if we were inside the law firm that provides assistance to so many criminals. As if we were standing behind the employees in Panama City, whose names are now so familiar to us, and looking over their shoulders at their screens.

Except that they cannot see us.

It's even more uncanny when these emails mention us – us at the *Süddeutsche Zeitung*. For example, in an email dated 9 March 2015, in which members of the law firm's staff forward to their colleagues our article about the raid on Commerzbank and Mossack Fonseca's involvement – more or less accurately transposed into Spanish by Google Translate. Or the email dated 19 February 2015, in which someone asks whether it's true that the convicted drug dealer Arturo del Tiempo Marqués is a Mossfon client. Some journalists had enquired about him the day before, it says. Those journalists were us.

So now we know that Panama is reading what we publish. But they don't know that we are reading their emails. . .

We shudder at the sight of an email from Mossack Fonseca's marketing department, warning about 'undercover journalists'. It urges all Mossfon staff to be vigilant.

In addition, we happen upon the agenda of the April 2015 Mossfon Corporate Strategy Meeting. The second item is 'Mossfon in the media' and 'the German case'. It's obviously us that they have in mind.

Mossfon appears to realize that the media are critical of its line of business – and for good reason.

[john doe]: Good morning.

[SZ]: Hello. All good?

[john doe]: So far. More data is on the go.

[SZ]: Okay

[john doe]: I think there are some companies in there that have a connection to the Syrian dictator, Assad.

[SZ]: We know the rumors that Mossfon allegedly worked for Assads people.

[john doe]: The rumors seem to be true.

[SZ]: Do you have company names?

[john doe]: Some. This should be a good start: Ramak Ltd., Dorling International Ltd., Cara Corporation, Seadale International Corporation, Hoxim Lane Management Corp., Lorie Limited, Drex Technologies S.A.

The last of these companies, Drex Technologies, sounds familiar. It already turned up in the HSBC Files. In our data we find a Drex Technologies S.A. folder numbered 537658 – Mossfon's internal reference. The folder contains 124 files: PDFs, emails, Word documents and photos.

This is the first genuine lead pointing towards Syria's dictator Bashar al-Assad. We examine the companies more closely, continue our investigations, and bingo! Mossack Fonseca apparently ran a whole web of shell companies associated with the brutal Syrian regime.

To make things clear: for obvious reasons, Assad is not mentioned in the documents, either as an owner or a director. Just try setting up an account or a company outside Syria in the name of Bashar al-Assad; it won't work. Dictators, mafia bosses and other criminals have so-called 'bagmen' for this kind of job. These are the foot soldiers who collect, manage and invest money for secretive bigwigs and bring it wherever it is needed.

Of the hundreds of thousands of Syrians fleeing their country, a large proportion are not running from so-called Islamic State but from Assad. Backers such as Mossack Fonseca and Assad's bagmen make sure that the regime doesn't run out of foreign currency. This cash serves to pay mercenaries and equip the dreaded Shabiha militia with weapons and vehicles, as well as allegedly enabling the production of poison gas and the operation of torture facilities.

We find the name of Rami Makhlouf, Assad's most important financier, dozens of times in our files. This is a man abhorred by the Syrian opposition. When the first protests broke out in 2011, the demonstrators didn't just burn pictures of Assad; they also destroyed branches of the telephone corporation Syriatel. Rami Makhlouf is Syriatel's owner. 'Makhlouf is a thief!' they cried.

Rami Makhlouf is probably the richest man in Syria. As well as Syriatel he also holds stakes in various banks, duty-free chain stores, an airline and much more. People in Syria have long since stopped asking what belongs to him and instead ask: what doesn't?

The *New York Times* wrote that Makhlouf was a 'symbol of how economic reforms turned crony socialism into crony capitalism, making the poor poorer and the connected rich fantastically wealthier'.

Rami Makhlouf, who was born in Damascus in 1969, is Bashar al-Assad's cousin. Makhlouf's aunt Anisa is the widow of the late president Hafis al-Assad, the current ruler's father. Rami and Bashar played together when they were young, and today they are close allies – one the head of state, the other the businessman on whose money and connections Assad can count at all times. The

US State Department classifies Rami Makhlouf as a 'financier of the regime', as one can read in a diplomatic cable sent in 2007 that was published by WikiLeaks.

As far as anyone can tell, Makhlouf's wealth has less to do with diligence and hard work than with unscrupulousness and brutality. 'Rami Makhlouf has used intimidation and his close ties to the Assad regime to obtain improper business advantages at the expense of ordinary Syrians,' said Stuart Levey in 2008, who was under-secretary for terrorism and financial intelligence at the US Department of the Treasury and who, in an ironic twist, now works for HSBC – the very bank that the ICIJ's HSBC Files investigation revealed had done business with Makhlouf for many years. In any case, Rami Makhlouf's ties to Assad are no secret. He is one of the regime's strongest backers – and as such, an international pariah with whom no one will do business.

Mossack Fonseca appeared to think differently. The law firm worked for years with the man who is said to shuttle back and forth between Dubai and Damascus, and understandably doesn't show his face in public in Syria.

[ ]

The oldest firm belonging to Makhlouf we can find in the data is called Ramak Ltd and was founded in 1996 in the British Virgin Islands. Makhlouf is only in his mid-twenties at the time. He takes over a string of Syrian companies, gets the better of his rival bidders and becomes richer and richer. The protecting hand of Assad's family is always over him. According to the US authorities, Makhlouf had in this way 'improperly benefit[ed] from and aid[ed] the public corruption of Syrian regime officials', and so in 2008 they include his name on their sanctions list.

Sanctions are one of the major weapons of international law. They are intended to force a country's government or ruling elite to back down and, for example, to cease persecuting their own population or pursuing hostilities against other countries, engaging in terrorism or genocide.

Sanctions hit countries where it hurts – in their coffers. The principle is fairly simple. The UN, EU or individual countries such as the United States try to figure out which people have money and influence. In Syria's case this is primarily Assad and his family. Next comes the inner circle: ministers, intelligence officials and financiers such as Rami Makhlouf, who also happens to be a relative. These names are put on the sanctions list to tell the world: Look here, doing business with these people spells trouble.

So US citizens have been banned from dealing with Makhlouf since 2008. Nothing from which he might profit may take place on American soil. Some lawyers even extend their interpretation of the rules so far as to say that it is forbidden to do business with him in US dollars. Anyone who breaches these rules will run into difficulties the next time they try to enter the USA. Sanction breakers also risk winding up on the list themselves, seeing their assets frozen or having their US subsidiaries confiscated.

Put plainly, it is better to have nothing to do with sanctioned individuals.

This is particularly important for Mossfon because the company also runs offices in Las Vegas, in Miami and in Wyoming, i.e. in the United States. Any businessperson in their right mind would therefore have severed all business ties with Makhlouf in 2008 at the very latest. Not so Jürgen Mossack and Ramón Fonseca. Makhlouf's name still features in Mossack Fonseca's papers after 2008 and indeed even after May 2011, when the European Union followed the US's example and imposed sanctions on Assad's financial backer.

On the other hand, this is exactly what shell companies are for: they are meant to conceal the identity of the ultimate beneficial owner. The oxygen that feeds firms such as Mossack Fonseca is secrecy, and that is one thing – if not the only thing – for which terrorists, arms dealers and dictators are willing to pay top dollar.

Sanctions quickly reach the limits of their power with shell companies, as sanctioned individuals can disappear fairly effortlessly behind their screens. Another of Rami Makhlouf's shell companies will simply do business in his stead and no one will be any the wiser, at least not at first.

It is therefore no wonder that the UN and the US Department of the Treasury have entire teams assigned to one single task – finding out behind which firms a dictator's financier or terrorists might be hiding. As soon as that is known, the firm can go on the sanctions list. Which is what happened to Makhlouf's Drex Technologies, the firm whose papers are now staring us in the face.

However, it takes four years for Drex to join Rami Makhlouf on the list. The explanation the US Department of the Treasury gives for this step in July 2012 is that Makhlouf is using the company 'to facilitate and manage his international financial holdings'. It is unclear how the US authorities reached this conclusion. What we see in the files is this: according to its deed of incorporation, Drex Technologies S.A. was established on 4 July 2000 with its official company headquarters in the British Virgin Islands. The name Rami Makhlouf appears a good dozen times in the company folder.

[ ]

It is not only Rami Makhlouf that we find, but also his brother Hafez, a brigadier and regional head of the Syrian civil intelligence service. Hafez Makhlouf, whom our data says is the sole owner of a company called Eagle Trading & Contracting Ltd, was at one time in charge of a notorious torture facility in Damascus.

What's more, experts suspect that he was responsible for poison gas attacks on the city of Ghuta, where hundreds of people were killed by sarin gas in August 2013. He has been on the US sanctions list since 2007 and on the EU's since 2011, yet the company belonged to him until at least 2013.[1]

We also find two other brothers. Iyad Makhlouf, a major in the Syrian Army and a secret service agent, whom the EU put on the sanctions list for alleged participation in attacks on civilians. And Ihab Makhlouf, sanctioned because he is vice chairman of Syriatel and supposedly provides funding to the regime to put down demonstrations. He is sporadically involved with several companies, but the data suggests that Hoxim Lane Management belonged to him alone.[2]

How can anyone do business with these people? That is the question a Swiss newspaper puts to Mossack Fonseca in spring 2015 (albeit focusing more on the technicalities than the morality of the matter). Its journalists spotted Rami Makhlouf's name in our reports on the law firm in late February 2015. To its direct question about Rami Makhlouf the paper receives the following response: 'Mossack Fonseca DID NOT KNOW that Mr Makhlouf or any other ally of Assad was indirectly using or abusing our services!'

Sorry? Mossack Fonseca did not know anything? In capitals?

Makhlouf didn't have just one firm with Mossack Fonseca but a whole web of offshore companies, and Mossfon says it knew nothing about them?

Put politely, that is not the complete truth. Put more precisely, it's a lie.

Rami Makhlouf demonstrably featured in Mossack Fonseca's files from at least 1998 as the majority shareholder of the offshore company Polter Investments, owning 70 per cent of the shares. Thus Mossfon must have known since 1998 at the latest that he was one of its clients. An email exchange from spring 2011 shows how Jürgen Mossack's law firm discusses such problem cases in-house.

Mossfon's compliance department – the department responsible for checking that the firm abides by all guidelines and laws in its daily business – asks the partners and managing directors whether they really want to continue to do business with Rami Makhlouf. It's a serious warning when someone is on the sanctions list and it would be better to steer clear of them, wouldn't it?

The Swiss lawyer Christoph Zollinger, who acts as a sort of junior partner in the firm, dismisses their misgivings. He writes to a colleague in an email dated 17 February 2011 that they can keep the Makhloufs as clients; after all, HSBC in London obviously doesn't have an issue with them.[3]

Mossack Fonseca has an internal debate about the problematic case of Rami Makhlouf, and it turns out that it also discussed him with HSBC – and yet Mossfon later claims that it didn't know Assad's financier was one of its clients?

The truth is that Mossfon helped, maybe for years, to ensure that the flow of cash to Syria didn't dry up.

This could have grave consequences for Jürgen Mossack, as our papers show that he was party to the decision about Makhlouf.[4] If we are correct in our assumption that he holds both Panamanian and German citizenship, that is. We have in any case found among the papers a copy of his German passport, which was valid until 2006. He has obviously kept renewing his passport since the 1960s, so why wouldn't he have done the same in 2006?

If he hasn't given up his German citizenship, he might come to regret it. German citizens face up to ten years in prison for breaching EU sanctions. In its reply to the Swiss newspaper, Mossack Fonseca tried to rebut the allegations about its dealings with dictators by stating that it would be pretty idiotic for Mossfon to do something of this kind. 'Who could believe that Mossack Fonseca would wilfully, deliberately or even accidentally tarnish a reputation carefully built up over thirty-seven years, by aiding criminals, dictators or money launderers' – and all, as Mossfon notes in all caps, 'FOR A FEW HUNDRED DOLLARS IN ANNUAL FEES?'

Indeed: who *could* believe it? Who could believe that Mossack Fonseca could be so 'idiotic', as they themselves put it, as well as unscrupulous?

We might also ask: who could imagine Mossack Fonseca could be so brazen?

For us this case not only means that we can establish a link between Mossack Fonseca and Assad; it also shows us the law firm's modus operandi. This is a company that will spread lies and, if necessary, twist the facts without the slightest qualm.

The Makhlouf case also demonstrates why the existence of anonymous shell companies poses an existential threat to millions of people. Because they can help dictators to circumvent sanctions imposed by the international community. Because they can help brutal leaders to plunder the countries they rule. And because they allow them to hide these stolen assets in shell companies, although the related account is often located in Switzerland or Luxembourg – in Rami Makhlouf's case at HSBC's Swiss office.

[ ]

Mossfon answered the *Süddeutsche Zeitung*'s enquiry in February 2015 by saying that it would not accept people on sanctions lists as clients. We therefore get hold of the UN, EU and US sanctions lists – a Who's Who of ruthless and genocidal dictators, terrorists and the companies they own or use. There are hundreds of names, each with many different spellings. We look for them in our data and are genuinely amazed.

So Mossfon doesn't deal with anyone on a sanctions list, huh? Pull the other one.

We find accomplices of African dictators, Central American drug barons, convicted sex offenders, each with an offshore company. There are so many of them that we soon lose track. We draw up lists and compare the details in our files with information from the EU, the UN and the USA. Below is a selection.

Bredenkamp, John Arnold

This South African-born arms dealer was subject to EU sanctions from 2009 to 2012 due to his 'close links to the Zimbabwean government'. The US Department of the Treasury views him as an associate of Mugabe's regime and imposed sanctions on Bredenkamp and twenty of his firms in 2008.[5]

Makhlouf, Ihab

Syrian president Bashar al-Assad's cousin was sanctioned by the EU in May 2011 because he 'funds the regime and helps to suppress demonstrations'.

Makhlouf, Iyab

Bashar al-Assad's cousin and a Syrian intelligence officer was put on the EU sanctions list because he was allegedly involved in putting down protests.

Makhlouf, Hafez

This brigadier and former regional head of the Syrian civil intelligence service was sanctioned by the EU, along with his brother, in May 2011.

Makhlouf, Rami

Said to be Syria's wealthiest man, he was sanctioned by the USA in February 2008, followed by the EU in May 2011.

N'Da Ametchi, Jean-Claude
The EU placed the banker on its sanctions list in 2011 because he allegedly provided 'funding to the illegitimate government' of the then president of Ivory Coast, Laurent Gbagbo.[6]

Rautenbach, Muller Conrad
The businessman and his firm Ridgepoint Overseas Development, managed by Mossack Fonseca, was subject to US sanctions from 2008 to 2014 due to his close ties to Zimbabwe's autocratic ruler, Mugabe. In 2012 the EU lifted the sanctions it had imposed on him in 2009.[7]

Stjepanovic, Savo
This Slovenian was sanctioned by the US in February 2015 because he allegedly belonged to an international steroid smuggling ring.[8]

Ternavsky, Anatoly
This Belarusian citizen was included in the EU sanctions regime from 2012 to 2014 because he was supposedly close to Belarusian autocrat Alexander Lukashenko.[9]

Timchenko, Gennady
The Russian-Finnish oligarch was placed on the US sanctions list in March 2014 in the wake of the Crimea crisis.[10]

Mossfon supplied such people with shell companies on a routine basis for many years.

Even if firms or their shareholders were in the crosshairs of the authorities and placed on their sanctions lists, Mossfon clearly did not always see this as a compelling reason to immediately break off business dealings, as the following cases illustrate.

Brodway Commerce Inc.

The firm was sanctioned by the US authorities in 2012. One of the company's directors was a Guatemalan woman, Marllory Dadiana Chacón Rossell, also known as 'Queen of the South'. According to the US Department of the Treasury she had once established one of the largest drug rings in Central America.[11]

Drex Technologies S.A.

The United States and the European Union placed this firm, founded in 2000 in the British Virgin Islands, on their sanctions lists in 2012 because it belonged to Rami Makhlouf.[12]

Kuo Oil Pte. Ltd

This Singapore-based company was sanctioned by the US from 2012 to January 2016 because it was said to have delivered over $25 million's worth of oil to Iran between 2010 and 2011, thereby breaching the trade embargo.[13]

Ovlas Trading S.A.

The US imposed sanctions on the company in December 2010 because of the alleged involvement of Kassim Tajideen, who it claimed was a major financial backer of Hezbollah.[14]

Petropars Ltd

The company was subject to US sanctions from June 2010 to early 2016 as part of the Iran embargo.[15]

Timpani Exports Ltd

This company, based in the British Virgin Islands, was sanctioned by the United States in November 2008 because it belonged to the aforementioned John Arnold Bredenkamp, who was a member of the Zimbabwean autocrat Robert Mugabe's inner circle.[16]

We also share our findings with the ICIJ. By now we are telephoning, chatting or emailing with Gerard Ryle almost every day. He asks questions and we answer. About how the data is structured, the tax havens that appear most frequently, the nationalities of the people whose passport photocopies we see in the papers: Gerard wants to know every detail. The only thing is that he still hasn't confirmed whether he and the ICIJ want to join the project. Meanwhile, we use every free minute to dig through the data, always emerging with new stories.

[ ]

Serious as most of them are (arms dealers and dictators are responsible for countless deaths, for instance), some cases are simply absurd. We have looked over and over again for the former Ukrainian prime minister Yulia Tymoshenko and her predecessor Pavel Lazarenko. The two of them are alleged to have creamed off millions of state dollars in the 1990s. Lazarenko was later sentenced to several years' imprisonment for money laundering, first by a Swiss judge and then by a US court. At the time the US investigators named as an 'unindicted co-conspirator' none other than Yulia Tymoshenko.[17]

So once more we enter 'Lazarenko' into our search engine and find, among other things, a fax bearing the personal signature of Pavel Lazarenko. Not from some point in the 1990s, but on 21 April 2005.

The absurd thing about this fax is that Lazarenko claims he had found out only a few weeks earlier that a certain Gateway Marketing Inc. – a shell company run by Mossack Fonseca – belonged to him. Now Lazarenko is asking for all the relevant documentation.

A shell company? Whoops!

Lazarenko sends the fax from California where he is living in a grotesquely outsized villa. There are countless pictures of the property with six pools on various levels.[18]

This adds another leading politician to our files. After the trails leading to Assad, Putin and the Kirchners, to the Icelandic prime minister and the former Nicaraguan president Arnoldo 'Fat Man' Alemán, it is Ukraine's turn.

It is now worth filing these cases in a specially named folder: 'Heads of state'.

[SZ]: There's a story about Mossack Fonseca and the Leak in a Swiss newspaper. The author has also questioned Mossfon.

[john doe]: Really? And what does Mossack Fonseca say?

[SZ]: They say: "Our organization has had no data leaked to date."

[john doe]: Ha! No leak! If there's no leak, I wonder why I need all this storage space for the data. . .

Of course we would love to know as much as possible about where our source got the data, but it's not critical. What is critical is that the data is authentic and socially relevant. There is absolutely no doubt that it is relevant and, after much crosschecking, its authenticity is fundamentally beyond dispute.

And yet the nightmare scenario of every investigative journalist is that he or she has been taken in by false data. The realization that no human could have faked such a huge quantity of data is only of limited reassurance, as it would suffice for one crucial document to have been doctored and planted there for the whole project to come under fire – even if 99 per cent of the data was genuine.

We have already compared our documents with court papers, public registers and other sources and have come across no anomalies whatsoever. Moreover, we have a secondary guarantee. We found out that German tax investigators had purchased Mossfon data a little while ago. By a roundabout route we were able to correlate that data with our own. Our data is a great deal more up to date and there is far, far more of it, but there are no inconsistencies between our data on offshore companies and the investigators'.

We keep turning over the same questions with ICIJ boss Gerard Ryle:

Who might have an interest in setting us up?

Who might wish to set us a trap, and how?

How can we test the trustworthiness of our source?

These and other questions always lead to the conclusion that the crucial thing is not the source but the material. *That* we trust, and this trust has been backed up by hundreds of crosschecks.

On this we agree with the ICIJ boss, who has by now officially announced that our data deserves its own ICIJ project.

We get down to planning.

[ ]

We have a problem, however: there is too much data. Neither of us is an expert in dealing with large volumes of data, even though we have worked on a number of similar projects before. The big difference, though, is that this particular data is not landing any old place, but on *our* computers. We can just about cope with storing and safeguarding the information. We buy external hard drives with half a terabyte of memory. We shunt files around, back them up and encrypt the drives.

The thing is we can't search it properly any more. Even in recent weeks it was only partially possible to do a search, because we were unable to run text recognition on the PDFs and photographed contracts. Our computer's search engine couldn't recognize the content of the text; it merely registered the file name and the fact that it was a picture file.

Now, with roughly 200 gigabytes of data, our computers have given up. IT experts explain to us that the computers have too little of just about everything you need to search large quantities of data – disk space, main memory, processing power.

We need a new computer, and quick. Our head of department and editor-in-chief agree to buy us a new, more powerful laptop. We are even authorized to bypass the strict central purchasing rule and order it separately, as our in-house expert says it will take four to six weeks until our special laptop is actually set up and in our office. If all goes well. We order one online instead and a week later the thing arrives.

Along with a few technical specifications the laptop has one major particularity: it has never been connected to the Internet before. Its wireless local area network (WLAN) is deactivated, and no LAN cable will ever penetrate its casing. This is known as an 'air gap'.

One of the many lessons of the Snowden leaks is that a computer is only relatively secure from hackers if it has never been connected to the Internet, i.e. if an air gap separates it from other systems. Intelligence services are now able to control even switched-off mobile phones, so it's a piece of cake for them to hack into a computer that has been connected to a WLAN. To bridge an air gap, however, a secret service agent would have to have physical access to the relevant computer, which would mean getting past the security guards at the entrance to the *Süddeutsche Zeitung*'s offices.

We sit down together every few days and consider how to proceed. We are only marginally inconvenienced by current reporting jobs: one of us is investigating a scandal about salmonella-infected eggs on the side; every few weeks, the other takes on another subject such as the 'no-spy' affair or the hack attacks on the German parliament.* Otherwise, our colleagues Hans Leyendecker and Klaus Ott cover our backs with an almost frightening output

---

* The 'no-spy' affair was a dispute about American spying on German soil.

of articles. Nobody would really know that the Brothers Obermay/ ier have been working for weeks on a new secret project.

By this time we have decided to concentrate initially on the international dimension. We want to work out the international relevance of the growing mountain of data before we start scattering it around the world.

Following the ICIJ's go-ahead, the leak machinery is just getting into gear. Gerard Ryle has brought the consortium's data specialists, reporters and organizers into the loop. Marina Walker, Ryle's deputy, is to lead the new project. An Argentinian, she has fifteen years' experience as an investigative journalist under her belt and has won just about every professional award going, including honours from Investigative Reporters and Editors Inc., the Overseas Press Club of America and the Society of Professional Journalists. Most importantly, though, Marina Walker is a fantastic organizer, so she's perfect for this project.

There is a never-ending list of questions to be answered. Which other media should we invite on board? How do we transfer the first documents? Which programs can we trust? Our investigations will unsettle a lot of people who have done business with Mossack Fonseca, and that makes us potential surveillance targets.

It all feels normal while we're discussing this kind of issue in practical terms; encryption is nothing new. However, we feel queasy every time we think of all the names in our data. We have already found many traces of people who have obviously had other people killed. Do we want to report these facts? Do we want to find ourselves in the sights of the Italian mafia? Or the Russian mafia?

Both these organizations have links to Mossack Fonseca shell companies. We come across the name of a Russian who was arrested for arms deals with the Russian mafia. One Italian man in the data is suspected of being the accountant of a branch of the mafia. Yet we still do not know the purpose of these companies.

When the ICIJ joint venture is up and running, though, we can count on the help of others and will be able to pass on such stories to our colleagues in Italy and Russia. Those colleagues will be better able to evaluate the potential danger involved. Leo Sisti of the weekly *L'Espresso*, for example, has been uncovering criminal machinations for over thirty years. He was the first to write about Silvio Berlusconi's offshore dealings and has published books about the funding of Al-Qaeda and the Sicilian mafia. And he's still alive.

[ ]

We are completely addicted to the Assad connection. We search for more people from the entourage of the man waging a war that has so far claimed over a quarter of a million lives – and we find them. A man called Suleiman Marouf appears as a shareholder in quite a number of our shell companies. Like Rami Makhlouf, he is reputed to be a good friend of Assad. The media have named him the Syrian dictator's 'London fixer', a middleman for his business there.[19]

A further minor detail: as emails published by WikiLeaks revealed, Marouf also purchased expensive Ming vases and Armani designer interior furnishings at Harrods for Assad's wife Asma, long after she was a persona non grata in Europe. One hundred thousand people had already died in the Syrian civil war and Asma al-Assad was stocking up on items in the Harrods sales.[20]

Ten months after Marouf was added to the EU sanctions list, Mossack Fonseca's compliance department called Mossfon's London office. After all, the Syrian still owned at least eleven companies, seven of which were apparently used to buy or run properties in Britain. The compliance department concluded that 'according to our risk assessment, these companies [are] high risk'. Mossfon employees run Marouf's name through World Check, one of several databases containing the names of every person with suspicious ties to politicians or criminals. The Mossfon people also google Marouf and find the same information as we did: he is 'Assad's man in London' and is on the sanctions list.

Despite this, Suleiman Marouf was retained as a client and is still one in 2015. Occasionally Mossack Fonseca's inaction works out nicely, for Marouf was taken off the sanctions list in 2014. Under pressure from Marouf's lawyers, the British Foreign Office had him removed from the sanctions list – 'for lack of evidence that would stand up in court'.

We also happen upon a company called Maxima Middle East Trading Co., which in January 2013 decides to open an account at the Syria International Islamic Bank. Long after Syria had descended into civil war, reports suggested that the bank supplied Assad's regime with money and helped it evade sanctions. In 2012 the financial institution was therefore placed on the US sanctions list – and yet Mossfon helped its client to open an account there.

Of course, our number one question is: why did this company want to open an account with this bank?

We study the company more closely, scour the documents one by one, search databases and question experts. We discover that Maxima Middle East Trading Co. runs an office in the free trade zone of Sharjah, one of the United Arab Emirates and an infamous hub of secret supplies to Syria. The US authorities do indeed regard the firm as the nexus of a complex network of companies that use fake papers to deliver oil to Syria. In December 2014 the US imposed sanctions on Maxima Middle East Trading Co. and its then managing director Ahmad Barqawi.[21]

The US Treasury Department suspects the company of having 'worked with a Russian oil and gas firm to obtain various types of base oil for transfer to [Syrian] government-controlled refineries [...] in Homs and Damascus'. It had thus helped other companies 'in their deceptive practices and facilitation of the movement of aviation fuel to Syria' – the fuel that the Syrian regime needs to bomb its own people.

A company by the name of Pangates International Corporation Ltd is also said to have joined in with Maxima Middle East Trading Co.'s operation. Pangates is also mentioned in our data – three times. Once as a company in the tax haven of Niue (a South Pacific island), once in Samoa and once in the Seychelles. In July 2014 the United States finally sanctioned the company for providing 'material support for, and goods and services to, the Government of Syria'.[22] And thus to Assad.

And yet in Mossack Fonseca's systems the company appears to have remained active for another year after it was sanctioned. Another year during which Mossfon apparently broke a US embargo.[23]

6

FROM THE WAFFEN-SS TO THE CIA AND PANAMA

259 gigabytes. 260. 261.

This makes our mountain of data the largest leak in the history of journalism. Larger than Offshore Secrets.

By way of comparison, the diplomatic cables published by WikiLeaks amounted to 1.7 gigabytes; the HSBC Files, based on Hervé Falciani's documents, 3.3 gigabytes; the Luxembourg Tax Files 4 gigabytes; the WikiLeaks Afghanistan protocols 1.4 gigabytes.

Of course, it isn't the size of a leak that matters. 260 gigabytes of meaningless files are, in the final analysis, no more than meaningless files. Also, it is very hard to imagine 260 gigabytes. Well, let us tell you: 260 gigabytes represent almost a million emails and several million pages of secret documents. We should be able to do something with that much information. But 'the biggest ever leak' should be a headline that captures people's attention if we go public with the results of our investigation one day.

'Do you really want to do it? Do you really want to publish something one day?' our boss Hans Leyendecker might quip at this juncture, having teased us for so long that we have in effect given up newspaper reporting and simply laze around on top of our hard drive. Yet he is the man who has made all of this possible and defended our 'laziness' to his superiors.

The size of the leak is also helpful in another way, because it allows us to interest ICIJ colleagues from all over the world. The bigger the leak, the greater the likelihood that individual journalists will find good stories involving their own countries; and the more colleagues join the investigation, the more stories we'll be able to bring to light.

The whole world. Our leak. Assad, Putin, Iceland, $500 million. It's utterly absurd, and the most amazing thing is that the source just keeps on going. He or she just won't stop.

The next day we phone Gerard Ryle. We tell him about the state of play and how the arguments for our ICIJ colleagues are getting ever better. He's happy, but he soon steers the conversation towards practical aspects. The ICIJ is going to send two data specialists to Munich: the Spanish journalist Mar Cabra, head of the ICIJ data team, and Rigoberto Carvajal, the head programmer from Costa Rica. The two of them will review our data critically and try to make sense of it. They will tell us how to tackle this data mountain and will bring with them a program that enables us to search it better. They will also take a hard drive back to Washington. Encrypted, obviously. Or to be more precise: encrypted and concealed.

This is how it works. Encryption programs such as TrueCrypt or VeraCrypt (both of which Edward Snowden says even NSA experts couldn't crack, at least until recently) are used to prepare an external hard drive so that it appears at first sight only to be encrypted. However, on this hard drive, alongside the visible encrypted drive, there is a second encrypted and invisible one. Should the FBI, customs or anyone else compel Rigoberto or Mar to plug in the hard drive and decrypt the drive, they will enter the password for the visible drive. This will then start up, and on it we will have saved a few folders containing some files that look secret and important, but actually aren't.

The presence of a second drive is neither visible nor verifiable.

It is not incredibly difficult to encrypt a hard drive in this way, but nor is it the easiest exercise in the world for people like us who have trouble memorizing a six-letter password. Our new passwords look something like this:

Nvc87sad5chj56586356%&fc8796c_ndnuc71dehdtg3%$654tz3

That isn't a joke. All of a sudden, entirely without warning, we have become nerds. But that's okay: it feels pretty good to do our bit for security. In any event, it's up to us to encrypt the hard drives until Rigoberto and Mar, whom we've known since Offshore Secrets, get to Munich.

[ ]

As the two data experts are setting off, we do some old-school investigating, visiting archive offices and leafing through yellowing documents. When we started to track how Jürgen Mossack ended up in Panama, we submitted a large number of requests to archive offices. We wanted to know if his father had been a Nazi and if he had had a particular reason for decamping to Latin America.

The first results of our requests have arrived. It turns out that Erhard Mossack was in the Waffen-SS. In the federal archives we find his service card, on which it says that Mossack was promoted to *Rottenführer*, or corporal, in September 1944.

We find out more from an FBI dossier. Erhard Mossack, born 16 April 1924 in Grube-Erika in the district of Hoyerswerda, joined the Hitler Youth at the age of fifteen and the Waffen-SS at eighteen. Fittingly, under 'distinctive features' it records a scar on the inside of his left upper arm 'where the blood-group tattoo was removed'. The blood-group tattoo was a virtually unmistakable sign of Waffen-SS membership, and therefore many SS soldiers tried to get rid of the tattoo in the final days of the war and beyond. According to the dossier, Erhard Mossack did in fact move in November 1942 to the SS *Totenkopf* (Skull and Crossbones)

Division, with which he fought in what was then Czechoslovakia, Finland and Norway. In January 1945, a few days after his promotion to corporal, he was sent to the Western Front and in March he was taken prisoner by US units. In December that year he managed to escape from a prisoner of war camp in Le Havre in France and battle his way back to Germany.

Then, in 1946, he was arrested in Offenbach. An informant for the US Counter Intelligence Corps (CIC) claimed that Mossack 'possessed a long list of names' connected with an underground organization of which Mossack himself was a member. The CIC assessed Mossack thus: 'Indoctrinated through and through with Nazi ideology. As a typical Hitler Youth leader, he still lives in his world of Nazi slogans and is a remarkable example of a German youth under Hitler.'

The big question is, why was the Waffen-SS man later allowed to enter the United States? That had, after all, been his stated aim when he signed off the register in Germany.

The answer is that Erhard Mossack obviously changed sides after the war. We discover this through a simple Google search. We type in 'Erhard Mossack' and at some stage we end up on a website that publishes US documents related to the Second World War, including a list of names of suspected Nazis who assisted the American intelligence services after the war. One of those names is Erhard Mossack.

That would explain the immigration permit – if, that is, he ever entered the United States and didn't travel directly to Panama. Whichever way, it is likely that the sheltering hand of the CIA facilitated his passage. Panama was regarded as a safe and pleasant haven for National Socialists, who were for a variety of reasons no longer welcome in the USA. The American author Eric Lichtblau cites a host of examples in his book *The Nazis Next Door*.

The case of Klaus Barbie, the 'Butcher of Lyon', who lived in Latin America under the pseudonym 'Klaus Altmann', is one example of the despicable way in which the US intelligence services went about recruiting Nazi informants. Barbie too was an occasional visitor to Panama.

There is a fairly unflattering CIA cable about Erhard Mossack's work as an informant. It would appear to be about Cuban agents, but the CIA doesn't seem too sure that Mossack is reliable or that his past won't catch up with him.

However, we have now established that Mossack did cooperate with the intelligence services. We know that because we have received a reply from the BND, Germany's foreign intelligence agency. We wanted to know if there is any material in the BND's archives pertaining to Erhard Mossack. There is, but the BND doesn't want to provide it, because a disclosure might, among other things, 'endanger the welfare of the Federal Republic of Germany or one of its regions'.

So far, so mysterious.

Unfortunately this is where Mossack's trail peters out. The one thing that is certain is that a 'Peter Erhard Mossack' becomes a director and chairman of a company called Union Alemana de Exportación S.A. (German Export Union), established in March 1965. One of the other directors is Luisa Herzog de Mossack, his wife. The documents show that the company rented office space until 1970, more or less.

Jürgen Mossack, their son and offshore king, tries to sell this company in 1989 for the sum of $20,000 to a London-based lawyer who is strangely desperate to acquire a company founded around 1960. The Union Alemana de Exportación S.A. was therefore five years too young and the sale did not go ahead.

Why, in 1989, would a London-based lawyer need an offshore company established in 1960? It can provide an impression of legitimacy – for example, that a company has been active for a long time. If you want to take part in a public tender, for instance, you often have a better chance if you've been in business for a while and not just for a few months. The specialist term for this is a 'vintage company'. Vintage, because the firms are supposed to look worn, like jeans. Still, we have no idea what Mossack's prospective buyer meant to do.

Due to the BND's stonewalling, the precise intentions and activities of the ex-Waffen-SS man who became a CIA informant with a BND file remain opaque. What does seem clear, though, is that Mossacks father and son followed a similar principle: never be too picky when choosing your business partners.

[ ]

At the beginning of May 2015 the two ICIJ data experts, Rigoberto Carvajal and Mar Cabra, land in Munich. They listen with fascination as we tell Erhard Mossack's story. Nazis are always news, the CIA is always news, but the two combined is fantastic.

Rigo Carvajal and Mar Cabra have rented a flat in Munich, and when we enter, it feels as if we've stepped into a pastiche of a hacker film. All the blinds are down, there are laptops on two tables and on all sides cables snake, external hard drives wink, screens flicker and computers hum. Scattered around them are USB sticks, coffee cups and rucksacks.

Mar and Rigo have broad grins on their faces. 'Welcome to the world of data,' says Mar. We place our laptops beside theirs and dive into this strange universe.

We hand over all the material we have so far, then tell them everything we know about it, starting with the fact that Mossack Fonseca has arranged its data very neatly. Every company Mossack Fonseca sets up is given a reference number. Next, a digital folder bearing this number is created in the system. Into this folder Mossfon's employees then clearly slide any information related to the company: certificates of incorporation, copies of the shares issued, a register of the directors and shareholders, contracts, scanned copies of official passports and, above all, emails regarding the company.

Mar, ICIJ's Spanish data chief, has enough energy for at least three normal people. She bounces around the room like a rubber ball, waving her arms about and talking virtually without pausing for breath – even when *we* are supposed to be explaining what we've got. She lets out a hoarse laugh, apologizes and says, 'Then why don't you say something? We're here for you!' At the same time, Mar is very structured. She writes a new to-do list every few minutes, drafts new time schedules and outlines best-case and worst-case scenarios. She's got everything, and everyone working on this project, under control.

Rigo, the programmer, generally sits there quietly and listens, but his eyes twinkle. Only occasionally does he ask a question, and we can see that his mind is working overtime. It's his job to analyse the data in a way that allows journalists to make the best possible use of it. At the end of every ICIJ investigation, no one knows the data as thoroughly as Rigo. He has to understand every ramification in order to be able to program perfectly the various tools everyone uses: a multi-level security database for secret documents, which can be accessed by every journalist participating in the project worldwide; a secure forum for everyone to communicate with each other; and a database exclusively for structural data that can be used to create visualizations. Every company and its related entities should appear in this, which means primarily the shareholders and the brokers. Rigo's idea is that every participating journalist should be able to find out in a couple of clicks if an individual has a stake in other companies and if so, which ones; and then which other individuals have a stake in those companies, and so on. An ever-expanding visualization, so to speak. Rigo is an enthusiastic advocate of representing complex networks of companies with graphics.

That's easier said than done, though, as in many cases the owner column merely reads 'The Bearer' or, in Spanish, 'El

Portador'. This is something we learned right at the beginning of the investigation: if offshore companies only issue a single bearer share, then the company's owner is the person who physically possesses that paper. The advantage of this is that it is very easy, without leaving any trail, to buy and sell companies, along with all the company's assets, whether that be a villa in Mallorca or a shipload of automatic rifles for a country in the midst of a civil war. It is simply impossible to determine to whom the company belongs: the information is often not even in Mossack Fonseca's internal folders, or only in one file among a thousand in a folder.

If we really do want to publish something some day – and that's what we've promised our boss – we're going to have to search faster and more effectively.

[ ]

We need a program like Nuix Investigator. Nuix is an Australian company that produces forensic IT software, which means that you can use it to sort and sift through jumbled data. It can even log unsearchable PDFs, pictures and scanned documents. We have thousands of those kinds of files, so Nuix is precisely what we need. But it costs a fortune. It's the type of software normally used by intelligence services, law firms, police forces and anti-corruption investigators around the world. 'No software other than Nuix can process large collections fast enough to meet the SEC's desired timeframes', is how Nuix advertises its products on its homepage. The US Securities and Exchange Commission (SEC) is the body that regulates the stock exchange and as such must deal with vast quantities of data. If Nuix can deal with that, it'll certainly be able to deal with our data.

Although Nuix is exorbitantly expensive, we and others in the ICIJ used it for Offshore Secrets. ICIJ boss Gerard Ryle is

Australian and he managed to persuade the company to support the consortium's work by providing several free licences.

Nuix does the same for this project. Mar and Rigo bring us a licence on a stick. So, a little awestruck, we sit there in front of our new laptop with 500 gigabytes of memory and let Mar and Rigo explain how Nuix works. On the surface it's very simple: a search field that is used like the Google search bar, a preview window and a list of results. But the results also show the file path, the environment and the tree data structure. What's more, you can export and save all the search results if you don't have time to analyse the search right away.

Anyone who has only ever worked with free search tools and then switches to Nuix will feel as if they've traded up from a soapbox on wheels to a Formula 1 racing car.

Nuix's basic principle is simple: the files you want to search are uploaded into the program as 'evidence' and automatically tagged – or as the pros say, indexed. This is relatively easy with Word documents and emails, but harder with PDFs and photo files – and there are already hundreds of thousands of those in our data by this point. The Nuix program must therefore first be able to identify if there is any text in the pictures. This is done by text recognition software called optical character recognition or OCR. Only when every document has undergone OCR is a negative search result truly a negative search result. Only then can you be relatively certain that Angela Merkel is not hiding in the data after the search for 'Angela Merkel' has produced zero hits.

That's as long as the name is not in a fax that has been printed out and later scanned or has been written using an old typewriter; if that's the case, OCR will not produce any hits. You can therefore only ever entirely exclude the possibility that someone has done business with Mossack Fonseca by examining every single page yourself.

Once Nuix has compiled an index of our data and OCR has

run through it, we are for the first time in a position to conduct a comprehensive search of our data – all 350 gigabytes of it at this point. Mar and Rigo fly back to Spain and Costa Rica respectively, and we sit down at our computers again. Only, what are we looking for? Helmut Kohl? Gerhard Schröder? Uli Hoeness?

[ ]

While working on the Offshore Secrets documents in late 2012, four of us sat in a windowless office for several weeks and threw random search terms at the system. The result was that each of us typed in names such as Franz Josef Strauß, Klaus Zumwinkel, Josef Ackermann and of course Helmut Kohl – not just once but twice or even three times. Who could remember whose name he'd entered ten days ago? Then we realized how ridiculous this was and started to make lists of the main German politicians, major business leaders and so on.

This time around, we approach our task strategically from the outset. Naturally, we use every free moment to search for names that interest us, but we also draw up detailed lists. We realize after Mar's and Rigo's departures that without these lists we'll soon lose track and that will mean wasting time – time we're bound to need later, given the size of the data mountain.

Basically, we make an inventory of public life in the Federal Republic of Germany. We list all the leading politicians, business executives, sportspeople and public figures. We look for the super-rich, criminals and swindlers, and we try to compile the names of as many individuals implicated in scandals as possible, meaning anyone involved in a major affair such as the Christian Democratic Union of Germany's donations scandal. Our data stretches back into the 1970s.

We want to use these lists later to fish in the data, because you can do that with Nuix. You feed in an Excel document filled with names and you get back an Excel document with the hits. The results are ranked by match percentage. 'Gerhard Schröder', for example, would be a 100 per cent hit, 'Gerhard Schrader' probably about 95 per cent, 'Gerd Schröder' 80 per cent and 'Gerhard Schroem' 60 per cent or below, so you often have to go through the lists of results manually, hit by hit.

Our final list for 'party donations scandals' includes 130 names, whereas the list of former Stasi officials and their suspected helpers totals 94,856 names.

Meanwhile, we keep on searching for terms that seem as if they might bring to light interesting internal emails. For instance, Mossack Fonseca has regular dealings with criminals and authorities track criminals. Maybe we should type in 'search warrant'?

Lo and behold, we get a long list of hits with 'search warrant'. One of these is related to a series of companies in the British Virgin Islands, which an organization called the Libyan Asset Tracing Committee suspects of being sham companies with whose assistance Gaddafi and his accomplices supposedly smuggled $150 million out of the country. Mossfon rejects this allegation, but it is obviously serious enough for the Financial Investigation Agency – a British Virgin Islands body not known for its zeal in such matters – to intervene. On 30 October 2013 the FIA issues a warrant to search the local Mossack Fonseca office.

What we barely ever see is any sign of consternation. One might expect, in internal emails at least, to read sentences like 'Damn, have we really been helping Gaddafi's henchmen to ransack their country for years?'

[ ]

A new lead. We create a new subfolder in the 'Heads of state' folder and call it 'Gaddafi'. The company names inside it sound quaint, romantic even: Wildwood Trades Ltd, Moon Silk Ltd,

Sirvent Star Corporation, Bristows Corp., Regency Belle Corporation, Seafire Systems Ltd, Sea Swells, Morning Star Technology Ltd, Pacific Mist Ltd, HC Nominees (BVL) Ltd and Albion International Group.

Studying these companies, we find several letters from the authorities. What emerges from them is that the investigators presume that the companies belong to a certain Ali Dabaiba. Under Gaddafi the qualified geography teacher was head of the Organization for Development of Administrative Centres, a gigantic public procurement agency.[1]

The exciting thing about this lead is that it's extremely fresh. We need more information.

[john doe]: Had some trouble sleeping tonight. I was thinking about how people will react to these revelations. It's very likely that some of the firm's clients will try to find me. And some of those clients have intelligence agencies.
[SZ]: Quite possible. Be careful.
[john doe]: I'm trying. Are you also taking precautions? The journalists involved here are not going to be particularly popular among the clients either.
[SZ]: We do what we can.

It's true that we're taking greater care with every passing week – as it becomes clearer that this data could send shockwaves around the world. At first, we only initiate those who absolutely need to know about our project: our head of department and the main editorial office. Our cooperation with the ICIJ is now official. Mar and Rigo have completed a preliminary analysis of the data we gave them in Munich. They've carried out some initial trials to determine how best to process it and make the scans searchable, and they have also set up an encrypted forum. We set up virtual meetings with Mar Cabra, Rigo Carvajal, Gerard Ryle and Marina

Walker every few days. We run through the data, our plans, the work to be done and which colleagues from which countries we should target and approach. Argentina is clear: *La Nación*. In Britain the *Guardian* and the BBC. In France *Le Monde* and Edouard Perrin, who revealed the Luxembourg Tax Files.

We need journalists in Russia too, but that isn't so simple. There aren't very many Russian colleagues who can write freely. And those who do risk a great deal: beatings, imprisonment, their lives.

The same is true for China. Mossack Fonseca now has ten offices in China, which is a sign that it has a lot of rich Chinese clients, yet including a colleague from China or Hong Kong is unthinkable.

Why?

In early 2014 we did a follow-up report to Offshore Secrets, an investigation, based on the same data, into Chinese owners of shell companies. We had left out this part the first time because Chinese names are so hard to verify. Then we found out from the Offshore Secrets data that China's ruling elite was conducting secret business in tax havens on a huge scale. We came across shell companies belonging to close relatives of leading politicians. Some of the country's wealthiest men and women were in there, as were executives of state-owned companies caught up in corruption scandals.

We worked with *Ming Pao*, a newspaper in Hong Kong at the time. We thought we realized how big a risk *Ming Pao* was running, but no one realized quite how big. On the one hand, the paper was in Hong Kong; on the other, criticizing China's elite is always a gamble, even in relatively liberal Hong Kong. In any case, *Ming Pao*'s editor-in-chief Kevin Lau was fired shortly before the planned publication and replaced with a successor who was kindly disposed to the regime. There were massive protests among the staff, but to no avail. Within hours of publishing our stories, most reports had been censored in China and the homepages of the *Süddeutsche Zeitung* – where we published the most important findings in Chinese – and of other ICIJ partners were blocked.

Far worse was to come. Shortly afterwards, Kevin Lau was attacked with a knife in the street one morning on his way to the car park. He was stabbed six times in the back and seriously injured, but survived the assassination attempt. His attackers fled the scene on a motorbike, but several Triad members were later arrested. They were the compliant henchmen – young men who were ready to kill journalists for a fistful of Hong Kong dollars. But the identity of those who masterminded the crime has still not been uncovered to this day. Some argue that the attackers were not supposed to kill Lau, but merely intimidate him.

The ICIJ has now brought Alexa Olesen onto our project. She was China correspondent for the Associated Press news agency and worked as a freelance journalist on Offshore Secrets. She's responsible for China-related subjects this time too and within days she has scored her first success: she finds the granddaughter of a high-ranking party member among the data, along with two Chinese billionaires and a film star.

Our German discoveries almost pale into insignificance compared with the international scope of our data.

By this point, the source has supplied us with a list of about 215,000 Mossfon companies. We forward this new list to the ICIJ. Mar Cabra, the head of the data team, loves lists. Using lists, you can impose order on the data chaos. Mar can see in which tax havens the companies named in the data are based, and in which countries their shareholders are resident. She can then prepare separate lists for individual countries – which will, at a later stage in the project, make journalists from those countries very happy indeed. These lists proved to be enormously helpful during the HSBC Files investigation. Rather than having to search through all the data, journalists could concentrate on the documents that concerned individuals from their own country.

Not all our colleagues across the world will be working under such comfortable conditions as ours. By this time, we have effectively been released from normal duty for six months to work on the project. We know from previous projects that colleagues in Africa and Latin America, for example, will be working on this investigation while also writing daily stories for their newspapers or producing topical TV programmes on all kinds of issues. Such lists will be invaluable to them – they offer a great starting point and will save weeks of searching.

It has now become clear that the data sent to us by the anonymous source over the past few months will be the biggest project the ICIJ has ever managed. Journalists from every continent will be involved in it. Day after day, ICIJ project manager Marina Walker is on the phone with one ICIJ member after another to tell them about the project: not too much, as the circle of initiates cannot grow too big at first, but enough to get them to bite – and to start investigating.

The project has now been given a working title: Prometheus, like the *Star Trek* starship. The names of ICIJ projects have traditionally been chosen by data specialist Rigo Carvajal. And Rigo loves *Star Trek*. The HSBC Files project was known internally at the ICIJ as 'Enterprise', the Luxembourg Tax Files as 'Voyager' and the investigation into the World Bank's questionable projects as 'Odyssey'. All *Star Trek* starships.

And now we have Prometheus.

[ ]

We have reached the end of May and the ICIJ members and media organizations who have already confirmed their involvement – including *Le Monde*, the *Guardian*, the Organized Crime and Corruption Reporting Project and the Swiss Sunday newspaper *SonntagsZeitung* – are still waiting for the official go-ahead for the project. But we are aiming to publish in November. Which means we'll have to get our skates on. It is time to organize an initial meeting, says Marina. A meeting in which we plan, discuss and allocate tasks; a meeting that will help our colleagues to estimate how much time and effort they wish to invest in the project. These initial conferences have become a part of the modus operandi at the ICIJ, a lesson learned from the Offshore Secrets project. Back then, all the important details were discussed by email and phone. A number of the project partners had never met face to face and – to put it mildly – not everyone demonstrated the same level of mutual trust and readiness to share information.

For that reason, every major project since then has started with a conference. The Luxembourg Tax Files project meeting was held in Brussels; the HSBC Files conference in Paris. Over the course of a day, the ICIJ explains what the project is about, and discusses issues such as the exchange of research results and planned publication dates with the assembled journalists. The Prometheus meeting was actually planned for May, or June at the latest, here in Munich. But then the mountain of data kept growing and it became clear that if we met in June, we still wouldn't really know the full scope of the data we had in our possession. So we keep postponing, over and over again...

But the source just keeps on sending more material.

We come up with a solution. We will hold two meetings. A big meeting in the SZ Tower in Munich sometime in late summer and a smaller one before the summer holidays for the benefit of all the media organizations that wish to put large teams on the case. Marina suggests the ICIJ headquarters in Washington as a venue.

We agree – even though the trip will do nothing to boost our department's meagre travel fund.

Julia Stein from the research department at broadcaster NDR will be joining us in Washington. She is also an ICIJ member and an amazing colleague. We have already worked with her on

Offshore Secrets, the Luxembourg Tax Files and the HSBC Files. By this point, Julia's team is already acquainted with the project, and more and more NDR colleagues are getting involved in the investigation. Another German broadcaster, WDR, will also take part – the *Süddeutsche Zeitung* established an association of investigative journalists with the two broadcasters in 2014.

Our two-man operation is suddenly beginning to look like a global investigation.

7

THE FOOTBALL FACTORY

While we continue to research individual stories as best we can, the pile of data continues to grow. 400 gigabytes. 500 gigabytes. 600 gigabytes. We have long lost all sense of scale. Initially, we kept track by converting the volume of information into the equivalent number of printed Bibles. But we stopped after a certain point. It's difficult to imagine a pile of more than a million copies of the Bible.

In the meantime, the ICIJ data team has set up a multi-encrypted forum, the iHub, to facilitate international cooperation. They could not have chosen a more appropriate name: over the coming months it really will become the central hub for all our work. It is where project participants will be able to share the results of their research and discuss how to proceed. It's a kind of Facebook for investigative journalists, with discussion groups for individual topics. You can even 'like' entries by colleagues within the system. Access is initially restricted to us and ICIJ staff. We first need to summarize the results of the research we have done so far. This will then serve as inspiration for the other journalists when they are eventually allowed access – which will be at the meeting in Washington, if not before.

A date has finally been set for that meeting: we will be flying to the US capital at the end of June. By that time, we want to have collated as much detail as possible regarding the biggest cases we have uncovered so far: Russia, Syria and Iceland. There is much work to be done.

[ ]

At the end of May a breaking news story tears us away from our research: FIFA officials arrested!

On the day before the 65th FIFA Congress in Zurich, police arrest six senior FIFA officials in a luxury hotel. Among them are two of the football governing body's vice presidents: Jeffrey Webb from the Cayman Islands and Eugenio Figueredo from Uruguay.

The arrests were instigated by a New York investigation initiated by the current US attorney general Loretta Lynch. The Americans are sending a clear message to the world.

And the world is stunned. Europe has been rather more passive, with prosecutors and officials turning a blind eye to FIFA's activities in the parallel world of sport. For years there have been more than just rumours about suspicious payments, bribed officials and bought tournaments. You only need to pick up a copy of *FIFA-Mafia*, written by Thomas Kistner, our colleague at the *SZ*. Or watch the documentaries of BBC journalist James Oliver, who is collaborating with us on the Prometheus project. Over the past few years he has filmed several programmes featuring FIFA scandals and corruption for *Panorama*, the renowned investigative current-affairs series on British TV. After a secret list of multi-million-dollar payments made by a shady sports marketing company was leaked to him, Oliver exposed a bribery scandal involving three members of the FIFA executive committee under former FIFA president João Havelange.

It was no secret that unsavoury deals were made at FIFA, but no one had done anything about what was clearly an intolerable situation. However, the Americans were now on the case and they showed in a very public manner that FIFA was by no means untouchable. By treating the organization as a 'criminal enterprise led by fraudsters', the prosecutors could apply specific laws to the case.

A brief wave of resistance emerges against President Sepp Blatter within FIFA and UEFA, the Union of European Football Associations, before he is then safely re-elected with 133 votes for a further term of office just two days after the arrests.

The New York investigators indict fourteen officials, on charges that include money laundering, fraud and corruption. The men are alleged to have built up, over a period of twenty-four years, a system that has allowed them to enrich themselves 'through corruption in international soccer'. They are said to have accepted bribes totalling more than $150 million.

[ ]

We get our hands on a copy of the indictment – public legal documents of this kind are freely available online in the USA, and very quickly. We discover that several shell companies played an important role in the system of receiving bribes that was allegedly used by those who stand accused. We systematically search our data for the names of the accused and for the shell companies mentioned.

It's not long before we find three of the fourteen indicted officials.

The name of the former Uruguayan FIFA vice president Eugenio Figueredo, one of the six officials arrested in Zurich, appears in connection with several companies.[1]

The Argentine sports broadcasting rights agent Hugo Jinkis, one of those suspected of paying bribes, appears along with his company Cross Trading S.A. which, according to the FIFA indictment, was used to process suspect payments amounting to millions of dollars. Jinkis and others are alleged to have sought to secure exclusive rights to South America's continental football championships, the Copa América and the Copa Centenario, through bribery.[2]

The third person exposed is Hugo Jinkis's son Mariano, who is listed alongside his father as a director at the same offshore company.

The first thing we do is go through the Cross Trading S.A. folder. The company was established in the Seychelles, in Niue and in Nevada: three companies all sharing the same name. As a result, there are three separate folders but not one of them contains a contract with FIFA. Unlike other shell company owners, the Jinkises do not work with nominee directors, which means they wouldn't have had to send the contracts for any business deals – as mentioned in the FIFA indictment – to Mossfon to be signed. However, we do find contracts with UEFA, an organization that has so far been curiously untouched by all the scandals.

[ ]

The contracts cover exclusive Ecuadorian TV rights to the UEFA Champions League, the UEFA Cup and the UEFA Super Cup – all for astonishingly low sums of money. The contracts are in Mossfon's possession solely because those responsible for them at UEFA sent the documents relating to these TV rights to the attention of Cross Trading S.A. in Niue, where the company was registered. Mossack Fonseca staff in Niue opened the letters, scanned the contracts and sent them on to the Jinkis clan by email. For a fee, of course.

In doing so, they inadvertently sent them to us too because Mossfon staff filed the sent emails neatly in the appropriate company folder.

At this point we decide to do something we have wanted to do for a while. We ask UEFA very generally whether it too has done business with the fourteen accused FIFA officials or companies associated with them – but without explicitly mentioning Cross Trading. We simply want to know whether UEFA only made deals with the Jinkises or whether it also did business with the others.

UEFA's answer reads: 'According to the persons responsible at UEFA, no business relationships have existed over the last fifteen years with the persons or businesses you name.'

That is, to put it mildly, very strange. We did not explicitly ask about Cross Trading, but UEFA clearly had business relations with Hugo Jinkis, who, as the managing director of Cross Trading, signed at least one contract using his real name.

Naturally enough, the Cross Trading contracts have now suddenly become even more interesting. They cover the Champions League for seasons 2006/7, 2007/8 and 2008/9, the UEFA Cup for seasons 2006/7, 2007/8 and 2008/9, and the Super Cup in 2007 and 2008.

According to the contracts, Hugo and Mariano Jinkis's company paid a total of just under $140,000 for all the exclusive TV broadcasting rights. That seems suspiciously low, even taking into account that European football rights in Ecuador will naturally only be worth a fraction of what broadcasters in Europe would have to pay. However, Ecuador does have a population of 15 million and the Champions League, with all its global superstars, is bound to attract a following there too.

We find a possible explanation in the FIFA indictment. The New York investigators claim they have proof that Hugo Jinkis and Mariano Jinkis paid bribes and kickbacks to senior officials at FIFA and other associations to obtain or retain cheap TV broadcasting rights for football tournaments, namely the Copa América and the Copa Centenario. They then sold on, or intended to sell on, these rights for a profit.

Here is one specific example from the indictment. In autumn 2011 Hugo and Mariano Jinkis are said to have invited three high-ranking Central American football officials to a house in Uruguay. It is alleged that the three officials promised to help Hugo Jinkis and his son acquire certain media marketing rights and that they were rewarded financially for this. One of the three is thought to have received around $250,000, the other two getting $100,000 each. This $450,000 came – according to the indictment – from an account owned by Cross Trading S.A.[3]

The question now burning on our lips is: did this go on at UEFA too?

[ ]

We discover that the Ecuadorian TV rights sold by UEFA to the Jinkis-owned company Cross Trading ended up in the hands of Ecuadorian media group Teleamazonas. But how much did Teleamazonas pay for them?

Via the ICIJ, we are in contact with colleagues in Ecuador who are carrying out investigative work – under rather difficult conditions. We explain the present situation to our colleague Monica Almeida at the Ecuadorian daily *El Universo*. Just a couple of days later she comes back to us with all the information we were after – and much more.

But let's take things in order.

Among the documents we have access to, we can see the contract between UEFA and Cross Trading S.A. concluded on 13 September 2006, which covers exclusive TV broadcasting rights for the Champions League in seasons 2006/7, 2007/8 and 2008/9. UEFA is paid a total of $111,000 for these rights. Monica accesses the contracts concluded between Teleamazonas and Cross Trading S.A. and discovers that the broadcaster paid Cross Trading S.A. $311,170 for exactly the same rights. Three times as much. Leaving Hugo Jinkis and his son Mariano $200,170 better off from just one deal with UEFA.

But there's more. The second contract we found, again between UEFA and Cross Trading S.A. and dated 23 March 2007, covers broadcasting rights for the UEFA Cup in 2006/7, 2007/8 and 2008/9, as well as the Super Cup in 2007 and 2008. Cross Trading S.A. pays UEFA $28,000 for these rights and – according to the documents from Ecuador – sells them on to Teleamazonas for $126,200. Four and a half times as much – a mark-up of almost $100,000.

We can only think of two possible explanations. The first is that there are incompetent people in key positions at UEFA – managers who do not know the value of their own products. That would constitute a serious case of mismanagement.

Or Hugo and Mariano Jinkis have concluded the same kind of deal with UEFA as they are accused of having done with FIFA; they have bribed people to secure cheap TV rights and they have sold them on for a profit; and they have even used the same vehicle to carry out the transaction: Cross Trading S.A.

If that is true, they have committed a criminal offence.

One indication that this second explanation may be the correct one is that UEFA denies ever having done business with the Jinkis pair. Again, just to be clear in case UEFA should ever claim they did not know who was behind Cross Trading S.A.: the words 'Hugo Jinkis, Director' are printed in capitals on the contract under Jinkis's signature.

In view of the contracts we are sent from Ecuador, UEFA's denial is even more absurd than we initially realized. The Ecuadorian broadcaster had also bought the UEFA rights for the previous three-year period in the same manner: via Cross Trading S.A. According to these contracts, Teleamazonas also bought the rights to the UEFA Champions League, the UEFA Cup and the UEFA Super Cup for the 2003/4, 2004/5 and 2005/6 seasons from Hugo and Mariano Jinkis for around $400,000. A similar sum to the other Teleamazonas contract we have in our possession.

We have reason to believe that this remarkable business model was also used in this earlier period: Cross Trading buys the rights from UEFA cheaply and sells them on to Teleamazonas for a much higher sum.

We calculate that Cross Trading would have sold on the UEFA TV rights at a premium of $600,000 in the years between 2003 and 2009.

So UEFA may have been involved in highly questionable and, at the very least, extremely disadvantageous business dealings with sports broadcasting rights agents indicted in the FIFA case – and it was denying it outright.

Welcome to the murky world of sport.

8

ON FISHING, FINDING AND FINE ART

The urge is too powerful. The urge to rummage manually through the mountain of data that has now passed the terabyte mark. We know it hardly makes sense now to search Nuix for individual people, terms or facts because we will merely have to repeat each search, which leads to nothing as soon as we acquire more data. But we just cannot stop ourselves. Whenever we can, we snatch half an hour on the laptop and cast our net into the sea of data that is growing larger and larger week by week. We go 'fishing', as our ICIJ colleagues call it. 'Happy fishing!'

The funny thing is, we almost always find something. Every time we spend more than twenty minutes entering keywords we find some kind of trail, something that sounds illegal, unusual, amusing or downright exciting. But we cannot follow these trails to their conclusion there and then because we simply do not have the time and each case is complicated in its own unique way. So we save everything that sounds promising in an encrypted folder on our computers, label it and then... it just lies there.

But sometimes what we find is so good that we immediately dive in more deeply. For some reason – you soon forget the exact flash of inspiration that drives you to try a particular approach when 'fishing' – we enter the word 'painting' and get hundreds of results. Not ideal because we hadn't planned on spending that much time on random searches. But one of the first hits refers to a painting by Amedeo Modigliani called *Seated Man with a Cane*.

Modigliani was an Italian painter who lived and worked in Paris at the beginning of the twentieth century, surrounded by contemporaries such as Pablo Picasso and Pierre-Auguste Renoir. A quick search reveals that he painted the image in 1918. As its name suggests, it depicts a man with a cane and it is worth several millions.

We can already see from the search mask preview that the file that mentions our painting is a court document. We call it up from the data and see that a Frenchman named Philippe Maestracci is taking the Helly Nahmad Gallery in New York to court over this very painting. Maestracci is claiming rightful ownership of the painting, which he says the Nazis stole from his grandfather. However, the Helly Nahmad Gallery claims that it does not own the painting, nor is it currently exhibiting it.

Helly Nahmad is the very rich son of the even richer David Nahmad, a billionaire of Lebanese extraction with an Italian passport who lives in Monaco. Helly Nahmad is a well-known figure in the world of New York's rich and beautiful. He runs the Helly Nahmad Gallery – a gallery for impressionist and contemporary art not far from Central Park.[1]

Art experts regard the Nahmads as the biggest buyers on the international art market. They store some of their collection – which includes several Picassos – in a high-security warehouse in Geneva known as the Freeport.

Within the same folder as the court document – the folder for an offshore company called International Art Center (IAC) – we find a fax sent in late 2011 by the wealth management department of a large bank. It asks Mossack Fonseca to have the Mossfon-appointed directors of International Art Center sign a document attesting that the company owns Modigliani's *Seated Man with a Cane*. Two documents are attached: a proof of purchase issued by

Christie's auction house in 1996 and what appears to be some kind of certificate of ownership. Research is so easy sometimes! Both documents name International Art Center as the owner and state that the painting is in storage at the Geneva Freeport, where works owned by the Nahmads are also stored.

A long article published in the *Wall Street Journal* in October 2014 helps us understand the bigger picture. The story, as told by the *Wall Street Journal*, begins in Paris in 1946 when the Jewish art collector Oscar Stettiner writes a letter to the authorities. In it, Stettiner outlines his claim to ownership of paintings that were forcibly sold under the Nazi occupation of France. Stettiner fled Paris in 1939, leaving behind his art collection. The Nazis appointed an administrator for his gallery and the collection, which included *Seated Man with a Cane*, was sold in four public auctions.

In 1947 a state investigator began checking Stettiner's claim for the return of the Modigliani painting. He came to the conclusion that a man called van der Klip had bought *Seated Man with a Cane* in 1944, and noted the address as Rue de Courcelles 36, Paris. In addition to the Modigliani, the buyer also purchased a carpet and a painting depicting Oscar Stettiner as a child.

It appeared that Oscar Stettiner was about to recover his painting. The investigator tracked down van der Klip and set up a meeting with him and Stettiner in a Paris courtyard, where the carpet was stored in a shed. Van der Klip was prepared to return it.

But the Modigliani wasn't there.

Van der Klip claimed that he had sold the painting to a Monsieur Mariage Eu de Saint Pierre, who was also present at the meeting. He, in turn, explained that he had sold *Seated Man with a Cane* to an American officer for 25,000 francs in October 1944. He claimed the two men had met in the Café du Rohan on the Place du Palais Royal, close to the Louvre. However, the investigators were unable to find a name or an address for the purported American buyer.

And so the Modigliani remained missing for almost fifty years.

The painting resurfaced at a Christie's auction in London in 1996, where, according to our documents, it was bought by International Art Center. The only information provided in the catalogue regarding the painting's provenance is that it was being offered for auction by an anonymous seller. International Art Center paid $3.2 million for it.

Twelve years later, in the autumn of 2008, *Seated Man with a Cane* was up for sale once more, this time at Sotheby's. By then, the value was estimated at between $18 million and $25 million. The catalogue stated that the painting was possibly from the collection of Jewish art dealer Oscar Stettiner. So there was a distinct possibility that the Modigliani was looted Nazi art. *Seated Man with a Cane* did not find a buyer at Sotheby's.

A little later, however, Mondex heard of the case. The Canadian art restitution company was established in the mid-1990s to track down artworks confiscated by the Nazis and return them to their rightful owners or heirs. For a contingency fee, of course. Mondex found Stettiner's sole heir in France, the eventual claimant Philippe Maestracci, and it started searching for the painting on his behalf. It needs evidence that Stettiner had really owned the Modigliani. The art detectives come across a photo of the painting in the Venice Biennale archives, with a caption stating that Oscar Stettiner loaned it to them in 1930.

The only question is: where is the painting now?

After the 1996 auction, the Modigliani was exhibited once at the Musée d'Art Moderne in Paris, once at the Royal Academy of Arts in London and twice at the Helly Nahmad Gallery in New York. Maestracci therefore begins with Nahmad. He has his lawyer send two letters asking Nahmad for a meeting to discuss *Seated Man with a Cane*. He wants the painting back. Both letters go unanswered.

So in 2011, Maestracci takes the Helly Nahmad Gallery to court in New York – these are the documents we first saw in the data. When we widen the scope of our search, we discover that the case is still pending at a higher court. We discuss the case with the ICIJ – after all, the organization is based in Washington, and New York is only a few hours away by train. Perhaps one of our colleagues has time to travel to the next court date.

Marina Walker tells us that Jake Bernstein, who won the Pulitzer Prize a few years previously for his work covering Wall Street in the run up to the financial crisis, has already been working on the story. He read our first forum post on the case and immediately began further research. Jake has also been in touch with the Mondex art detection agency and the claimant's lawyers.

We search PACER (Public Access to Court Electronic Records) for information on the Modigliani painting stolen by the Nazis. PACER is a very useful online database. For just a few cents per item, you can access documents from almost any court case in the USA: defence documents, prosecution documents and applications to produce evidence. Virtually all the paperwork produced over the course of a court case is there.

We look for the Philippe Maestracci v Helly Nahmad Gallery case.

In a report that is dozens of pages long, Maestracci's lawyer traces the painting's journey from Oscar Stettiner to the Nazi-appointed intermediary, from John van der Klip to the Helly Nahmad Gallery. The report appears to be conclusive and well documented.

But Helly Nahmad affirms in writing that his gallery did not 'at any time' own the Modigliani. He merely borrowed the painting for a single exhibition at his gallery. Furthermore, Nahmad's lawyers present a document from Christie's showing that the painting was sold in 1996 to the Panama-based company International Art Center, not to the Helly Nahmad Gallery.

Maestracci can offer no counter-argument and he withdraws the lawsuit in 2012.

In 2014, he – or a court-appointed administrator for the 'estate of Oscar Stettiner' – makes another attempt. The defendant this time is not only the Helly Nahmad Gallery, but also International Art Center, which allegedly owns the painting, as well as Helly Nahmad and his father David. The IAC and the Nahmads are all represented by the same star lawyer, who declares that International Art Center is the painting's sole owner. 'Not anyone else in the world, including defendants Helly Nahmad Gallery, Helly Nahmad or David Nahmad, owns the painting.'

That is true, from a strictly legal point of view. But our data reveals the following: International Art Center S.A. was founded in 1995 by Giuseppe Nahmad, who is David Nahmad's brother and Helly Nahmad's uncle. In 2008 he reassigned half his IAC shares to David Nahmad. And we find a document dated 22 October 2014 that is signed by David Nahmad in his role 'as sole shareholder'. The same David Nahmad who in 2015 claimed through his lawyer before the Supreme Court of the State of New York that the painting was owned solely by IAC.

So we see how the painting's ambiguous ownership status leads the heir of the Paris art dealer to bring legal proceedings against the wrong party twice and how the Nahmads profit from the opacity of their offshore business structure.

We were keen to discuss IAC and *Seated Man with a Cane* with the Nahmads but our request for a meeting remains unanswered as this book goes to press. Meanwhile, the New York lawyer who represented them and IAC in court stated in an interview that the question of who owns IAC was 'irrelevant'.

That, sadly, is true. Even if the claimant ultimately succeeds in asserting his claim against IAC, he still might not get his hands on the painting. Enforcing a US judgment against a Panama-based shell company can be hard work. One lawyer with whom we discussed the case at length concluded his assessment with the words: 'Have fun. . .'

[ ]

There are just a few days until our meeting in Washington and we have our flights already booked. We will be heading to Washington at 11.40am on a direct flight from Munich with United Airlines.

The flight could be a little tricky because we will be taking the data with us on the journey. We have more than a terabyte now, which means that we will have to encrypt a hard drive, set up a hidden area on it and upload the data.

We are familiar with that process but until now the hard drives have always been transported across the Atlantic by others. This time the hard drive will be in our luggage and knowing that is not likely to help us relax.

What if we are detained? David Miranda, the partner of Edward Snowden's confidant Glenn Greenwald, was detained by British police in Heathrow at the height of the NSA affair. Officials searched his luggage. 'They were threatening me all the time and saying I would be put in jail if I didn't cooperate', Miranda later said. He eventually revealed the passwords to his hard drives.

What if the same thing happens to us? What if the US authorities know about the data? Data the police, intelligence services, tax authorities and stock exchange supervisory authorities would surely be interested in. Data that may well reveal state scandals.

Would we be cool-headed enough to reveal only the external password to the US police? Without sweating, or stuttering, or indicating in some other way that there is more information on the hard drive?

In short: we are a little nervous.

9

A VIEW OF THE WHITE HOUSE

Landed safely in Washington.

It's time to take a deep breath and stay cool. Don't think about the data in the suitcase. Everything is fine, we tell ourselves. We're just two normal journalists from Germany. But we still feel uneasy as we walk towards the baggage claim area.

The worst thing that could happen is that a customs official is standing there with the hard drive from our luggage.

The good thing is that we *cannot* actually grant anyone access to the data. The password to the secret section of the hard drive is forty characters long and we deliberately did not bring it with us, not on the computer, not on our phones or hidden on our bodies. We only have the password for the section of the hard drive that we have packed with boring old folders for the bene-fit of US Customs. We will be sending the ICIJ the password for the secret hard drive by encrypted message once we return to Germany.

Unfortunately, we have a long wait before we even reach the US Customs and Border officials. The queue for the customs desk is enormous. The zig-zags of people waiting patiently go on and on endlessly. It's a miracle that people don't snap and go berserk on a regular basis here at Washington Airport. Low ceilings, thousands of passengers inching forward slowly, all sweaty and exhausted from their journeys, stressed adults and bawling kids wherever you turn. And at the end of the queue, an army of police and customs officers waiting to decide whether it was all in vain.

It must be hell for anyone who has even the slightest phobic tendency. And it is not ideal for anyone who fears they might be picked out by customs officers and questioned about the stolen data in their luggage.

We edge forward at an agonizingly slow pace. At a certain point we become separated by the queue, or more precisely by a customs officer who points us in different directions. We follow his directions. At the counter, we face some brusque officials, probing gazes and a professional nod. But no questions. We collect our luggage and that is it.

The data has arrived on US soil.

[ ]

It is late afternoon and we go straight to the ICIJ in the centre of Washington. The ICIJ offices are on 17th Street Northwest, not far from the White House. There, on the second floor, they have workstations for about ten journalists. We sit down to a meeting with ICIJ Director Gerard Ryle, his deputy Marina Walker and the head of data Mar Cabra to discuss the final details for the following day.

Marina smiles at us and asks: 'Are you two ready for your presentation tomorrow?'

We nod amiably.

We have not had long to work on our presentation. Marina only told us a week beforehand that we would be presenting the project ourselves. ICIJ staff had given the presentation at the preliminary meeting of the Luxembourg Tax Files project in Brussels, with a few contributions from Edouard Perrin, the first journalist to see the leaked data. There was also an expert present to explain the secret advance tax rulings of large corporations. The preliminary meeting of the HSBC Files project took a similar course, with ICIJ staff explaining what it was all about: the treasure trove of data leaked by whistle-blower Hervé Falciani at HSBC in Geneva. Our two *Le Monde* colleagues who lifted the veil on that story, Gérard Davet and Fabrice Lhomme, just sat at the table smiling and answering questions. But we are expected to give a presentation. In English. In Washington.

We were a little anxious when we put together the first PowerPoint slides in Munich. Marina Walker's email did nothing to alleviate that nervousness: 'Bastian and Frederik: Please prepare thoroughly for the presentation so that you both inspire and help the other journalists.'

Marina is great. She is the one who runs the show when it comes to these international collaborations and it is she who ensures that all the journalists involved know how important virtues such as punctuality, exactness and reliability are. And, as you see, Marina can be very direct.

But she is right. Some of our forty colleagues making the journey have only a vague idea of what's going on: a leak, secret offshore data, an intriguing initial scent. It is our job to get them excited.

We take Marina's email as the impetus to go through our presentation a third time on the plane. And then a fourth time. When we arrive at our hotel after the chat at the ICIJ, we go over it again.

[ ]

Shortly after 9am the following morning, after an overpriced breakfast and a sweat-inducing walk in the muggy 30°C heat, we are standing in the First Amendment Lounge on the thirteenth floor of the National Press Building in Washington DC, in a conference room with a view of the White House. Before us are colleagues from all over the globe: Spain, Italy, Britain, Argentina,

Costa Rica, the USA and many more countries. They include some of the world's best investigative journalists, such as James Ball from the *Guardian*, Jake Bernstein, and Uri Blau from Israel, whose stories have sparked national crises in the past.

They are all sitting around a long table listening to what we have to say.

Our plan in the First Amendment Lounge is to try to grab our audience's attention immediately by outlining the magnitude of the leak:

- The biggest leak ever, with 1.5 terabytes of data already on hand and the mountain growing steadily.
- An eerily up-to-date leak. The most recent emails are just a few days old.
- Detailed information concerning about a quarter of a million offshore companies.

We had asked a colleague from the layout department to design a graphic that put the various leaks into perspective: our 1.5 terabytes, Offshore Secrets' 260 gigabytes, and the WikiLeaks files, most of which were just a few gigabytes in size (but which were very influential nevertheless). When presented in that context, our haul really does look very impressive and the room quietens down immediately.

We have won over our audience and after a few minutes we have forgotten our nervousness. We talk and talk and talk. We talk about Putin's alleged best friend, about the Icelandic prime minister, about Bashar al-Assad's cousin, about the mysterious German and the $500 million in gold in the Bahamas account. As we talk, we can tell from our colleagues' faces that we won't have to work very hard to persuade anyone to get on board with Prometheus.

We basically talk non-stop from 9am until lunchtime. We explain the structure of the data, where the different information is to be found, what the best way to search is and what the problematic areas are.

In the afternoon we draw up a plan of action: when to publish, what specific topics to search for and which stories to tackle in groups. The great thing about this collaborative project is that we have expanded the expertise of our department at the *SZ* overnight. There is hardly anyone who knows more about FIFA than James Oliver; the Argentines know all the ins and outs of the Kirchner story; and our Icelandic colleague will be a much better judge of the Gunnlaugsson case than we could ever be. But we are even more delighted by our colleagues' reactions. We were already convinced of the importance of 'our' leak and that it called for international collaboration. But it is good to hear it from the mouth of a Pulitzer Prize-winner nevertheless. And to see that the BBC, the *Guardian* and *Le Monde* are equally excited and are putting teams on it then and there. TV colleagues from the French press agency Premières Lignes and US broadcaster Univision are there with cameras to film the conference and to interview us.

[ ]

The meeting in Washington changes the way we view our work. It is no longer our small project. It is now a mammoth project and we will have to take care not to sink under its weight. After all, we will be at the centre of a globally coordinated research project. Other publications may be set up to handle such assignments, or could at least quickly adjust, in terms of staff, equipment and costs. They say that the *Spiegel*, when it got its hands on WikiLeaks, drafted thirty members of staff to sift through the documents. Thirty people!

The *Süddeutsche Zeitung* is not prepared for that kind of project in any shape or form. How could it be? Our desk is currently staffed by four people – and those four are expected to contribute to day-to-day reporting.

We do not have an employee who is an expert on data journalism. There is no one on the team who is fluent in Spanish, although more than half the leaked documents are in that language. We do not really have a budget for additional staffing or for extensive upgrades to our technical equipment. All we have is the absolute trust of our head of department and the support of our Editors-in-Chief Wolfgang Krach and Kurt Kister. Wolfgang Krach was previously an investigative reporter at the *Spiegel* and he has never lost his passion for big research stories.

We head in a swarm of reporters from the National Press Building to the restaurant the ICIJ has booked for dinner. The route helps to further elevate the celebratory mood, leading as it does directly past the White House. From there we continue to Farragut Square and up Connecticut Avenue to the Dupont Circle – the area of Washington we know so well from TV series such as *House of Cards* and *The West Wing*.

After the meal we try various rare beers on the terrace of a pleasantly quiet restaurant. One after another, colleagues – investigative journalists to the core – take a seat next to us to learn a little more about the source. By now we are accustomed to the standard reaction to our answer when they ask whether we really have no idea who the source is.

Are they really anonymous?

We smile.

Yes, really.

We smile.

That is the truth.

[ ]

Our third day in Washington is a work day. The ICIJ machine is rolling, the course has been set. All that is left to do is to decide on the exact coordinates. Which are the most important cases? When should we break the story? Which subjects should we tackle together?

We sit in a small conference room surrounded by data journalism experts – what the ICIJ agenda called a 'Geeky data meeting'. Our colleagues are discussing the best way to filter, sort and browse the data using special programs. We sit on the sidelines smiling amiably.

The one thing we quickly grasp is that a large number of research paths are closed to us as long as we search the data using conventional approaches.

We need a real expert.

[ ]

Christophe Ayad, a French colleague, takes us to one side at this meeting. 'Look here,' he says, 'I've found Alaa Mubarak in the data, the son of former Egyptian president Hosni Mubarak.' We have found the next case involving a president. Ayad tells us that he discovered the name of the autocrat's son in the documents of a company called Pan World Investments Inc.

We pull up the relevant company folder from the data and click through the documents, year by year, document by document. Nothing unusual, simply a normal offshore business: a certificate of incorporation issued in the British Virgin Islands in 1993, fee invoices, the occasional change in nominee directors. That's all.

It seems as if it is still business as usual even in 2011, when Hosni Mubarak is deposed by the Egyptian people and his sons Alaa and Gamal are arrested. The sons are regarded by Egyptians as a prime example of a rapacious elite that enriches itself at the expense of the population at large, sucking the state dry in the process. They are put on trial. Shortly before our meeting in Washington they are convicted of embezzlement. And so, reality and data converge.

Alaa Mubarak, the now convicted despot's son, has been the ultimate beneficial owner (UBO) of Pan World for two decades. He retains that position despite the Arab Spring, his father's fall from power, his own trial and the negative headlines in the global media. Only in 2013, when the financial authorities in the British Virgin Islands request information about Pan World, does an interesting dialogue develop between Mossack Fonseca's compliance and legal departments. The authorities want information... missing information.

Alaa Mubarak's name should have triggered alarm bells. His company, Pan World Investments Inc., should have been classed as 'high risk' in an internal review. Instead, Mossfon still rated the shell company as 'low risk' in 2012 – one year after the events of the Arab Spring. Now the head of the legal department warns that they should under no circumstances admit this to the authorities. It would be an admission that 'our risk assessment formula is seriously flawed'.

After all, Alaa Mubarak is not just some politically exposed person (PEP), writes a colleague from Mossfon's compliance department. He is a sanctioned person, an international outlaw. The EU put the former Egyptian dictator's son on its sanctions list in 2011 'for misappropriation of state funds'.[1]

Surely such a circumstance would be noticed immediately by a company that assured us in February 2015 – in answer to a query relating to the Commerzbank raid – that it adhered strictly to the 'Know Your Customer' guidelines and that it not only carries out due diligence procedures for all new customers, but that it also makes 'periodic checks and updates on existing customers'.

Know your customer?

One Mossfon lawyer writes to her colleagues in August 2013: 'The truth is we did not identify the beneficial owner in the beginning (as we should have done).' Mossfon had the son of a dictator on its files and even had a copy of his passport – but apparently it had no idea who he was.[2]

In our Washington hotel we stumble upon a spreadsheet drawn up by a Mossfon employee. It is a list of all the Mossfon companies in the Seychelles, sorted according to whether Mossfon knows the beneficial owner or not. The result? Of the 14,086 companies, Mossfon knows who the real owner is in only 204 cases.

That is a sad commentary. And it shows how irresponsibly Mossack Fonseca skirts its responsibilities. These companies could be owned by any manner of criminal – murderers, mafiosi, dictators – and Mossfon is glad to be at their service.

10
SPARKS FLY

When we arrive back in Germany on 3 July 2015, our email inboxes are full and three-quarters of the messages share the same subject line: 'XY has posted a new entry on the forum. Click here to read it.' These emails are notifications sent from the encrypted forum set up by the ICIJ for the research work. The Washington meeting has clearly inspired our colleagues and the research results keep flowing in for days. In the meantime, Marina has recruited additional journalists for the project and they are all busy entering terms into the search engine that combs through our data. About seventy journalists are now on board.

The latest findings include a Uruguayan presidential candidate, an arms smuggler with links to the Iran–Contra affair,* a Peruvian intelligence chief, a Russian billionaire and a company embroiled in a murder conspiracy. All excellent stories.

We are still stunned by some of the discoveries. One of our American colleagues happens across Kojo Annan, son of the former UN secretary-general Kofi Annan. According to the

---

* The Iran–Contra affair was a political scandal during the Reagan administration in the United States, involving the illegal funding of Nicaraguan 'contra' guerrillas fighting the Sandinista government, using funds from the illegal sale of arms to Iran.

documents, Annan Junior owns two shell companies in the British Virgin Islands and a third in Samoa.

We read up about the case and see a guest article written by Kofi Annan for the *New York Times* in 2013. The title of the article was a plea: 'Stop the Plunder of Africa'. Annan's article is a scathing attack on those who are exploiting the African continent – an exploitation facilitated by anonymous shell companies and corporations that relocate their headquarters to tax havens. Annan cites Nigeria as an example.

Which is ironic.

Until at least 2015, the co-owner of one of Kojo Annan's companies in the British Virgin Islands was the son of a prominent former senator from Nigeria. We cannot tell from the data exactly why the company was established. When contacted by the ICIJ, an adviser of Kojo Annan's stated that he manages his companies 'in accordance with the laws and provisions of the relevant jurisdiction'. Any tax liabilities were paid in the relevant countries. The purpose of the companies was simply to manage 'family and business matters'.

A few years previously, Kojo Annan had been involved in some controversial business, namely the scandal surrounding the Iraqi Oil-for-Food Programme. Annan was working for a company that was awarded a multi-million-dollar contract to supervise the delivery of UN relief aid to Iraq (Kofi Annan was the secretary-general of the UN at the time). A British newspaper had already raised critical questions about this back in 1999. The payment methods used by the company to remunerate Kojo Annan had also been discussed at the time. A commission chaired by the former chairman of the Federal Reserve Paul Volcker later concluded that there was 'no evidence' that Annan Senior had profited financially. Neither did it find evidence that Kojo Annan had broken the law, although he had been uncooperative with the commission. Annan's adviser notes in a letter that it is clear from the report 'that the commission presents no evidence or findings of any kind whatsoever that Kojo Annan ever spoke with anyone in the UN or ever tried to influence anyone in the UN to award contracts to any company he was connected with'.

[ ]

We are fascinated by the way our data comes alive without us having to do anything at all. Ping – a new result. Often overnight, due to the time difference between us and the Americas. The data is now being fished twenty-four hours a day; at any given moment at least one of our colleagues is sitting at a laptop entering new names into the search mask in one time zone or other. We come back from lunch and someone has discovered another head of state or government. When our European colleagues are mining the data, we see the new results coming in live, hour by hour. A number of the findings are spectacular:

The president of the United Arab Emirates.

The former prime minister of Jordan.

The family of a former South American dictator.

The Palestinian deputy prime minister.

There is also a trail leading to Nawaz Sharif, the current prime minister of Pakistan. Sharif had also been prime minister on two separate occasions in the 1990s. In a critical report, the World Bank names two companies in the British Virgin Islands that Sharif is said to have used for questionable business deals: Nescoll and Nielson. Sharif is believed to have bought luxury homes through these companies, including in London. State funds transformed into a private villa in the blink of an eye. We find both companies in the data. The documents reveal that the owner, at least until 2012, was Mariam Safdar, née Sharif: Nawaz Sharif's daughter.[1]

We always try to read up on cases to get an understanding of what they are about, and to help us decide whether we can provide assistance or whether we should get involved. We know best the exact structure of the data as we have been working on it for months. We are often able to advise our colleagues on how to get more out of the files.

[ ]

At about this time, the end of June and the beginning of July, a large amount of rebuilding work is going on in our SZ Tower on the outskirts of Munich: walls are torn down and new ones erected, offices are merged and boundaries abolished. The project is called 'One *SZ*' and its objective is to finally merge the editorial teams of the print and online editions. Until now, there have been, in some cases, up to ten floors separating the two editorial teams. Now, however, the politics desk of the newspaper will be on the same floor as the politics desk of sz.de. As part of this restructuring, our department is being moved from the twenty-fifth floor to the twenty-fourth.

Neither of us two cares which floor we are on. At the moment we don't need to get in touch quickly with the newsroom or the special reports desk. As our head of department Hans Leyendecker says when he wants to annoy us: we don't even write any more in any case.

As part of this move, he arranges for us to get a room dedicated to the project. A 'war room'. Waist-high filing cabinets around the walls and wipeable magnetic boards hanging above them. The door, an all-glass one like every other door in the tower, is covered with plastic film. Access is limited to employees of our department and neither security nor cleaning staff are allowed in. Nor are our editors-in-chief.

It is exactly what we need. The project now has a concrete place in the real world. As a first official act, we hang a piece of paper with the project name on the wall: Prometheus. We then make a list on one of the whiteboards. A list of trails leading to current and former heads of state and government.

First the country, then the connection or position:

Pakistan, current prime minister.[2]

Iceland, current prime minister.[3]

Syria, cousin of the current dictator.[4]

The list comes to a dozen or more prominent figures. It motivates us every day and it helps us to retain some semblance of order over this madness.

The heads of state are just the high-profile part of our story. We have also discovered known CIA defence contractors, offshore companies that manage oil deals for the Iranian regime and very wealthy supporters of US presidential candidates.

It is not always clear whether Mossfon staff are fully aware of whose money it is they are taking. But their business model tacitly accepts that, with their help, whoever it is can conceal their tracks.

Members of the Sicilian mafia? In the data. Associates of the Russian mafia? In the data. Supporters of the Mexican Sinaloa drug cartel? Intelligence officers? In the data. Gambling fraudsters? White-collar criminals? Bank robbers? All in the data.

This would all be great, if only we didn't have a tiny little problem. We can't actually search the data ourselves. At this time, the middle of July, our colleagues across the world have access to a few hundred gigabytes of the material. That is sufficient to make some great discoveries but by now we have 1.7 terabytes of data here. And our technical equipment is struggling.

Nuix, the program given to us by the ICIJ to analyse the data, takes up a lot of memory. It is normally used by clients who have very powerful computers, from large corporate law firms to global news services. Companies where money is no object. We have a €1,500 laptop, which is rather sumptuous for journalistic purposes.

But our laptop is overwhelmed by the indexing and text recognition work on the 1.7 terabytes of data. Rather than a display counting down how many documents remain to be processed, all we see is a rotating circle indicating that the computer has come to a stop. Nothing is happening.

The laptop freezes repeatedly.

What a nightmare.

We head to the main editorial office and explain that we need a new computer. Again. We need more memory, more processing power, more terabytes. More more more. We gather opinions and advice from the ICIJ data team, the Nuix experts and other specialists in the field.

Of course, we could simply rely on the help offered by the ICIJ. Its data team could index everything we receive, run it through the data recognition software and put everything in order. But we want to be able to work with this data in two years' time, here in the office. We are going to have to manage by ourselves.

In the end, we choose a computer with 64 gigabytes of main memory. As a point of comparison, a normal laptop has 4 gigabytes, or 8 if it's a good one. We also order four hard drives, one of which is an SSD. We don't know much about technology but we have picked up a few things. The SSD abbreviation means that the hard drive is faster than a normal one.

We have to assure colleagues from IT and purchasing several times that there was no typo, we really did intend to order the 'mega workstation' – a computer that is used in the office as a server but not for writing articles.

The editors want the computer so it is pushed through. Computer number two.

Until the supercomputer arrives we are left sitting in front of a mountain of data we cannot sensibly search through. And there are so many trails we would like to be following. Old trails such as the $500 million Siemens man and Putin's best friend, the cellist. And new names are appearing every day.

[ ]

Jake Bernstein is on a roll. He has already tracked down half the Middle East in the data, including the prime minister of Qatar.

Now he has found Ayad Allawi, who was the Iraqi vice president from 2014 until 2015.

'Every time you post something in the forum, it's another head of state,' comments ICIJ Deputy Director Marina Walker dryly on the forum.

Jake finds Allawi's name in documents relating to two companies in the British Virgin Islands and two further companies based in Panama, which have since been dissolved. He even finds a copy of Allawi's passport.

Allawi is the son of a wealthy Shiite family of merchants. Originally a member of Saddam Hussein's Ba'ath party, he left Iraq in the 1970s. He was involved in the exile opposition movement, allegedly worked with the CIA, and attracted attention even before Saddam Hussein's fall by hiring prominent PR advisers and seeking to establish contact with influential politicians and journalists in the USA and the United Kingdom. Money doesn't seem to have been an issue for Allawi.

There is one vexing aspect to the case. One of his shell companies, which has since been dissolved, was owned by him and by the children of a former Lebanese prime minister. It is a peculiar team, even for the Middle East: the former Iraqi vice president and the children of a former Lebanese prime minister in joint ownership of a shell company. Allawi had even been interim prime minister of Iraq for a few months when the company was founded in 2005.[5]

This discovery gives us a sense of déjà vu. After all, we have already discovered current and former heads of state from Jordan, Kuwait, Palestine, Pakistan and Qatar in the data.

It is remarkable how many Arab heads of state move their money abroad – every single one of them, more or less. Over the course of our HSBC Files investigation, we discovered Swiss bank accounts owned by two kings, a former Egyptian trade minister and the brother-in-law of Tunisia's former dictator, Ben Ali.

Now, with our data, we are again finding it hard to keep track of the countless emirs, dictators, princes and sheikhs. A number of these govern in countries that display stark levels of inequality. They enjoy unimaginable luxury while at least part of the population is living a hand-to-mouth existence. A number of African and Middle Eastern countries are being sucked well and truly dry by their corrupt elite.

Dozens of foreign accounts and shell companies owned by Arab autocrats were discovered during the Arab Spring but that was only a fraction of the total in existence. The Libyan government is still searching for Muammar Gaddafi's secret millions. It is a bitter realization for the people: even if they succeed in overthrowing a corrupt leader, it is highly unlikely that they will ever retrieve the state funds he has squirrelled away abroad.

Why is it so easy for dictators and their families to hide their amassed wealth? Because they can use this system of anonymous companies. Or to put it another way: because people like Jürgen Mossack and Ramón Fonseca help them to cover their tracks.

The World Bank and the United Nations highlighted the issue in a comprehensive report in 2011. Their analysts investigated 213 cases of corruption that went to court across the globe. No fewer than 150 of these cases involved at least one shell company that helped to conceal the identity of the beneficial owner of the assets. The cases involved a total of $56.4 billion.

[ ]

'Ping' – the next big name.

Deng Jiagui. The name will not mean much to readers in the Western hemisphere but Deng Jiagui is the brother-in-law of the Chinese president Xi Jinping. Very close relatives. According to the data, Deng Jiagui owned two offshore companies between 2009 and 2011: Wealth Ming International Ltd and Best Effect

Enterprises Ltd, both based in the British Virgin Islands.[6] That is controversial because of all people, his brother-in-law, the Chinese president, announced a few years earlier that he would crack down on greed and corruption. Both in the lower ranks, the 'flies', and in the upper echelons, the 'tigers'.

Back in 2004 he called on China's politicians to 'rein in your spouses, children, relatives, friends and staff!'

Perhaps he should have had a word with his brother-in-law.

The case is also interesting because there have been so many revelations concerning Chinese politicians using relatives as beneficiaries when they have wanted to hide away the wealth they have accumulated.

We come across other princelings, as the close relatives of the powerful Chinese elite are called. They have often been the subject of negative headlines in recent years, involving stories about Ferraris, wild parties, arrogant behaviour, drunken accidents and rapes. The most prominent case among them involves the daughter of former premier Li Peng, who is known as the 'Butcher of Beijing' because he was the one who sent in the tanks to crush the protest in Tiananmen Square in 1989. According to the documents, Li Peng's daughter Li Xiaolin and her husband established the Cofic Investment Ltd company in the British Virgin Islands through a Geneva law firm in 1994.[7]

The Chinese president's brother-in-law and the daughter of the former premier – two more trails to current and former heads of state and government, two more names for our list in the 'war room'.

[john doe]: I'm thinking about making contingency plans if I have to travel suddenly . . . Anywhere in particular you think I should avoid?
[SZ]: China maybe. The brother in law of the current prime minister and the daughter of a former prime minister are in.

[john doe]: Really? Wow – didn't know about those. Well I wasn't planning to show up in China anyway.

[SZ]: At least.

[john doe]: At least I won't be stranded at the Moscow airport like Snowden. Visiting Russia right now would be a very bad idea, as things currently stand.

'Ping'.

A post by our colleague from *Le Monde*. He has discovered a five-page list in the data that was compiled by and emailed to Mossack Fonseca staff members in 2010. A list that reveals the real owners of dozens of companies. A list full of Russian names.

But these are not just any old names.

The list includes a close relative of a very well-known Russian oligarch.

It includes the son of Sergey Chemezov, who runs the Russian defence company Rostec and who knows Vladimir Putin from their KGB days in Dresden – he has been on the US sanctions list since 2014.[8]

And there is more to come: two brothers, Boris and Arkady Rotenberg, who are among Vladimir Putin's closest associates, and are probably two of the Russian president's most important business partners. They too are on the sanctions list.[9]

These names will keep us busy for weeks. During the Washington conference we established a special working group that would focus on Russia. This group includes journalists from the BBC, the *Guardian*, the Swiss *SonntagsZeitung* and the Organized Crime and Corruption Reporting Project (OCCRP), whose team includes Russian colleagues, some of whom are still reporting from inside Russia. We will be subjecting these sensational names to further scrutiny as part of this team.

It is clear that the Russia story is going to be huge.

11

FEAR AND TREPIDATION

[john doe]: One more thing: I'm going to need a warning or some kind of message a few weeks before all this is all published.

[SZ]: No problem

[john doe]: Just before publication I may want to tell my family about it. I haven't decided yet, it might actually increase the risk involved. And I also will be telling a few people I trust just in case something happens to me or one of them.

[SZ]: This could put those people at risk.

[john doe]: I know. They are at risk anyway, in a sense. I will not tell them everything — just as much as they need to know, and most importantly, how to reach Süddeutsche Zeitung in a worst-case scenario. But if something happens to me or I disappear, I want there to be at least one person who actually understands why.

[SZ]: Okay.

[john doe]: When is publication planned for?

[SZ]: Spring. We don't make November, it's all too much.

[John Doe]: Spring?!? Who knows if we'll all still be alive by then. . .

[SZ]: We will. We will.

[john doe]: Are not you afraid? You are supplying ammunition that will be used against very powerful people. Your name will be on the byline and all over the papers. Not mine. (Hopefully.)

We are asked this question increasingly by colleagues who are in on the story. Aren't we afraid?

As long as we don't think about it, no, we are not. But when we do think about it? Yes, somehow we are.

Maybe not fear exactly. It is more a sense of unease that we have not felt while researching previous stories. Why would you be afraid when investigating – as we have – the General German Automobile Club (ADAC), a scandal-plagued Bavarian egg producer, the Catholic Church, or even German arms companies? Germany is a very civilized country when it comes to offering resistance against the press, at least as long as you are not writing a story on neo-Nazis or Salafist groups who are prepared to resort to violence. Investigations against journalists – such as the case of the Netzpolitik.org blog – are very rare, and journalists are not normally arrested, beaten, kidnapped or killed.

This project, however, goes well beyond anything we have ever worked on by a factor of ten. Or fifteen, even. In any case, one of the reasons we like the international cooperation so much is the security it offers us. By this point, more than 100 journalists have access to our data. There would not be much point in bumping us off, we of all people, because it would not do anything to stop the coverage. Quite the contrary – it would only attract even more attention to the story.

Having said that, we are the ones making the data available to the ICIJ and, through it, to dozens of media institutions across the globe. If someone wanted to make an example of journalists in an attempt to stop the growth of such collaborative projects between trouble-some reporters, we would be a reasonably good place to start.

Unfortunately, we have found plenty of shady figures in the data who presumably wouldn't lose any sleep if they sent round a gang of thugs to deliver us a message.

[ ]

By now, we have discovered three companies linked to Sergei Roldugin, the cellist and Vladimir Putin's friend. In addition to International Media Overseas, which we came across in the early days of our research, we have now discovered two companies called Sonnette Overseas Inc. and Raytar Ltd. All three companies are registered under the name of the man who claimed in a 2014 interview that he was not a businessman, let alone a millionaire. So we are curious to find out who owns it all.

These companies are part of a complex network of shell companies in which other figures from Putin's circle, as well as a number of less well-known bankers and businessmen – almost all of whom are from St Petersburg, the city in which Putin began his ascent – are involved.

The Mossack Fonseca documents concerning these offshore companies expose deals involving shares in several big Russian companies. Large sums of money change hands. Unbelievably large sums.

Many experts, mainly Western ones, believe that the Russian president, whose declared income in 2014 was 7.65 million rubles ($119,000), holds stakes in important major companies through nominees. The Russian analyst Stanislav Belkovsky estimated Putin's wealth at more than $40 billion back in 2007, although he was unable to prove it. Several similar estimates of Putin's wealth are making the rounds. They only differ over whether Putin is worth $10 billion, $40 billion or $200 billion USD.

Is Putin behind these companies? It would make sense.

Our international Russia task force, made up of a handful of reporters, is working its way contract by contract and company by company through the convoluted network of businesses linked to the cellist. The group exchanges research results on a weekly basis and will have an opportunity to discuss their discoveries face to face in a few weeks when all project partners meet in Munich. We are already coming across some peculiar documents: backdated contracts, loans that will probably never be repaid, mysterious transfers. We add together all the money we see flowing through the accounts of the companies in the Roldugin network and arrive at a total of more than half a billion US dollars. And we are not even finished with the research yet.

It is possible to imagine all kinds of things going on in Russia since the fall of the Soviet Union. But that a cellist such as Roldugin is running operations worth hundreds of millions of dollars? Unlikely.

There must be people behind him who are far more powerful.

This takes us back to the question of fear.

When the Russian edition of *Forbes* magazine first published a list of the 100 richest Russians (several of whom we find in our data) in 2004, the magazine's chief editor was shot dead outside the *Forbes* offices just a few weeks later. The Russian journalist Anna Politkovskaya, who made her name reporting on Russia's war in Chechnya, was murdered in the stairwell of her Moscow apartment building in 2006. Those who ordered the killing were never caught. But every Russian knows the date the crime was committed: 7 October 2006, the date of Vladimir Putin's fifty-fourth birthday.

There it is again, that vague sense of unease. But what about Roman Anin and Roman Shleynov, our Russian colleagues who have now been on the ICIJ team for a few weeks? Roman Anin started as a sports reporter with the *Novaya Gazeta* newspaper, which is well known for its critical stance towards the Russian government. Within a few years he had made a name for himself as one of Russia's toughest investigative reporters, having probed and exposed corruption and cronyism in the military, in politics and in business. Anin published the construction contracts for the Winter Olympics in Sochi – contracts that were lucrative for many of Putin's acolytes. He knows that he is in danger and that there are no guarantees.

At least four of his colleagues at the *Novaya Gazeta* have been murdered since 2000.

Anin now works for the OCCRP network and other media. Most recently, he has been working on 'Comrade Capitalism', a series on Russia's corrupt elite, for the Reuters news agency. The other journalist is Roman Shleynov, who is working as an investigative journalist at the *Vedomosti* daily newspaper, a joint project by the *Wall Street Journal*, the *Financial Times* and a Russian publisher. Shleynov is also a member of the OCCRP. Over the last few years he has reported widely on the scandals that have accompanied Putin's rise to power.

Our two Russian colleagues cannot access our multi-encrypted forum because you would need a smartphone, among other things, to do so. A piece of smartphone software is part of the complex encryption system. Roman Anin and Roman Shleynov do not use smartphones for security reasons – Anin has discovered spyware on his phone in the past. We only exchange research results with them via encrypted emails. Safety first.

[ ]

We too force ourselves to maintain discipline regarding our data and devices. All hard drives are encrypted as a matter of course and all external hard drives are stored in a safe. Some of the hard drives are kept in the editorial office and the others in a secure location elsewhere. We have special security measures in place in our project office. The new computer is even given its own lockable housing, which, in turn, is chained down so that you cannot simply walk off with the whole unit. We also paint all the housing screws with glitter nail polish.

That's right: glitter nail polish. Our children would be envious, if they knew. A security expert advised us to do this because we would see it immediately if someone tampered with the housing. Single-colour nail polish can easily be painted over. But you would quickly notice if they tried that with glitter nail polish.

However, these measures can only keep the data safe. Glitter nail polish won't be much help if someone decides to pay us a visit.

But what steps should we take? We do not feel the danger is so acute that we should be wearing bulletproof vests. But we do suggest to colleagues working with us on Prometheus that they should at least block public access to their address at the registration office. In Germany, you can simply walk into a registration office, pass yourself off as a journalist and ask for an address – and you will usually get it.

We know this from experience because we once discovered the name and a photo of one of us on a neo-Nazi website, a kind of 'wanted poster'. Feel free to pay Obermaier a visit, it said. Since then, the name is no longer on the doorbell nameplate and the authorities have blocked the address for all external enquires. This is the standard approach from now on.

But just to reiterate: we live in Germany, a paradise for most investigative journalists. For our ICIJ colleagues in Africa, the Middle East, Eastern Europe and Latin America, the results of this research will be far more dangerous. And the threat omnipresent. An Egyptian colleague received a call from the intelligence services around the time the HSBC Files story was published in February 2015. Woe betide you, warned the voice at the other end of the line, if you report on the following stories. A list was read out. The colleague had understood the message… and he heeded the warning. We would have too – we're not crazy.

That story, as we understood it, concerned a certain Middle Eastern royal family. This time the data includes almost every ruling dynasty in the Middle East, along with African despots, Eastern European oligarchs, Latin American rulers, members of international mafia networks and a host of other criminals. Some members of the ever-expanding Prometheus team will not be able to report freely – or if they do, they will face serious problems.

[ ]

Khadija Ismayilova cannot even take part in the research – she is behind bars in an Azerbaijani prison. We worked with Khadija on Offshore Secrets in 2013; she investigated offshore holdings owned by relatives of the Azerbaijani president Ilham Aliyev. At the time, Khadija worked for Radio Free Europe, which has since ceased broadcasting, and the OCCRP, which has members from Southern Europe, the Caucasus and Central Asia. They do what local media no longer dares for fear of reprisals or economic pressure: investigate, expose and publish explosive stories.

According to Khadija's Offshore Secrets investigation, several relatives of the Azerbaijani president had holdings in shell companies. It appears that his two daughters, Arzu and Leyla, established three offshore companies in the British Virgin Islands in 2008. What's more, the data revealed that the president and his wife Mehriban – who is a member of parliament – also set up their own offshore company in 2003: Rosamund International Ltd.

Exposing financial affairs of this kind is a hazardous business in Azerbaijan. In 2016 Azerbaijan ranked 163 out of 180 in Reporters Without Borders' Press Freedom Index.

Despite being threatened several times, Khadija Ismayilova was undeterred. In 2013 she was arrested and detained briefly. When she returned from a journey to Europe in 2014 she was held for several hours by customs officials at Baku airport. The authorities demanded to see the content of her USB stick. Since they had no legal grounds for making their demand, she refused and called the police. She later reported that the USB stick was actually empty – for Khadija it was a matter of principle.

She was arrested again in December 2014. One of the charges: inciting her ex-boyfriend to suicide. An absurd accusation, say observers, friends, colleagues. 'Khadija Ismayilova is an inconvenient messenger, and her arrest fits squarely among the Azerbaijani government's concerted efforts to silence dissenting voices,' declared Human Rights Watch. 'This step is the last link in endless attempts to silence the free media in Azerbaijan – Khadija Ismayilova is one of the last independent voices in the country,' says Amnesty International.

In summer 2015 she was sentenced in Baku to prison for seven and a half years. A few minutes after the judgment, the OCCRP posted this on its website: 'Today, the Azerbaijani government sentenced Khadija Ismayilova to seven years and six months in prison. They think this will stop us from reporting. They are wrong.'

And indeed, Miranda Patrucic, who works with Khadija at the OCCRP, discovers the family of Azerbaijani president Ilham Aliyev in our data. Khadija Ismayilova's reports were correct. Not that we ever doubted her. But the documents we now have before us show that she had only scratched the surface.

Our data shows that Aliyev's wife and – no small irony – the Azerbaijani minister for taxation had a stake in the country's biggest corporate conglomerate, Ata Holding, via a Panamanian trust. The group includes banks, technology companies, travel agencies and insurance companies. In fact, there is hardly an industry in which the conglomerate is not involved. According to the documents, the group's profits were diverted, at least for a certain period of time, via a complicated network of British and Panamanian companies and trusts, with a part of it eventually ending up in accounts owned by Aliyev's son and two daughters.[1]

Our OCCRP colleagues also come across two hitherto unknown companies owned by Aliyev's daughters. The companies are called Kingsview Developments Ltd and Exaltation Ltd. According to the documents, the latter was established in January 2015 to conceal a British property valued at more than $1 million.

12

THE SIEMENS MILLIONS

While we attempt to follow all the trails leading to the various heads of state and keep up to date with developments on the forum, we are still hunting Hans-Joachim K., the German former Siemens employee, to whose Bahamas account $500 million in gold was apparently transferred in November 2013. We have spent so much time searching online for him and the missing piece of the puzzle, and we have had photos of the slim figure with sparse hair and glasses in front of us for so long, we have started to feel that we actually know him. He was CEO of Siemens in the Andes region at the turn of the millennium, and CEO of Siemens Mexico from 2003 to 2009. No small fish, by any means. We also know that he now works as an independent consultant – we have seen video footage of his public appearances, we have gathered personal information about him. But something is missing.

We go through all the money transfers to and from his account at the Bahamian branch of Société Générale. We have clearly overlooked something. Then we see it. Next to the confirmation of an incoming transfer of about $50,000 in the spring of 2013, there is a note saying 'Transfer from Gillard Management'. A new lead.

We find a company called Gillard Management in our data and the man who requested its incorporation at Mossack Fonseca in the summer of 2007 is indeed Hans-Joachim K. But his is not the only name in the company's digital folder – there are also three other former Siemens employees here, some of them very senior figures: a former managing director of Siemens' Mexican subsidiary, a former Siemens employee now resident in Ecuador, and a former commercial director at Siemens Colombia. All three have, like K., managed slush funds in Latin America, as court documents on the Siemens Affair reveal.

Four of the Siemens employees involved in the slush fund scandal appearing in a single offshore company?

We need more background material. We saw in the indictment against former Siemens boss Uriel Sharef that proceedings were also brought against K. We get hold of the files and work our way through hundreds of pages. They describe how a whole team of Siemens managers in Latin America siphoned millions of euros from the company's official channels and managed these funds in parallel with the legitimate accounts – common practice until about ten years ago, it seems. This money was used as a slush fund that could be freely dipped into at the managers' discretion – for example, to pay 'advisers' who would then forward the money to others.

Three of the four men we now find in the data admit when interviewed – mainly in ambiguous terms but sometimes more specifically – that they transferred Siemens money back and forth from one offshore company to the next via accounts at a number of banks. Several million euros were deposited for a period of time with Casa Grande Development, a company we discovered months ago – a slush fund for Siemens in Colombia, Ecuador, Venezuela and Peru. As the CEO of the Andes region from 2001 to 2003, K. was responsible for Siemens activities in these four countries. Our documents now show not only how these secret accounts were restructured with Mossack Fonseca's help, but also how approximately $32 million was transferred back to Siemens via Mossfon's trust department after the Siemens Affair came to light.

Well now. That Siemens set aside hidden accounts expressly for bribes is not news. But it is strange that we find practically nothing on Gillard Management in the investigation files on K.'s case.

Why was the company still active years after the Siemens Affair was exposed? Where does the money come from? What is it being used for?

The story of Gillard Management begins on 28 August 2007. A Mossfon employee notes that a colleague 'met with Señor K. (one of his long-time clients)' in Panama on that day, and that they agreed to set up an offshore company whose bank account would be managed by Mossack Fonseca. The money would be sent 'possibly from Luxembourg, Germany or Switzerland' – they were expecting about $2.2 million.

The secrecy surrounding Gillard Management is impressive. By this point, after a few months working with the data, we must have examined hundreds of companies. But we have not come across such a clandestine spectacle as this. The Siemens people only very rarely sign their emails and Mossack Fonseca staff members use abbreviations almost without exception. Hans-Joachim K. is 'Señor K.', his Siemens colleagues operate under the names 'L.L.' and 'Mr P.'. Furthermore, Mossfon instructs its staff members not to send any documents to Hans-Joachim K. – everything must 'stay here within the company until we are given new instructions'.[1]

'Señor K.' is thereby adhering to the golden rule of shady business deals: leave nothing in writing.

In addition, an anonymous and encrypted email account is to be set up for K. 'to facilitate communication with us'. This is done through a company that presents itself to the world via its website as a normal import–export company. In reality it is owned by Mossack Fonseca. In Gillard Management's digital folders we see two anonymous email accounts from which messages are sent. One is under the codename 'Azkaban', the other under 'Bruni'. Azkaban is the name of the prison for convicted magicians in the magical world of Harry Potter. Bruni is, as we discover when wading through the investigation files, the first name of Hans-Joachim K.'s mother.[2]

An anonymous email account?

We find the explanation in an internal Mossfon memo. The clients are keen to handle this business with 'the highest possible degree of confidentiality'.

The money is to be transferred to the newly founded company. And to ensure that there are no trails, it appears they do all this indirectly, via a trust deed with Mossack Fonseca.

However, Gillard Management needs an account and for that the company needs a 'beneficial owner'. The Siemens employees nominate their retired colleague from Ecuador, normally known at Mossfon as L.L. An account is to be opened at the Swiss branch of Berenberg, a Hamburg-based private bank with whom Mossack Fonseca has had positive experiences over many years. However, Mossfon needs to present Berenberg with a character reference of sorts for L.L.

This task is undertaken by a German Mossack Fonseca employee, the managing partner in the department of wealth management, Mossfon Asset Management S.A. (MAMSA). He drafts a letter in which he claims that 'the credit to be deposited' is L.L.'s 'life savings and inheritances from his parents'.

How extraordinary. This same Mossack Fonseca employee had been told clearly in one of the first emails regarding the incorporation of Gillard Management that the money transferred to the account was coming from another source. And if the account really was for 'life savings and inheritances from his parents', why was the money in this account later transferred to Siemens?

This business construct also appears to have been regarded as unusual internally at Mossack Fonseca at the time. A senior member of staff talks about 'delicate transactions' and warns that

Mossfon is exposed to 'significant risk' through this company. He does not, however, ask that the client be refused – merely that they demand higher fees. In the end, they decide to refer the decision over this new client – 'Mr L.L.' – to the firm's partners. This is by no means standard practice. The management team must decide, and that it does. Jürgen Mossack approves the new client in a one-line email.[3]

Once the company has been established, the Siemens colleagues – as we see from the data – pour millions into their account at the Berenberg Bank. They even open two additional accounts, one at Société Générale Singapore, the other at the Panama-based Financial Pacific. They have their reasons for doing this. At a meeting in a shopping centre in Panama City in February 2008, K. and L.L. explain to their Mossfon contact that they are worried about the Swiss account. Another Swiss account held by them has just been frozen by the authorities over suspicions of money laundering.[4]

By this time the public prosecution investigation into the Siemens Affair, launched at the end of 2006, is already well under way and Hans-Joachim K. is gradually coming under increasing pressure. The investigators have long discovered that Siemens Latin America was using slush funds – K. had held management positions in this region almost continuously since 1996. He decides to come forward to the authorities of his own volition. At 1pm on Tuesday, 10 June 2008, Hans-Joachim K., accompanied by his lawyer, turns up at Munich's department of public prosecution. He talks to the investigators for almost three hours.

On the same day, just a few hours after the interview, K.'s German Mossfon contact, noticeably disappointed, writes a circular email. He has received 'some bad news from Mr K. today' and he explains that the Siemens money would now be returned to Germany after all. This means that 'we'll be losing this money and losing Gillard as a client'.

Interesting to note that the news is clearly *not* that Mossack Fonseca has helped to conceal millions of dollars of illicit Siemens funds.

The news, rather, is that the opportunity to return this money has come up and that Mossfon will lose that business as a result.

K. and his Mossack Fonseca adviser decide that K. should come to Panama as soon as possible to discuss over lunch at the Hotel Bristol how to proceed. They come up with a plan. First, all three Gillard Management bank accounts are to be closed. Then, the money is to be transferred to Siemens via Mossfon's trust department, and Gillard Management dissolved.[5]

That sounds commendable, and Hans-Joachim K., in his statement at the Munich public prosecution department, evidently comes across as being trustworthy. In 2012 the Munich prosecutors close the embezzlement case (Section 153a of the Code of Criminal Procedure [StPO]) against him, in return for a payment of €40,000. The case is closed despite the severity of the crime. K., like almost all his Siemens colleagues, had always stuck to the story that they had given away millions to 'advisers' to foster business. Did these 'advisers' then bribe politicians and other decision-makers? K. claims he does 'not believe that this money would have been "shared" with contracting authorities'.

K. also repeatedly emphasizes that he had always made attempts to return the illicit money to Siemens. Hans-Joachim K. had indeed contacted Siemens' compliance department in late 2006, reported the slush funds, and asked how he could integrate these into the regular accounting system. Shortly before that, in November 2006, there had been large-scale raids at Siemens.

In July 2010 Hans-Joachim K. receives an official certificate from Siemens declaring that 'all monies managed by Mr Hans K. and declared by him recently as part of the internal and public prosecution investigations have been transferred to Siemens AG accounts'.

The only question is: how could Siemens possibly know how much money had really been squirrelled away in slush funds? In police interviews, the balances of individual accounts vary between $35 million and $55 million depending on who is being interviewed at the time. The public prosecutor makes no secret of the fact that it can neither say where all the Siemens millions that ended up in the slush funds came from, nor whether all that money really found its way back to Siemens after the scandal was exposed. When questioned, K. emphasizes that he 'never pocketed any of the money'. The public prosecutor – for lack of evidence to the contrary – follows his version of events and decides in favour of the accused that he has facilitated 'a full and complete repayment'.

We review this assessment using our documents.

As part of the repayment, about $4.1 million is returned from Gillard Management's main account at the Panamanian bank Financial Pacific, which is mentioned in K.'s interrogation records in the Bavarian State Office of Criminal Investigation file, to regular Siemens accounts. The payment reason stated is ambiguous: debts from 'past business transactions' between Gillard Management and Siemens. But the account is not empty as a result; it still has a balance of about $2 million. This money later finds its way to a new Gillard Management account at Andbank, a private bank in the microstate of Andorra.

Only in 2012, when the investigation against him has been closed, does Hans-Joachim K. have Mossack Fonseca share out the money. By that point he is working as an independent consultant and has not been a Siemens employee for three years. The lion's share – a little more than $2 million – is transferred to a numbered account at UBS in Zurich. A UBS banker is named as the recipient. In the summer of 2010 this man was, according to the investigation files, one of K.'s 'client advisers' at the bank when K. had UBS transfer about €40 million from other secret Siemens accounts back to Siemens.

The $2 million was almost never transferred to the numbered UBS account. Mossack Fonseca's compliance department raised objections for several days. It did not have sufficient information regarding the recipient, let alone a copy of his passport, which was an internal requirement. International anti-money laundering guidelines specify special precautionary measures where suspiciously large sums are involved. But K.'s designated adviser within the company dismisses all these concerns.

According to our documents, the law firm's management team is informed by email of the transaction and approves it. Despite that, a Mossfon employee asks once more what the money is actually for. A little later, K.'s adviser contacts Mossfon and says he has spoken to his client but the latter has 'no idea... what the recipient is doing with the transfer'. The money may be used 'to open a new account' or it 'may be distributed'.

What is astonishing from the vantage point of the present is that there is no mention of the money being returned to Siemens. And somehow the transfer still takes place even though Mossfon clearly has very little information about the recipient. The $2 million is sent to Zurich and Mossack Fonseca makes a commission of about $75,000.

We enquire at UBS whether the bank was aware of these transactions, whether the account was really held by the UBS employee, and whether this matter had been investigated internally. Not surprisingly, we are told that the bank 'cannot comment on individual customers or transactions for legal and regulatory reasons'. UBS could neither confirm nor deny that the account was owned by the client adviser.

We also reach the client adviser, who has since left the bank. He tells us amiably but firmly that he cannot comment on the matter other than that he never profited personally from the Siemens money.

That stands to reason. Why would a banker allow suspicious

funds to be transferred to an account at his bank of all places? But if the banker did not receive the money, who did?

Siemens? We can all but rule that out. By 2012, the process of returning the money had long been completed according to Siemens and K. When we ask, Siemens explicitly confirms that the only slush fund money returned to the company after 2010 came from frozen accounts in Switzerland. Gillard Management's accounts were not based in Switzerland and they were never frozen.

We are still not getting anywhere.

But we do discover something of significance. After the bulk of the money is gone from the peculiar numbered UBS account, $70,000 still remains. K. sends instructions by email to have $20,000 transferred to his former Siemens colleague L.L.[6] The Mossack Fonseca adviser notes, as if with a conspiratorial wink, that the 'bank has already been informed' that the other $50,000 is being 'paid into a friend's account'.[7]

This 'friend' is Hans-Joachim K. himself. This is the transaction that drew our attention to Gillard Management in the first place, the 'Transfer from Gillard Management' in the spring of 2013.

When interviewed by the public prosecutor in Munich a few years previously, K. claimed that he never 'personally took money from the accounts'.

We finally get hold of Hans-Joachim K. on the phone. He explicitly states that he knows nothing about Gillard Management – even though he told the public prosecutor the number of one of the Gillard bank accounts. Neither does he know anything about these money transfers. However, he claims that his email account was hacked in 2014 and that we have been taken in by false information. K. even emails us the case reference number and a check reveals that it is genuine. However, the case was never solved. More importantly, the transactions we see in the documents were carried out well before 2014 and K.'s emails come from several email accounts.

K. deflects most of our questions by referring to the hacked email account he had reported. When we finally confront him regarding his contact at Mossfon and his suspected accomplice, K. ends the conversation. We receive no answer to our email outlining in detail our suspicions that he distributed money from the Siemens fund among dubious recipients.

But the Gillard Management account is not the only account that still had money in it. Casa Grande Development, the company named in the court files, also had substantial funds at its disposal. A large proportion of the $32 million that was returned to Siemens via Mossfon came from Casa Grande. There was still about $750,000 in the account even after 'full' repayment had been made.

One of K.'s former Siemens colleagues – called 'RPS' internally at Mossfon – appears to have been after this money. 'RPS' is surprisingly open with his German Mossfon agent regarding all this. He writes telling him that his 'old comrades' had left him with a 'financial deficit' of more than half a million dollars and that they 'refused to acknowledge a single penny of it'. 'I need cash urgently.'

He arranges for $420,000 to be transferred and asks them to state 'Property tax' as the reference. The invoice, however, states 'Consultancy and administration services' as the reference. How strange. Especially as he then 'borrows' another $100,000 – we can see no repayment to Casa Grande in our documents. There follows a request for $45,000, which he needs because of 'over-indebtedness', and which should carry the reference 'Transfer duty'. Then a further transfer of $40,000 to 'offset cash deficit'. And so it continues.[8]

In total, we see about $2.8 million transferred from former Siemens slush fund accounts long after the repayments are allegedly complete.

In March 2013 K.'s $50,000 is transferred to the Société Générale account in the Bahamas – the same account in which, according to our documents, $484 million in gold appears in November 2013. The account remains active afterwards and we see regular inflows and outflows of high sums.

In one of the last data packages our source sends us, we find a statement by Mossfon wealth management for Hans-Joachim K. According to this document, dated late 2014, the sum of almost $500 million in gold is no longer in the account. The transaction remains a mystery.

Was it a typo? Did a Mossfon employee click on the wrong currency by mistake? Was it an erroneous transfer? Or has K. long transferred the money to another account himself?

When we ask him about this $500 million, Hans-Joachim K. initially explains to us by email that he 'has never experienced such an absurd situation'. He does not say whether the account is owned by him. He later confirms on the phone that this is indeed his account and he also confirms other payments into the account that are listed in the same document. But he insists that no astronomical sums of that kind have ever been transferred into the Bahamas account and he goes on to explain again that he has been hacked and that our information has been falsified. We ask him for the account statements covering the period in question and Hans-Joachim K. says he will have his bank issue a summary. We are still waiting for these statements at the time of going to press.

But we do receive something else – spectacular new information. Someone from within UBS credibly assures us that the $2 million transfer to the numbered Swiss account at UBS had indeed taken place. The source provides details we had not revealed to them, including the sum, the date of transfer and the sender, namely Gillard Management. But the source gives a different name for the account holder. According to their information, the numbered account is not owned by the UBS banker but by Hans-Joachim K. himself!

Even though the name of the bank employee was clearly stated as the recipient in the Mossfon transfers? Our source at UBS explains that it is largely irrelevant what name is given as the account holder. In the vast majority of cases, only the account number is checked in money transfers, not the name. We ask several banking experts and they all confirm that the name of the account holder is not the crucial factor, only the account number matters. In this case, that number – according to our source at UBS – was the number of Hans-Joachim K.'s account.

If that is true, he would have simply moved the remainder of the illicit Siemens money to his account once the investigation against him had been closed. The $2 million was previously in an account that K. himself had declared to the public prosecutor to be a slush fund account.

We send K. another email in which we ask him in detail about the $2 million we suspect him of embezzling. No answer. In another email, we ask him about the numbered Swiss account. Hans-Joachim K. is no longer responding to our questions.

13

'REGARDING MY MEETING WITH HARRY POTTER. . .'

[john doe]: What do you think will happen to the firm, once this is all published?

[SZ]: I think the firm will face problems. Anyone in this business of keeping secrets has to expect big trouble. Not only with its customers.

[john doe]: What about Jürgen Mossack and Ramon Fonseca? Do you think they will actually go to jail or get extradited, or try to escape and hide somewhere?

[SZ]: Not really. Panama has its laws fairly well adapted to this type of business, if we understand it correctly. Apart from the sanctions violations. But the Panamanian authorities would also have to really want to go after them – which is to be doubted.

[john doe]: But Jürgen Mossack is German. . .

[SZ]: He probably should not travel much. But if he stays in Panama, he will have to fear probably little.

[john doe]: Sad, but I think you're right. Do you as a journalist not get upset seeing people like this get away with it?

[SZ]: We do. But law enforcement is not our job. . .

It is now August and the mountain of data has grown to more than 2 terabytes. Over these past months, the two of us have clicked through hundreds of companies and thousands of emails. And we have a further 100 or so colleagues in more than fifty countries conducting their investigations. By this point, the Prometheus investigators have opened and examined tens of thousands of company folders. The image of Mossack Fonseca that is emerging contrasts starkly with the image the law firm is keen to convey. The documents we and our colleagues view suggest that the company is not your standard law firm that is, inevitably, unlucky enough to have the odd client or two who act outside the law. It is, rather, a company that talks publicly about fine-sounding concepts such as compliance and due diligence; it that is in reality nowhere near as clean as it would have us believe.

A good example of this is Mossack Fonseca's role in the Siemens Affair and the Latin American slush funds. In all this Mossfon plays a supporting role only; the Siemens directors are clearly the driving force behind the plan. But Mossack Fonseca not only helps the directors to funnel illicit money into clean channels; it also shows in passing what all the talk about supposedly cast-iron principles is really worth – not much.

When Mossack Fonseca has come under attack from journalists in the past, the company's standard line of defence has been that it has no contact with end clients, that it does not carry out bank transfers on behalf of end clients and that it is committed to the 'highest standards' of due diligence. It would never support or tolerate unlawful acts.

We are still dumbfounded when we read statements like these even though we should be familiar with such excuses after all these months. But the confidence with which Mossack Fonseca whitewashes its affairs staggers us every single time.

The Mossfon advisers knew the acting Siemens managers – end clients – personally. We know they met in a Panamanian hotel and shopping centre. We have proof that Mossfon advisers carried out bank transfers on behalf of individuals and various shell companies. They, as 'third parties', have even opened, managed and closed accounts for hidden Siemens slush funds. As late as 2012 they transfered about $2 million to a numbered UBS account without paying more than lip service to due diligence procedures.

One Mossfon employee's objection that the Siemens manager Hans-Joachim K. was embroiled in a bribery scandal is brushed aside by his colleague at Mossack Fonseca, who says that is water under the bridge. Yet the million-dollar sums sitting in companies owned by those former Siemens managers came from exactly those same 'waters'.

In this case alone Mossack Fonseca ignores so many warning signs it is almost incredible. The parties concerned were at times reluctant to provide sufficient information about themselves, they used multiple accounts, they acted conspiratorially, they gave conflicting explanations about the origin of the money and they had even been investigated for financial crimes. Any bank employee with even the slightest level of authority learns to interpret the signals money laundering experts warn about. And it is not that they are naïve at Mossack Fonseca: we discover that one Mossfon subsidiary even offers seminars on how to combat money laundering.

Despite that, Mossfon staff members repeatedly ignore the signs.

The Siemens case demonstrates how little Mossfon cares about whether questionable things go on at the companies it administers. Mossfon staff members were aware of the dubious Siemens funds by the summer of 2008 at the very latest, but they did not drop the client. On the contrary, it appears that Mossack Fonseca even helped to transfer money back and forth: K.'s agent at Mossfon gave the Berenberg Bank false information regarding the origin of the money and Mossfon employees transferred this money from one account to the next, and finally to the accounts of Hans-Joachim K. himself and another Siemens colleague.

Mossack Fonseca did all this while skilfully concealing tell-tale details by using code words, abbreviations and anonymous email addresses.

But the Siemens case is not the only one in which Mossfon staff members operate in such a clandestine manner. We find dozens of cases in which Mossfon's wealth management department supplies end clients – with whom the firm purportedly never has contact – with anonymous email accounts. These email addresses end with '@tradedirect.biz', an email service we have never heard of previously. On its website, www.tradedirect.biz, the company offers 'global trade and professional consulting', supposedly with a focus on 'international exporting and importing'. There is only one link, which flashes on one side of the screen: 'secure email'. When you click on it, it leads you directly to the log-in page of a standard Outlook server. Very similar to the one we have at the *Süddeutsche Zeitung*, incidentally. But whose system is it that you are logging in to?

A little more research in the data reveals the answer. The internal email server belongs to Mossack Fonseca. After further research we discover that Trade Direct International, whose email domain is used for clandestine correspondence by so many Mossfon clients, is actually part of the Mossack Fonseca cosmos. According to our data, Jürgen Mossack and Ramón Fonseca hold the Trade Direct International shares through a dummy corporation called Serena Services LLP, which is based in the UK. The website that purports to offer import–export services appears to be no more than a façade.[1]

We find internal emails that give clear instructions on how clients can log in to these accounts. These emails include client account addresses featuring codenames (e.g. 'winniepooh@tradedirect.biz'), screen names ('Winnie the Pooh'), user names ('winnie') and passwords ('win48491'). In theory, we could now log in to dozens of secret email accounts. But of course we don't, despite the great temptation.

[ ]

Some of the fake names are quite bizarre. Alongside 'Winnie the Pooh' we come across boy wizard 'Harry Potter' and 'Daniel Radcliffe', the actor who made his name playing the role. Other aliases include 'fighter', 'panama', 'oktoberfest', and even 'father', 'daughter' and 'son'.

It gets even better. The Mossfon advisers actually address their clients in emails by these fake names, as if they were in a bad spy movie:

'Dear Harry'

'Hi son'

'Hello father'

Our favourite line comes from an email to 'Winnie the Pooh': 'Regarding my meeting with Harry Potter. . .'

Incidentally, 'Harry Potter' is a successful American lawyer, as is 'father'. 'Winnie the Pooh' is a company director. And 'fighter'? He is a former boxing world champion. . .

These client emails, sent via the internal Mossfon server, arrive in the inboxes of Mossfon staff members with only the fake names displayed, which means that we have to check who 'father', 'Harry Potter' or 'Bruni' really is each time. It is also striking how many of these clients who use anonymous email addresses provided by Mossack Fonseca's strange Trade Direct company seem to have problems with undeclared money. Even more interesting, however, is the fact that Mossack Fonseca advisers often appear to be fully aware of these problems. . .

Here are a few examples:

A client gets in touch because he wants to cash a couple of cheques worth about $100,000, but without leaving 'a trail' to him or his company. Any bank trainee would, at this point, be asking: well, why would you want to do that?

But the Mossack Fonseca advisers simply get creative and seek to offer the client the best possible solution. One of the suggestions made is to put the money in an anonymous trust, which then buys shares in a company, which makes a donation to the client.

Alternatively, one of the Mossfon lawyers advises, they could set up an offshore company and include a clause in the statutes stating that 'this company named ABC also trades under the names XYZ and BLA'. This would allow them to open a bank account under one of these other names.

A Mossfon adviser comes up with an equally unusual suggestion for two other clients. Client A wants to move a substantial amount of money out of the US. Client B wants to move his money discreetly from Singapore back to the US. Mossack Fonseca's plan is that the two clients should transfer the money to each other. Client B sends $800,000 from his account in Singapore to a Swiss account belonging to client A, and client A sends money from his account in the US to client B's account. This would leave the two with $800,000 exactly where they want it. The Mossfon agent explains, however, that they would have to come up with 'another reason' for the transfer from client A to client B within the US. A kind of 'services agreement', perhaps, whereby client A pays client B for services – ones that are never rendered?

Mossfon really suggests issuing a fictitious invoice. A how-to guide to deception.

Mossack Fonseca's pain threshold is astonishingly high. It even advises 'daughter' to issue the reference letter to Mossfon, concerning a transfer to Switzerland, because Mossack Fonseca 'is a law firm. This would avoid creating the impression that you are moving money abroad.' Mossfon is helping to construct a façade and it promises it will 'try to somehow avoid compliance'.

What was that? Avoid compliance?

If such examples appeared only occasionally, they could perhaps be explained as the isolated failures of individual employees. But these are not isolated cases. We see time and again how Mossack Fonseca cooperates in cases involving suspicious transactions and requests.[2]

[ ]

We come across the case of another former Siemens director who seems to have used Mossack Fonseca to transfer money discreetly from Switzerland to Panama. His name appears in emails received by Mossfon in late November 2012, a few days after a new tax treaty falls through between Germany and Switzerland, which would have allowed tax evaders to remain anonymous and avoid prosecution. A client adviser at the Andorran Andbank states that they wish to use Mossfon's escrow service – i.e. to transfer money elsewhere via Mossack Fonseca.

An email exchange in December 2012 reveals that the client has accumulated quite a fortune through business deals in the USA and Sweden. A little over €2 million and 1 million Swiss francs are sitting in a number of Swiss accounts. According to the emails, the former Siemens director wants to transfer this money to an investment account with Andbank in Panama. We also discover a copy of his passport, valid until 2014, among the documents, and a testimonial by a Zurich asset manager, according to whom the ex-Siemens man has been a client since 2008 and is a 'reputable and trustworthy person'.

The money appears to be transferred in several instalments from one account – which is, according to our documents, not in his name but in that of a shell company – to a trust company, which in turn transfers it to Andbank Panama, to another trust company. This company is owned by Mossack Fonseca. The instructions received by Mossack Fonseca state that the money should be transferred from Mossfon's account to the 'end client's' immediately. However, it is vital that the name of the account holder does not appear on the transfer.

In this way a total of about €3 million was moved from Switzerland to Panama in December 2012 without the former Siemens manager's name being visible to anyone on the outside. The final recipient is, however, explicitly named in internal communication at Mossack Fonseca.

Why did this 'reputable and trustworthy person' transfer this money from the Swiss account to an investment account in Panama by such a circuitous route? Why was a much more complex and expensive method chosen? For the secretive bank transfer, Mossack Fonseca charged a fee of 0.5 per cent of the transferred amount – about €15,000 for moving a total of €3 million. €15,000 for a service that could have been completed using a standard transfer, which is free at many banks.

But, of course, a standard transfer – and therefore also the former Siemens director's name – may have been visible to the tax authorities.[3]

[ ]

Mossack Fonseca's core business is not trust services such as the one used by this former Siemens director, but the large-scale sale of dummy companies and trusts to institutional intermediaries. These intermediaries pass on the companies to their respective customers – 'end clients' as Mossfon refers to them. This bread-and-butter aspect of the Mossfon business does not always involve astronomical sums of money and they do not require Harry Potter email addresses. Your average estate agent, dentist or businessperson can simply park their money in these companies to minimize their tax liabilities. In reality, Mossack Fonseca usually knows very little about these people. Internal Mossfon documents reveal that in thousands of cases they do not even know who owns the offshore companies.

But one thing Mossfon often does know all too well is the reason why many banks and asset managers need these shell companies. In their roles as salespeople, Mossfon staff members regularly meet their clients, especially the regional shell company salespeople, in countries such as Switzerland, Luxembourg and the UK.

Mossack Fonseca employees submit written reports on these meetings – there is a special field for this purpose in the firm's internal computer system. The reports we have access to could hardly be clearer.

There are dozens of entries on banks whose clients have 'undeclared funds', and who are therefore 'very sensitive' when it comes to confidentiality. Writing about one client, the advisers note that their end clients 'usually want to hide their money from ex-wives and the taxman'. And so it goes on. There are also countless reports in which they freely admit that the European interest income tax introduced in 2005 will boost business with this or that client. The tax is only applicable to accounts held by EU citizens, not to accounts held by Panamanian companies. The introduction of the tax functioned as a kind of turbo boost for business at companies like Mossack Fonseca. The share of accounts held through offshore companies rose by ten percentage points in Switzerland alone. The number of private individuals registered as account holders sank accordingly. There is reason to suspect that many people established shell companies so that their accounts were no longer held in their name, but in the name of a company whose real owner is very difficult to identify if any questions are asked.

In Mossfon memos from recent years we also regularly come across slightly despondent notes regarding certain banks that no longer administer hidden accounts and that are therefore unlikely to require Mossack Fonseca's services.

In many cases, we have seen how Mossfon is just as unlikely to refuse banks, many of whom hardly bother to conceal their roles as accessories, as they are the end clients. Instead, Mossfon staff members are all too often happy to assist in word and deed. They explain which tax haven would be best for various purposes, what kind of business construct offers optimum protection, and they repeatedly swear that the real owner's highly sensitive data is in good hands with them at Mossfon. One Mossfon client adviser reassures a Swiss client who is worried about the security of his data after the Offshore Secrets revelations by informing him that Mossfon uses a 'state-of-the-art' data centre and that all communication is encrypted to 'the highest possible security standards'. Mossfon also promises other clients that all the sensitive data held at Mossack Fonseca is safe and that it will never leave Panama.[4]

But exactly that has now happened. And we, the journalists, are not the only ones who have data. According to information we have received, the German tax authorities recently paid €1 million for documents concerning about 600 Mossack Fonseca companies thought to be owned by German citizens. In the spring of 2015, investigators not only searched offices belonging to suspected enablers and accomplices such as Commerzbank on the basis of this data, but they also – according to our information – carried out raids on about 100 Mossfon end clients.

The documents seized by investigators during these raids function as counterparts of the entries within the internal Mossfon system – one set reveals an intention to evade taxes, the other set proves that taxes were evaded.

So the proof that Mossack Fonseca enabled German citizens to evade taxes is ultimately produced by government authorities.

Some German banks, among them Commerzbank and HSH Nordbank, have already agreed to pay large fines for their dealings with Mossack Fonseca, so that legal proceedings against them are closed. Commerzbank paid €17 million and HSH Nordbank paid €22 million. These figures consist of financial penalties and the return of unlawful profits from illegal business deals. These banks would, presumably, not have agreed to pay these sums if they had not helped people to evade taxes.

Incidentally, Commerzbank in particular was initially very wary of working with Mossfon. Staff at the bank expressed concern that secret deals could be leaked or that nominee directors could disappear with their clients' money. Mossack Fonseca explained the system over and over and finally suggested a particularly safe option: bank clients could conceal their money in offshore companies under the protective cover of an anonymous trust. This would give clients 'the advantage, when asked by the German tax authorities, of being able to truthfully answer no to the questions listed above regarding the account holder, beneficial owner and authorization'. In plain English, it means clients would be able to inform the tax office that they do not own the account and that they have no access to it. This is because the account belongs *pro forma* to the company, and the company belongs *pro forma* to the trust – which, in turn, appoints the client as a beneficiary.

This tip came, according to a letter we have in our possession, directly 'from our senior partner, Mr Jürgen Mossack' – Mossfon's German director.[5] Over the past few years, Mossack Fonseca has attracted the attention of public prosecutors time and again in relation to investigations involving companies set up by Mossfon. In April 2008, for example, a slightly panic-stricken employee at the Mossfon branch in the Seychelles sends an email to the headquarters in Panama. She says that the attorney general of the Seychelles has just informed her that investigations are under way against four companies administered by Mossfon, and that this was now the sixth case in just a month. The woman is clearly afraid of 'what might happen if the cases go to court', and asks whether 'there is a kind of exclusion of liability that prevents Mossack employees from being investigated'.

We have not actually seen any cases in which Mossfon is investigated as an accomplice. Ultimately, public prosecutors have invariably concentrated their energies on the principal offenders, i.e. the individuals or organizations who approach Mossfon seeking assistance to conceal their money.

Until now.

According to information we have received, the German tax authorities are now conducting an investigation into those

responsible at the Mossack Fonseca law firm, on suspicion of facil-
itating tax evasion – and Jürgen Mossack is among those under
investigation.

It seems the investigators are querying whether employees of
the Panamanian law firm knew more than they would have those
on the outside believe.

Unlike the investigators, we are no longer asking that question.
We know they did.

And so Mossack Fonseca's central line of defence collapses.

Of course, everyone knows at heart that offshore companies
are often established for exactly this purpose. But since Mossack
Fonseca has decided to put on this act, we have to play along and
expose the game for what it is. In correspondence with us,
Mossack Fonseca compared itself to a wholesaler who has no
idea what the end client does with the goods they sell. But
in reality, the law firm knows exactly what goes on within a
number of these companies. In many instances, Mossfon is responsible for the upkeep of the 'goods' and even for the accounting.
In those cases in which Mossfon nominee directors 'manage'
the company, Mossfon is often directly involved in questionable
business deals.

In February 2015 Mossfon informed us that every individual
granted authority to sign on behalf of a company was first subjected
to a 'World Check'. High-risk individuals would either not be
accepted as clients at all, or would not be granted authority to sign.
But we see one case in the data involving a senior South American
director at a national oil company. Alarm bells ring when the
check is carried out, and the Mossfon employee informs the oil
manager's lawyer that they cannot issue him with the authority to
sign for the company. What they could do, however, is issue his son
with the authorization. . . in which case it would be crucial not to
mention anywhere that the authorized representative is the son of
the true owner.

We know the image of the wholesaler is completely inaccurate yet Mossfon continues to try to promote it. It is the method employed by the law firm to attempt to distance itself from its 'ethically challenged' end clients, as Jürgen Mossack called this kind of clientele in a lobbying letter to the British Virgin Islands' financial regulation authority. He could just as well have written 'criminals'.

It would appear to us that Jürgen Mossack and his partners face ethical challenges of their own.

14

A SECRET MEETING
WITH ALPINE VIEWS

We have an odd profession: that's worth mentioning here. For months on end, we've been sitting in front of our mountain of data and have barely told a soul at the *Süddeutsche Zeitung* about it. So far, that hasn't been a problem. We don't usually walk around the building telling everyone about our investigations anyway. But now, on this Tuesday in September, it starts to get really odd. Hundreds of reporters from all over the world have made their way here to find out more about Prometheus. This means that our colleagues from the *SZ* hear us speaking English with our colleagues from the BBC in the lifts and see the South Korean team filming outside, in front of the high-rise building. Our colleagues from the *SZ* stand behind Ritu Sarin from the *Indian Express* at the turnstile in the entrance hall and sit down beside Florian Klenk, our Austrian colleague from *Falter*, who some know personally and many know by sight, in the sunshine in front of the SZ Tower's cafe. In short, it's obvious we have visitors. Even the *Guardian*'s new Editor-in-Chief Katharine Viner has come here to find out about our project.

So what do we tell our colleagues when they stop us in the lift, cafe or foyer to ask us what's going on today?

Er, well. Some kind of meeting? A type of conference?

We worm our way out of the conversations and feel awkward about it. The feeling only subsides when we remind ourselves why we're being so secretive and full of our own self-importance: because someone, somewhere in the world, is fearing for their life. Our source.

Nevertheless, word spreads throughout the building about the meeting. We bring several colleagues into the loop because they will have important roles to play in the project at a later stage, for example the editors from the foreign affairs department, with their wealth of knowledge and correspondents all over the world. But we can hardly invite anyone to the meetings with our colleagues from the ICIJ. We simply don't have the space. The ICIJ has managed to get partner after partner on board; the aim is to have journalists in every country we've got good hits for, or where we expect to find some. Initially, forty people signed up. This figure quickly rose to sixty, then eighty – in the end, 104 journalists come together for the discussions.

We're meeting in the SZ Tower's Sky Lounge, a room that's only really meant to hold eighty people. But what were we to do? Uninvite colleagues? The room is spread over two floors and surrounded only by windows on three sides. From here, you can see the mountains in the distance, the city with its towers and turrets, and the Allianz Arena, lit up in blue to signal that 1860 Munich are playing at home.

We close the blinds so we can use the projector. While Kurt Kister and Wolfgang Krach, our editors-in-chief, welcome the guests, we quickly test the WiFi on our phones. It's working, we can get started.

The big ICIJ meeting in Munich. Two days of Prometheus.

[ ]

For days now, Hans Leyendecker, our head of department, has been in exceptionally high spirits; he's unashamedly proud of what his 'young people' are up to. And it's hardly surprising; it's not all that often that the *Guardian* editor-in-chief and hundreds of other top journalists call in. But in the past few days, we've been so busy making sure we've got enough bottles of apple juice, discussing where the lunches are going to be handed out and organizing another projector for the South America working group that we haven't had the time to get excited about it. On top of that, we've had to keep adding people to our reservation in a Bavarian beer hall in the centre of Munich; we'd promised our colleagues that they'd be able to drink beer out of massively oversized glasses and that they'd get roast pork and dumplings to go with it. The day before the meeting, we got together with the ICIJ team from Washington to discuss the agenda for the two days.

And then the conference kicks off. We talk about the leak (current status: 2.4 terabytes, 8 million files, 200,000 shell companies) and the findings to date (thirty-five links to heads of state), and our colleagues from the ICIJ present the specially designed research platforms, for all those who hadn't been there in Washington in July. We're fascinated to hear about the discoveries made by our colleagues who have been working with us on the project for a while and the potential repercussions in their countries. Two hundred journalists from more than sixty-five countries are now working on the project, and not all of them enter all of their hits on the forum. So this is also an opportunity for us to catch up on the most recent developments in our investigation.

Leo Sisti from Italy reports on links with the mafia, Jake Bernstein from the ICIJ explains that he has found numerous other world-famous art dealers, and Ewald Scharfenberg from Venezuela talks about all the *Chavistas* he has found in the data, referring to socialists and supporters of the recently deceased party leader Hugo Chávez. Our Icelandic colleague Jóhannes Kr. Kristjánsson introduces his research findings: in addition to the current prime minister, who we had already found at the start of our investigations, Jóhannes has also discovered the owners of one of Iceland's three failed banks, who have since been jailed. And so it continues. In the afternoon, the deputy editor of the *Guardian*, Paul Johnson, puts his thoughts into words we won't be forgetting in a hurry. His newspaper, Johnson explains, has been involved in a number of fantastic projects: WikiLeaks, the Snowden Files, Offshore Secrets. 'But nothing of this magnitude. It's simply incredible.'

[ ]

Once the major international stories have been presented, the second part of the meeting begins: we split off into project groups. Several topic areas – Russia, FIFA, the arms trade – are too big for one editorial team to work on alone. To some extent, the groups already exist, but it's easier to exchange information when you're sitting opposite someone in person than by writing encrypted emails or posting on the forum. For example, we hear from our two Russian colleagues, Roman Anin and Roman Shleynov. A few days ago, they joined our small working group on Russia, which, since our meeting in Washington, has been digging up anything it could find to do with Russia. And it's found a fair bit.

First of all, of course, there's Sergei Roldugin, the cellist and godfather of Putin's daughter, in whose company network we have already found more than half a billion dollars. Then there are Putin's (since sanctioned) judo friends Boris and Arkady Rotenberg,[1] as well as Putin's cousin Igor and one of Russia's richest men: Alisher Usmanov. The oligarch amassed a fortune through raw material and media businesses, temporarily owned several per cent of Facebook and is still a major shareholder in Arsenal Football Club. Mossfon itself views him as a 'highly risky' client, but has still decided to hold on to him for the time being.[2]

The list goes on. All of these names are especially interesting because they are associates of Putin, who himself has condemned the offshore system as 'unpatriotic'. It doesn't exactly create a good impression, having so many people from his entourage appearing to be involved in this unpatriotic offshore world.

Roman Shleynov tells us about another case that he's currently researching. It involves the company Earliglow Ltd, which was established in the British Virgin Islands in 2010. In the company records, Roman discovered an interesting document that states that Earliglow is a 'non-direct shareholder' of a Russian company called Svyazdorinvest.

Around 2010, Svyazdorinvest was awarded a contract by the Russian state-run company Rostec to build a fibre-optic cable between China and Russia. Estimated order volume: $550 million. A mega-project.

Rostec's director, Sergey Chemezov, is an old friend of Putin's from the KGB, and he too is on EU and US sanctions lists. A graduate of the Russian General Staff Academy, he was once stationed with Putin in Dresden, and later became one of the Russian head of state's most important middlemen. He awarded a multi-million contract from the state-run company he manages to a company owned, in part, by his son. In any case, this is how it appears to us. And it gets even better: according to our documents, the daughter of the vice president of Rostec holds indirect shares in Svyazdorinvest through Earliglow.[3]

It looks as if we have hit upon part of 'Russia Ltd', that gigantic self-service shop disguised as a democracy that experts have been criticizing for years. Karen Dawisha, the author of the recently published *Putin's Kleptocracy*, refers to it as 'kleptocratic authoritarianism'.

Roman Shleynov is telling us about this story in detail for the first time now, because neither he nor Roman Anin have had access to the forum so far for their own safety.

After some consideration, we come up with the following solution together with the ICIJ: they will both get smartphones here
in Germany for use specifically in this project. And they will
immediately dispose of them if they suspect that a Trojan could
have been installed on them. Journalists working in Russia who
publish texts that are critical of Putin regularly report break-ins in
their offices and homes. It goes without saying that offices and
homes are bugged. The two Romans won't be using their new
smartphones to make any phone calls.

So we go shopping with them. We drive to a nearby electrical
store and pay with cash, so that it can't be traced back to us.

[ ]

During the meeting, we use every opportunity to call for caution.
It would only take one remark to the wrong person and Prometheus could be exposed. Mossack Fonseca would be warned, as
would the clients. They would then have plenty of time to work
out a counter-strategy, and we wouldn't even be halfway through
our investigations. The whole project would be in jeopardy.

That's the worst-case scenario.

The best-case scenario is as follows: in spring 2016, hundreds of
journalists from all over the world go online on the same day, at
the same time, with the story about the Panamanian law firm
Mossack Fonseca, and it's the first anyone has heard about this
team investigation.

In Munich, we spend a long time discussing questions such as
the exact publication date and the name we should give the
project, that is to say which catchword we should use for the
publications. We don't manage to answer either question definitively. Most people agree that we want to aim for publication on a
Sunday evening, so we can set it up as a topic for the whole week,
and that the middle of March or the beginning of April would be

a good time. But with 200 journalists from more than sixty countries, there are lots of limitations. No newspapers are published in
Russia on 7 or 8 March: Women's Day. Not an option. On 13
March, three state elections are being held in Germany. Not ideal
at all, as the papers will be full of election results. The Easter holidays fall in the week of 20 March, and on 3 April presidential elections are being held in Peru.

Whew! We postpone the decision.

The same goes for coming up with a name. Should it be
#globalleaks or #offshoreuncovered? #panamafiles or #theshell-
game? #shadowland or #hiddenmoney? We don't reach a consen-
sus, but end up with twenty new suggestions instead.

The discussions drag on. But that's the price you have to pay
when so many colleagues are involved. The mix of TV and newspaper journalists is also an issue. The TV people need moving
images from Panama, and they want to film them as soon as possible, because everything needs to be edited and they're always in
such a rush at the end anyway. But we don't want two dozen TV
teams turning up at Mossack Fonseca's offices in the next couple
of months and filming 'very inconspicuously'.

[ ]

Rita Vásquez stands up and asks for the floor. She's the deputy
editor-in-chief of *La Prensa*, the Panamanian newspaper that wants
to report in Mossfon's home country. Rita, our local partner, says
what we'd already been thinking: Panama is a small country and
the offshore industry is an industry whose representatives are
always on the lookout for investigative journalists. She believes
that if even just a small camera team were to turn up and start
asking strange questions, it wouldn't just make the people at
Mossfon nervous. That's because everyone knows everyone else
and the branch is closely connected with politics. Take Ramón

Fonseca, for example, who is the adviser to the president. She manages to convince our TV colleagues. We don't want to make the industry nervous already.

When Rita Vásquez talks about the offshore industry, we all pay special attention. She knows the branch like no one else, not only because she lives in Panama, one of the control centres of this industry, but above all because she used to be the manager of a Panamanian offshore branch in the British Virgin Islands herself. She doesn't want to talk about her past, but her experience and knowledge will help us to better understand Panama. A country that's the perfect location for Mossack Fonseca, despite all the legislative amendments. And, incidentally, for a whole host of other law firms that make their money through offshore companies.

It's not going to be easy to develop an understanding of Panama, or should we say: of the part of Panama that helps so many criminals, dictators, corrupt companies and tax evaders hide money. Of course, Panama is no longer the 'narcokleptocracy' that US Senator John Kerry, the later presidential candidate, called it in 1998, referring to the surprising proportion of the drugs trade that was passing through Panama. But still, as the British author Nicholas Shaxson quotes a US official saying, 'The country is filled with dishonest lawyers, dishonest bankers, dishonest company formation agents and dishonest companies.' A report published by the US State Department in March 2014 is somewhat more objective, but equally harsh. According to this report, Panama is still an 'attractive target for money launderers' who launder dirty money there accumulated through the drugs trade, corruption and tax evasion. 'Numerous factors hinder the fight against money laundering,' the report continues, including 'the existence of bearer share corporations, a lack of collaboration among government agencies', and 'a weak judicial system susceptible to corruption and favouritism'. Panama also features on the blacklist of tax havens published by the EU in June 2015.

[ ]

A few days after our colleagues left, the president of Panama, Juan Carlos Varela, announced his arrival in New York. He was set to give a big speech. We watch it online: Varela strides up to the lectern in the large hall of the United Nations, rustles his papers together and starts talking. Sixteen minutes. It's meant to be an attempt to turn the tide. 'Panama is committed to expanding its international cooperation in the field of fiscal transparency and advancing toward the automatic exchange of information on tax matters on a bilateral basis,' Varela says.

Varela, of all people, whose adviser is the offshore tycoon Ramón Fonseca, wants to put an end to the existence of tax havens? That's how it seems, in any case. What else could the automatic exchange of information mean, other than putting an end to the tax haven of Panama?

Are we writing about something that's no longer going to be current at the time of publication? Are we striking out at a country that's just decided to radically reform? Well, on the one hand, our data relates not only to Panama. Mossfon manages and/or establishes companies in the British Virgin Islands, the Seychelles, Bermuda, Samoa, British Anguilla and the US states of Nevada and Wyoming. And on the other hand, there's the question of just how credible Varela's announcements are.

[ ]

A short time later, we find out that we're not the only ones to have taken note of Varela's speech.

[john doe]: I just heard about the President of Panama speaking to the United Nations. Do you think he will pull this off and actually open up the country's data?

[SZ]: Hard to believe.

[john doe]: That would be a problem for Mossack Fonseca, right?

[SZ]: If it would be consistently implemented: yes.

[john doe]: And Ramón Fonseca is a consultant to Varelas administration.

[SZ]: Jep.

[john doe]: So that's never going to happen. . .

A couple of days later the source passes us a letter that those responsible at Mossack Fonseca sent out to its clients – banks, law firms and asset management companies – after Varela's speech. Obviously based on the assumption that its clients were as alarmed by Varela's speech as we were, albeit for different reasons, Mossfon attempts to reassure them. 'We would like to assure you', it states, that *'no changes to the existing laws and regulations'* were announced in Varela's speech.

No changes? Hadn't Varela promised greater transparency and the automatic exchange of information? In some way, yes. But Mossack Fonseca is confident that it will all be solved the Panamanian way. A potential 'exchange will have to be designed in such a fashion', it writes, that 'it cannot be abused in a way that inhibits the competitiveness of some countries at the expense of others'.

When reading these sentences, you mustn't forget that Ramón Fonseca is not only one of the president's closest advisers, but also the deputy leader of the governing party. Such a person has the president's attention, and such a person could, in case of doubt, also have the influence required to moderate unpopular legislation. Of course, only in order to maintain Panama's competitive position.

That letter from Mossack Fonseca goes on to say that President Juan Carlos Varela will continue to defend 'the interests of the country'.

The interests of Panama. We wouldn't be surprised if these just so happened to be congruent with the private interests of cabinet member Ramón Fonseca. And in some ways, they are: the more money law firms like Mossfon bring into Panama, the better. At least, that had been true until now.

15

MOSSFON HOLDINGS

One of the outcomes of the meeting in Munich is that we give Mossack Fonseca our full attention again for a few days, concentrating on the firm's various businesses, which are behind everything we've found out so far.

There's only one problem: there isn't just one firm. There are several. Dozens.

Time and time again throughout the course of our investigations, we and our Prometheus colleagues have come across strange companies that seem to belong to the Mossfon universe. It's just not very easy to prove it, because the shares aren't usually held by Mossack Fonseca or the partners of the law office, but instead by Mossfon Holdings, which isn't usually recognizable as Mossfon Holdings at first glance. It's complicated.

Mossack Fonseca disguises not only its clients' ownership statuses to the outside world, but also its own. Objectively, this has the advantage that if one of its companies encounters legal problems, Mossfon can comfortably distance itself from the subsidiary company. Former US Senate investigator Jack Blum describes this tactic in *Vice* magazine. The trick is not only used by Mossfon but also by numerous other companies and involves working as 'seamless, vertically integrated top-down organisations', Blum explains, 'until the minute that a cop or investigator comes along. Then they disintegrate into a series of unconnected entities, and everyone swears they don't know anything about anyone else in the system. It's like a jigsaw puzzle that's assembled but suddenly falls apart when someone starts investigating.'

However, Mossfon manages all of its own companies itself, and we have the records as well. It just takes a great deal of painstaking work to follow up every lead at every individual company. Just like Russian matryoshka dolls, there's always another company that we have to open up, and then another and another until we eventually find the final one, the smallest doll. The link to Jürgen Mossack.

The most recent example is the Mossfon subsidiary in the US state of Nevada. A lawsuit has been going on there for a few years, initiated by Paul Singer, the owner of the hedge fund NML Capital, a side show to his dispute with the Argentinian government. Singer wants to prove that the late president Néstor Kirchner and his wife, the former president Cristina Kirchner, took about $65 million out of the country, allegedly with the help of 123 offshore companies founded by Mossack Fonseca. The Kirchner family denies these claims and, to date, no evidence has been provided to support them. Since Paul Singer's lawyers have no powers to acquire the internal documents in Panama, and the majority of these firms were registered in Nevada, a suit is being filed in the US state for disclosure of the ownership status.

And in fact, from the start, Mossack Fonseca's strategy was to distance MF Corporate Services (Nevada) Ltd. Jürgen Mossack himself even declares in a statement dated 8 July 2015 – under oath – that Mossack Fonseca and MF Nevada are separate companies, there is no parent–subsidiary relationship, and Mossack Fonseca doesn't have access to the 'internal affairs or daily operations' of MF Nevada.

When we check the data, we find an email conversation that suggests the opposite is true. According to this, in autumn 2014, employees at Mossack Fonseca are worried that MF Nevada's offices could be searched. According to the emails, its lawyers in Nevada are warning that this could happen. Such a search would obviously be a huge problem. Someone at Mossfon writes that this is because the investigators would 'easily find proof that we're hiding something'. This 'something' is namely the close connection between Mossack Fonseca Panama and MF Nevada. So they forge a plan, the 'aim of which is to ensure that MF Nevada can't be associated with Mossfon'.

The procedure is as follows: the sole employee in Nevada, Patricia A., is to carry out her day-to-day work 'as if she were a mediator; that's actually exactly what we want to achieve'. As a result, employees in Panama decide that A. should get a new telephone 'so that it's not possible to see that she has direct access to the entire Mossfon address book'. The new telephone – which later emails attest to her having received – shouldn't record calls that she makes either.

The next problem is the internal system that Patricia A. has access to. It needs to be 'hidden from the investigators'. However, after some deliberations, it's determined that that's not an option. So Mossfon Panama decides, after consulting a manager, to remove her access. But that's not enough. The investigators could, if they were to search Patricia A.'s computer, determine that she recently used the internal system. These traces can be found in the local log files, so someone called Francisco should 'clean' these logs 'remotely'. And the office itself is also being cleaned up: 'When Andrés [*referring to a Mossfon employee*] came to Nevada, he cleaned up everything and took all the documents to Panama,' one of the emails explains.

In the mafia, there's a special name for the people who discreetly remove all the traces after the act: cleaners.

As a quick reminder: Jürgen Mossack declared under oath that Mossack Fonseca wasn't controlling the internal affairs or daily operations of MF Nevada.[1]

On the other hand, hadn't Mossack also stated that there wasn't a parent–subsidiary relationship? After some effort, we find an application to open an account from MF Nevada, in which Mossfon discloses the ownership structure. According to this, all shares in MF Nevada are held by an offshore company by the name of Tornbell Associates, 45 per cent of which belongs to Jürgen Mossack, 45 per cent to Ramón Fonseca and 10 per cent to their Swiss junior partner, Christoph Zollinger.[2]

Mossack's claim that MF Nevada isn't a subsidiary company of Mossack Fonseca is typical of how the law firm and its representatives attempt to cover up the facts.

In addition, Mossfon is still trying to protect its clients from the hedge fund holder Paul Singer, who's filing the lawsuit: staff send emails to the administrators of affected Mossfon companies, in which they state that they 'can only reiterate' their advice not to, as far as possible, own any part of these special companies. In theory, these could be seized, the people at Mossfon write, in the event that the court is ultimately able to force Mossack Fonseca to disclose all information.

Now we have exposed MF Nevada as a company belonging to the Mossfon Group, we try to approach the search for companies associated with Mossfon in a systematic fashion. We compile a list of all the companies we know belong to Mossack Fonseca. We reach a total of thirty-seven. There are many others we have our suspicions about.

[ ]

We then strike lucky: our colleague Jan Strozyk from NDR finds an Excel file that helps us considerably. It's a type of 'Mossack Fonseca at a glance'. Since Mossfon evidently wants to take out an insurance policy, the people at Mossfon have provided a summary of their entire universe in a couple of tables. And listed the companies that belong to it. Dated: 2014.

Presumably it was part of the terms of the insurance policy that Mossfon had to explain how it earns its money and which companies are involved in the process. The irony is that Mossack Fonseca evidently also took out a type of insurance policy against white-collar crime with the same group. We investigate what exactly the insurer understands that to mean, and find a definition. According to the definition, this insurance policy protects companies 'against the financial effects of fraud (by employees or third parties), theft (including burglary and hold-up) [authors' note: *from outside, at the expense of Mossfon*] and electronic fraud. The risk includes "internal" damage as a result of employees abusing the trust placed in them by the company, as well as "external" damage.'

We can't rule out the possibility that Mossfon is insuring itself against exactly what is happening at the moment: internal data ending up in the hands of journalists.

In any case, the document provides us with the first reliable overview of the company. It reveals that Mossack Fonseca had almost 100 companies with a range of business objectives in the 2013 financial year, as well as more than 100 associated companies that were functioning as shell companies.

According to the document, there are a total of twelve holding companies functioning one level above the Mossfon subsidiaries, and these are all listed in the Excel file. In total, there are well over 200 companies.

Mossfon isn't just a law firm; Mossfon is an octopus with many legs!

But is this really the entire company network? We wouldn't bet on it. What we do discover is that Mossack Fonseca also provides services such as the registration of yachts and aeroplanes, legal advice in the field of intellectual property, asset management, investment banking, custodian services and the letting of virtual offices. Other companies are responsible for real estate, bank accounts, telephone lines, vehicle fleets and accounts. And of course, there are companies specifically for offices in other countries as well. So if such a Mossfon establishment were to run into legal problems, say because it was managing another company that was involved in fraud or breaking sanctions, the Panamanian headquarters would be able to distance itself from the offender at any given moment. This is precisely the aforementioned tactic described by the US special investigator Jack Blum.

We also learn from this overview document how high Mossfon's turnover is, namely $42.6 million in 2013. A figure that leaves us a bit baffled. Of course, it doesn't have especially high expenses. The nominee directors, for instance, only earn around $5,000 each per year. But despite that, we would have expected Mossack Fonseca to have made a bit more, considering its somewhat sketchy procedures and the potential risk involved.

The document also breaks down exactly which corporate divisions have which percentage share of the profit. It is hardly surprising that the majority of it is generated by the companies that dedicate themselves to the core business: the establishment and management of offshore companies. But the areas in which companies from the Mossack Fonseca Group work together directly with end clients also make up a significant part, namely around 12 per cent. According to the document, Mossack Fonseca had a total of 588 employees in 2013, of which 342 were employed in Panama, 140 in Asia and 40 in the British Virgin Islands. It also had six employees in Colombia, three in Samoa, five in Luxembourg and eighteen in El Salvador. You might think that this many employees would result in huge costs, but the level of wages in El Salvador, Panama and the British Virgin Islands is much lower than in Europe.

[ ]

By its own account, in autumn 2015, Mossfon has almost fifty offices in more than thirty countries. More than thirty of these offices are subsidiary companies and the remainder are 'partner offices' with a legal status that is unclear to us, but similar perhaps to franchisees.

In the midst of the 200 companies, you could almost overlook an inconspicuous company that, until recently when it changed its name to Mossfon Executive, was called International Outsourcing. The company, based in Panama, had twenty employees in 2013, including those whose names were familiar to us after all those months dealing with the Mossfon data: nominee directors, front men and women ostensibly leading 'their' companies.

They are the people who always appear in the public eye; you can even google them. They are the ones who crop up in the international media, because offshore companies that make the headlines use their signatures. They are the ones under the biggest pressure: they are the faces and the names of thousands of companies. Their names end up on sanction lists, in bills of indictment, blogs and newspaper articles. And if in doubt, as our experts from Panama explain, they can even be taken to court for the activities of shell companies.

It's easy to imagine why they're not employed by Mossack Fonseca directly.

[ ]

One of Mossfon's nominee directors is Leticia Montoya. She was the director of Casa Grande Development, which administered slush funds for Siemens in Latin America, and the company with which the Nicaraguan ruler Arnoldo 'Fat Man' Alemán and his assistants allegedly shifted millions. The list of director posts she has held or holds would be a long one; in total we see her name more than 25,000 times in the Panamanian company register alone.

In words: twenty-five thousand.

This figure doesn't include all the posts that Montoya holds or held in shell companies outside Panama. The total number is suspected to be considerably higher.

Leticia Montoya must wonder how she manages to carry out her duties as the director in such a tangle of companies.

But who is Leticia Montoya, the queen of the nominee directors?

According to a copy of her passport, she was born in Panama in March 1953, is a Panamanian citizen and her full name is Leticia Montoya Moran. She didn't go to secondary school, according to our sources she speaks very little English, and she lives in a poverty-stricken area outside Panama City. This is hardly surprising because although Mossack Fonseca earns millions from its operations with nominee directors, it doesn't let the exposed nominee directors, of all people, have a share in it: we almost feel a pang of sympathy when we read in the memo that Leticia Montoya – who has, according to an internal statement, been working with Jürgen Mossack since October 1981 – at times earned just $400 per month.

A quick calculation: Mossfon charges around $450 a year for the nominee director service. In many cases, Mossfon appoints three nominee directors per company, which works out at $150 per nominee director. Leticia Montoya's annual salary was, at least for some time, $4,800.[3] If she were the director of just thirty-two active companies, she would bring in exactly her annual salary. However, Montoya is in fact the director of more than thirty-two companies. Many more. In a statement from 2012, she's listed as the director of 3,143 shell companies. This means that she brought in almost $500,000 in 2012 alone. That's 100 times her salary.

[ ]

The nominee director system essentially requires three documents in order to function, and we find thousands of these papers in the data. The front man or woman, known as the nominee director in offshore jargon, assures the true owner that they will follow their instructions and that they don't have any claims against them or the company ('Nominee Director Declaration'). They then give the true owner, the beneficial owner, a 'power of attorney' that makes them the de facto director. In the third and final document, which isn't filled out by default, the nominee director submits their resignation ('Resignation Letter'). The nominee director signs this letter and passes it on to the real owner, but doesn't enter a date, meaning that the real owner can get rid of the fake one at any time, even with retrospective effect. The nominee director is often deprived of their rights from the very start.

For everyday use, Mossack Fonseca repeatedly instructs its nominee directors to sign all sorts of blank documents. These are often applications to open accounts, but they are sometimes also templates for shares, in which the client just needs to enter the name of the company. As a result, everything can happen very quickly if necessary; Mossfon Panama doesn't need to specifically bring in the nominee directors to sign the documents as they have already been signed.

And it gets even more absurd: in the data, we find file after file containing masses of blank, signed pages. Empty white pages, with the signatures of three nominee directors in various combinations. Sometimes the signatures are at the bottom of the page, sometimes in the middle and sometimes at the top. These white pages could, in theory, become anything. A purchase agreement, a new power of attorney, the closure of a company.

[ ]

Jürgen Mossack also held director posts and functioned as a front man. As 'Jurgen Mossack', he has held or holds around 1,500 former or current director posts. If you include the entries made in the company register under the names 'Jurgen Mossack 1', 'Jurgen Mossack7058', 'Jurgen Jurgen Mossack' or other variations, you can add a few more on top.[4]

We find an email from 2008 that states that Mossack himself – and his first wife – shouldn't be used as nominee directors any more. His staff now carry out this job for him. And if they happen to make a mistake, or if a nominee director gets taken to court, Mossfon has taken measures to ensure that this won't affect the bigger picture: if someone does initiate proceedings against the company in which most of the nominee directors are involved, they will end up at the Mossfon satellite company Mossfon Executive, one of more than 200 Mossfon companies.

What was the image again that the former US investigator Jack Blum used? A jigsaw puzzle that suddenly falls apart as soon as someone starts investigating.

This is the system that the entire Mossfon universe seems to go by. Since Jürgen Mossack and Ramón Fonseca have their own companies, for instance for the trust business, asset management of clients, foundations and most of the offices, an investigation or lawsuit would always affect a subsidiary first. However, it won't initially be recognized as a subsidiary company because it's held by an offshore company that, in turn, is held by a foundation.

It is almost inevitable that Jürgen Mossack and Ramón Fonseca pursue this principle of small, loosely associated units in their private lives too. They have both placed their assets in a network of companies, most of which appear to have a manageable function. One of Jürgen Mossack's companies owns a couple of *fincas*, another one a penthouse, one his helicopter hangar, one his helicopter, one his teak plantation, one his gold, and another still his yacht, the *Rex Maris*, 'king of the sea'. His firm has undoubtedly made Jürgen Mossack, the son of the German adventurer Erhard Mossack, a very rich man. A rich man with a penchant for offshore companies: he even has individual companies for his cars, one for his Mercedes, one for the Volvo, one for the Mazda and the Chevrolet Tahoe.[5]

The central element of his private asset planning seems to be a foundation called The Mossack Family Foundation. Most of the shares of his private offshore companies belong to it, and it appears that profits from Mossfon's activities also flow into it. The primary beneficiary of The Mossack Family Foundation, which was established in 1997, is Jürgen Mossack. Children and stepchildren are also listed as subordinated beneficiaries. Mossack is currently on his third marriage; it all adds up.

The Mossack Family Foundation, like many of the foundations sold by Mossfon, holds a discreet account in Switzerland.

But the family doesn't only profit from the company. The family has actually been part of the company for a long while: a daughter and son from Mossack's first marriage have been working for their father for many years. It appears that his daughter was most recently working as a client adviser and his son as a lawyer. Mossack's first wife was evidently a nominee director for a while, Mossack's two stepdaughters from his second marriage did or do also work at Mossfon, and his third wife, originally from Cuba, worked for Mossack Fonseca as a lawyer.

A company is also assigned internally within Mossfon to Jürgen Mossack's brother Peter, the Panamanian honorary consul near Darmstadt. It's not clear whether Peter Mossack actually uses this company. In February 2015 he told us that he had no idea about his brother's activities.[6] We even found evidence in the Mossfon archives that Jürgen Mossack's mother and his father Erhard Mossack, a former *Rottenführer* in the Waffen-SS and later CIA informant, have a company.

The family, *la familia*. The company. All is one.

16

SPIRIT OF PANAMA

So far, we have underestimated the importance of one of the Panamanian law firm's key figures. This becomes clear when we investigate Christoph Zollinger in more detail. At the very start of our project, we'd thought that Swiss-born Zollinger was one of three partners in the law firm, simply because, together with Mossack and Fonseca, he was asked to approve any especially difficult decisions faced by Mossfon's employees, such as whether a dubious client should be kept or not. The three men then usually replied in brief one- or two-line emails, and the matter was resolved.

But after the Commerzbank raids in February 2015 and our corresponding reports, a profile of Zollinger was published in the Swiss newspaper *Tages-Anzeiger* at the end of April 2015, in which he was quoted as saying that he left Mossack Fonseca in 2011, and had never been a partner in the law firm. In response to enquiries from the newspaper – whose sister publication *SonntagsZeitung* has since also joined Prometheus – Zollinger not only wrote that he had 'never been a partner or co-partner of MF Panama', but also that he had 'never been an authorized signatory', and specifically 'not for documents or for bank accounts'. He adds that he had never been 'a proxy or had any other power of attorney' and had 'NEVER been a member of the Board of Directors'. And he hadn't been a shareholder of Mossfon either.

Someone who vehemently and publicly denies their involvement in this way had better be in the right. If only because it would be rather embarrassing if they were found to be lying. So after the *Tages-Anzeiger* article, we decided initially to go by the assumption that Zollinger was telling the truth. However, we planned to investigate him in more detail at a later date. There was still plenty of time, but there were simply too many other things that seemed more important.

That said, there aren't many stories that are quite as interesting as his. After completing his law studies, Zollinger travels around the world, and in 1995, he settles in Panama, first of all working for an Internet provider and eventually joining Mossack Fonseca in 1997, initially as an assistant to the two founding partners. He quickly works his way up and joins the management team in 2004. He gets Panamanian citizenship, marries a Panamanian and later becomes special ambassador of the Foreign Ministry.

In 2010, during a visit to Switzerland, Zollinger has a go on a bobsleigh at St Moritz. He's so inspired by the sport that he clearly decides to emulate the protagonists in the film *Cool Runnings*. In the American comedy, a Jamaican bobsleigh team attempts, against all odds, to compete in the Winter Olympic Games. The film is based on the true story of the Jamaican bobsleigh team that took part in the 1988 Winter Olympics in Calgary. So Zollinger decides to set up a bobsleigh team of his own, finds sponsors such as Adidas and BMW, engages a world-class trainer and recruits pushers for his bobsleigh, the 'Spirit of Panama', via a TV casting show. A wave of support sweeps across the country and even the president publicly wishes the team luck in achieving its ambitious goal: to reach the 2014 Winter Olympics in Sochi. The story of the exotic Swiss/Panamanian bobsleigh team not only receives an enthusiastic response in Panama and Switzerland, the *Spiegel*'s children's magazine also publishes an article about the 'dream on runners'. The team, which is run by Zollinger and Eduardo

Fonseca – Ramón's son – also considers itself to be good at racing, until Christoph Zollinger injures his foot and the team fails to qualify. It's the end of a dream.

[ ]

Zollinger is back on our radar when we find a document containing a reference to the owners of Mossack Fonseca & Co. S.A. In the document, dated 21 May 2008, Christoph Zollinger is named as having a 10 per cent stake in the company. It doesn't state whether these shares are held directly or indirectly. The remaining 90 per cent are divided equally between Ramón Fonseca and Jürgen Mossack.

From this document, it seems very likely that Zollinger was, at least in 2008, an indirect shareholder of Mossack Fonseca & Co. – something he denied in the *Tages-Anzeiger* interview in April 2015. In March 2016, we confront him about this again, and get the same response. Zollinger does, however, admit to being 'referred to colloquially as a partner' and to having signed emails 'accordingly'.

We go through other important Mossfon companies and it doesn't take long before we find what we're looking for, and namely in holdings, that is to say in companies, the shares of which in turn belong to other companies.[1]

- According to our documents, Christoph Zollinger holds 10 per cent of the shares of Tornbell Associates, which holds shares of companies such as the US Mossfon company in Nevada. It is likely that Zollinger holds these shares indirectly.
- Christoph Zollinger holds 10 per cent of the shares of Baysel Invest, which holds the Mossfon private banking division Mossfon Asset Management. When asked, Zollinger confirms

that he had been a shareholder of Baysel and explains he 'didn't know' the company.

- According to our data, the private foundation Panaswiss Foundation, one of the three Panamanian foundations linked to Zollinger, holds 10 per cent of the shares of MF Private Holdings Ltd, a Mossfon holding company. Zollinger comments: 'My foundation was the beneficiary of a foundation that owned MF Private Holdings Limited.'

We stop here and turn instead to the question of whether Zollinger was represented on the supervisory board. After just a few minutes we have a Word document up on the screen, in which his posts as director at several of the law firm's companies are listed. This document is dated March 2015, which means that before the *Tages-Anzeiger* started its enquiries, Zollinger was the director of Mossack Fonseca & Co. S.A., the trust department, the private banking department and the holding company Beechfield Corp.

Mossack Fonseca employees even sent out brochures as recently as May 2015, in which Zollinger is presented as a member of the Mossfon supervisory board, complete with photo and CV, alongside Fonseca and Mossack.

We find Zollinger's quote again: 'I have NEVER been a member of the Board of Directors.'

At the start of March 2016 we ask Zollinger about his posts as director. He now denies having been a director and instead explains that he 'left the board of the companies referred to' in the past few years.

Next point: in the spring of 2015 Zollinger told the *Tages-Anzeiger* that he left Mossfon in 2011. This is astonishing, because we find various emails from that very spring of 2015, sent from his Mossfon email account. In March 2015 Zollinger still holds a number of posts as director. According to our data, he sent the most recent letter, in which he explains that he wants to stand down from these posts, shortly after we reported about the Panamanian law firm's wheeling and dealing in the *Süddeutsche Zeitung* at the end of February 2015. And we find emails from July 2015 written by an employee called Andrea N., with the signature 'Assistant to Ch. Zollinger'. In an internal email sent the same month, the Mossfon personnel department provides a headcount of its employees. Mossack Fonseca & Co. S.A. is listed with 260 employees, and 'C. Zollinger' with '2'.

In this context, Zollinger explains that he actually left his role as Mossfon's chief operating officer in 2011, but that he 'kept an MF email address for the MF projects I'm in charge of' and that he now has no functions 'except for an ad-hoc, external advisory role'. He also reports that he has not had 'any employees' since 2012.

Furthermore, in the *Tages-Anzeiger*, Zollinger claims that Mossfon 'never advised end clients', even though he himself is the director and shareholder of the private banking division, and that is precisely what it does, day in, day out.

We confront him about this as well. Zollinger explains that he was talking 'about the activities of Mossack Fonseca & Co.' in that discussion with the *Tages-Anzeiger*. Previously, he had also claimed that the *Tages-Anzeiger* had 'exclusively' asked about Mossack Fonseca & Co., which was not the case according to our information. When asked about business with end clients, Zollinger said, 'Mossfon Trust and Mossfon Asset Management aren't part of the classic law business. They advise direct clients, which their websites also acknowledge.'

What we see here is yet another example of attempting to split up the Mossfon Group by means of legal hair-splitting.

Zollinger recently told the *Tages-Anzeiger* that one of the reasons he left the Mossfon Group was that he 'couldn't identify with the offshore business as such' and that he didn't want to have to 'assume responsibility for potential offences committed by third parties through no fault of his own'.

Everything we find in the data suggests that Christoph Zollinger was one of the law firm's leading forces. At least, it was he who strongly advised keeping Rami Makhlouf, the cousin and financial adviser of the Syrian leader Bashar al-Assad, as a client – against the advice of Mossfon's own compliance department.

Today, Zollinger admits he made a 'wrong' judgement about that; it's something he regrets.

We had almost finished this chapter when our colleague Julia Stein from NDR sent us a link to a YouTube video. A Mossfon corporate film. In minute eight, an off-screen voice formally announces that Christoph Zollinger became an 'official partner of the Mossfon Group' in 2004.

17

THE WORLD IS NOT ENOUGH

In the late 1990s Joachim zu Baldernach – who's not really called that – finds himself unable to locate his Bahamas-based company. Strictly speaking, Baldernach, who comes from a family of billionaires, hasn't actually misplaced the company, but rather the anonymous bearer share for all 5,000 shares of the shell company, which was established in the early 1990s. But this bearer share is, effectively, the company. Offshore companies rarely have offices or employees; they don't usually even have their own letterbox. So Baldernach rather reluctantly sends a fax to the Mossack Fonseca branch in the Bahamas, enquiring into how he can get a new bearer share. The problem for Mossfon is that there's no way of knowing whether Baldernach hasn't actually sold, lent or pledged his share, and with it the company. After all, that's why anonymous bearer shares are so sought after by shady operators: you can sell your offshore company at any time without leaving a trace.

So what would happen if Mossack Fonseca were to issue a new bearer share for all 5,000 shares, only for someone to turn up the next day with the original, missing certificate? That someone would then be the legal owner of the offshore company. Our data reveals that, in the end, Joachim zu Baldernach signs a letter of indemnity for Mossfon. In it, Baldernach asserts that he has not transferred, lent or in any other way used the share, and Mossfon is released from any liability risk that could potentially arise in connection with the new share.

Joachim zu Baldernach gets a new share. The offshore company once again belongs to him.

But why did Baldernach, a descendant of one of the richest German families, have a Bahamas-based company at all – and especially one that he's only been a registered shareholder of for a few years? A company that used to be completely opaque, with nominee directors and anonymous bearer shares? For tax reasons? Did he want to protect his assets? Or was it simply for practical or legal reasons?[1]

Joachim zu Baldernach's offshore company was mediated by a consulting firm based in Geneva, which markets itself as a firm that coordinates international structures for tax minimization. Our documents indicate that Baldernach used it to carry out real estate transactions in South America, and we can say with certainty that his offshore company owned another company, which in turn held a yacht.

In the mid-1990s, Baldernach used his shell company to open a bank account in Switzerland, and around ten years later, he opened one in Luxembourg too. Two countries renowned for the discretion of their banks.

The most recent activity of the Bahamas-based company seen in our data is the sale of a luxury yacht – the nominee directors signed the associated contract. Joachim zu Baldernach had decided to buy himself an even bigger yacht, a mega-yacht tailor-made to his own specifications. By all appearances, this yacht is also held by a shell company in another tax haven.

All perfectly organized by a professional family office. But is it normal to set up one offshore company here, one there, and another over there?

In the world of the mega-rich, the answer is evidently: yes.

[ ]

At some point towards the end of the last century, a parallel universe emerged in which the 'uber-wealthy', a term used in America to describe the richest of the rich, park their assets somewhere offshore, simply as a matter of course. The number of very rich and very famous families in our data who have parked part of their assets in shell companies is in three figures. The asset managers of all the family offices, exclusive private banks and large VIP departments of the major banks assist with this. If you ask anyone employed in this secretive industry why the money almost automatically ends up offshore, you will be told that it certainly doesn't have anything to do with tax avoidance or tax evasion.

The Danish sociologist Brooke Harrington can confirm this. She knows the ins and outs of this business, having spent two years training as an asset manager, as well as two years living in this world. She sat alongside her colleagues in expensive hotels, training sessions, aeroplanes and conferences. Her inspiration for this long-term field project was the legendary US scientist John Van Maanen, who trained as a policeman in the 1970s in order to fully understand that world and to gain the trust of his interlocutors. Like Van Maanen, Harrington also discovered that once she was accepted into the group, people were less reserved about talking to her. Her interlocutors began to reply to her more directly and clearly, meaning that Brooke Harrington is in the unique position of being able to describe what drives the asset managers of the super-rich. Harrington explains how the 'uber-wealthy' pay their assistants generous fees so that they are freed of obligations 'that the rest of the world consider to be part of everyday life'. These may include taxes, debts and court rulings, but it doesn't stop there. Harrington adds that one of the tasks of the asset manager can be to 'remove personal assets from the grasp of governments', and to remove them from the grasp of ex-wives, unsatisfied heirs, angry plaintiffs or creditors in the process.

According to Harrington, the offshore industry is not only about avoiding unwanted taxes, but also about avoiding unwanted laws, regulations or obligations.

In democracies, this statement can be made a bit more specific: taxes, laws, regulations or obligations that the citizens have agreed on, and which ought to apply to everyone equally.

However, this doesn't appear to have been the case for a while.

'At the commanding heights of the US economy,' Nobel Prize-winner and *New York Times* columnist Paul Krugman writes, 'hiding a lot of one's wealth offshore is probably the norm, not the exception.'

By all accounts – and as we have been discovering for months in our leak – it's similar in the rest of the world. We find some of the richest Indian, African, Australian, Russian and Chinese people, billionaires from the USA, Europe, Latin America and the Middle East. We find more than fifty billionaires from the *Forbes* list of the 500 richest people of 2015. And Mossack Fonseca is just one of several major providers of offshore companies; we're a long way from seeing the overall picture.

The French economist Gabriel Zucman tried to make a projection about the percentage of global assets lying in tax havens. He arrived at 8 per cent, around €5,900 billion. Zucman estimates that tax isn't paid on about three-quarters of this. Leona Helmsley, the wife of the property tycoon and billionaire Harry Helmsley, once expressed this concept more directly, with genuine pride: 'Only the little people pay taxes.' However, the US court saw it differently and sent her to prison for tax evasion.

But taxes are actually just one of many incentives for going offshore. The British author Nicholas Shaxson, one of the best tax haven experts in the world, summarizes it in his book *Treasure Islands: Tax Havens and the Men who Stole the World* as follows: 'Offshore is a project of wealthy and powerful elites to help them take the benefits from society without paying for them.'[2]

Nicholas Shaxson also writes that the offshore world is the 'biggest force for shifting wealth and power from poor to rich in history'. In fact, according to the charity Oxfam, the top 1 per cent of the global population has more wealth than the rest of the world put together. It's hardly surprising that a booming industry has formed around this 1 per cent, existing solely by adding to this tremendous wealth. Part of this industry is represented in our data, involving almost every country and thousands of companies. It's the family offices, asset management companies, banks, investment advisers, tax experts, and of course Mossack Fonseca itself.

All for the 1 per cent.

[ ]

One per cent.

From that figure, an established political term has evolved to denote the richest 1 per cent of a country. In the US, the term was turned on its head to provide the slogan of a political movement: 'We are the 99%'. This was chanted by supporters of the Occupy Wall Street movement; '99%' was scrawled across placards and banners. It was an outcry against the excesses and omnipotence of capitalism, the type of outcry that's rare today. In his bestseller *The Unwinding*, US author George Packer describes, precisely and without getting worked up, how the financial elite have dominated the US economy, the absurd repercussions this has for the rest of the country and why citizens who weren't previously especially politically engaged suddenly got involved in the Occupy Wall Street movement: because they felt betrayed by 'them up there'.

By men like Sanford I. Weill, the founder of what was once the biggest bank in the world, Citibank. The banker, with his aristocratic appearance, is considered to be one of the figures who was jointly responsible for the banking crisis of 2008 that was caused by irresponsible deals. Sanford I. Weill is a hate figure of the Occupy Wall Street movement and was, of course, a Mossack Fonseca client. He held a shell company called April Fool with the Panamanian law firm. He gave the same name to his sixty-metre yacht, because Sandy, as he's known to his friends, met his wife Joan on 1 April 1954.[3]

That's the world of the 1 per cent.

[ ]

The '99%' slogan unites the average employee with the cleaner, the homeless person with the single-parent bus driver and the free-lance graphic designer with the building worker. What they all share is a sense of anger about the fact that normal people have to fight for their livelihood every day in times of crisis, while the 'uber-wealthy' are busy thinking about what name to give to the offshore company that they use to stow away their new super-yacht, penthouse or shares.

There's a website where the '99%' vent their anger. There you find, for example, a young woman holding up a piece of paper to the camera that reads, 'I'm 30 years old, married and have a child. Everything was going well for us, but then at the end of 2006, I became pregnant and had to stay in bed for four months due to pre-eclampsia. During this time, I was fired. 2011: We've sold all our possessions to give our daughter what she needs. I can't find another job. Our house has just been sold in a forced auction. I AM SCARED. WE ARE THE 99%.'

Why are we telling you this? Because so far, we haven't found anyone like this woman in our data. And it wouldn't be too wild to assume that we won't be finding people like her in our data in the future.

The more complicated and opaque offshore structures are, the more expensive they are. But even so far as standard shell companies are concerned, assets need to be large in order to make them worthwhile. Financial service providers overseas charge high fees each year, on top of which come fees for lawyers who take care of the details, and perhaps another account in Switzerland; all of it ideally for a number of years. And on top of that, sometimes it's difficult to get the money there, and a roundabout approach is required.

That's how Mossfon sees it too: a Mossfon employee writes to an interested party from Germany, telling him that 'the vast majority' of its clients are 'so-called high-net-worth individuals', who may have assets 'of more than $500,000'. The Mossfon employee alerts the individual to the fact that 'structures that require the highest degree of confidentiality and professionalism can often cost many thousands of dollars each year'.

Not a problem for the super-rich. And there are richer people still: in the world of asset managers, 'ultra-high-net-worth individuals' are those who can generally be expected to invest at least $30 million. There are currently around 103,000 people who fall into this category, and the number is increasing year on year.

This group certainly includes a large number of sheikhs from the Middle East, who own companies managed by Mossfon. In June 2009 one of these companies, Marshdale S.A., purchases the legendary 87-metre yacht *Ecstasea* from a Russian oligarch for several hundred million dollars. According to the documents at our disposal, staff at Mossack Fonseca are a bit unclear about who the owner of Marshdale is. Until one colleague explains that it seems as though 'the ultimate owner of the company is His Highness Sheikh Abdullah bin Zayed Al Nahyan from the Royal Family of Abu Dhabi, the foreign minister of the United Arab Emirates'.[4]

[ ]

And what about the German billionaires and super-rich?

We find them too.

We see, for example, a number of men from the boardrooms of the biggest German companies buying offshore companies in the British Virgin Islands to hold their villa in Mallorca or the Caribbean, or because the former owner only wanted to sell the villa to them that way. One of them even sends us excerpts from his tax return to prove that foul play wasn't involved. Another is quick to tell us on the phone that he would 'happily pull his trousers down' because he's got nothing to hide, and invites us to a meeting with his tax adviser.

Of course, in addition to other advantages, these structures also provide tax benefits. If you want to buy a house in a country like Spain, you have to pay 10 per cent land transfer tax. This tax, however, isn't applicable if you don't buy the house itself, but instead buy the shares of the company that owns the house.

We also see numerous members of the wealthiest German families who, via Mossack Fonseca, are investing in other continents or hold or have held some of their possessions offshore, for example works of art. Industrialists and princes, brewery owners and entrepreneurs, countesses and barons. In general: nobility. Habsburg, Stauffenberg, Wittgenstein, Bismarck – members of all these families have connections to Mossack Fonseca.

In the Panamanian company register alone, so many German aristocrats crop up that you might think someone had emptied the German nobility register there. And they are not the only ones: when we investigated the Panamanian company register for the *Süddeutsche Zeitung* in 2013, we discovered a concentration of prominent names that was almost uncanny: among others, Ferdinand Piëch, multiple Porsches and Silvia Quandt were registered as directors of companies in Panama. At the time, Piëch and the Porsches explained that the companies were part of a structure that was never used, and which didn't provide any tax advantages either; Quandt told us she couldn't explain why her name was found there.

We also find the Bahamas-based company Longdown Properties in Mossfon's company register. This company is the reason Helmut Linssen, the former finance minister of North Rhine-Westphalia, was forced to leave his office as treasurer of the German Christian Democratic Union in 2014. The information was originally found on a tax CD and in 2012, criminal proceedings against him were initiated, which were later dropped. In the relevant years, his offshore structure had cost more than the assets he had parked there – which had been deposited in the 1990s via a Luxembourg bank – had earned in interest.[5]

[ ]

Nicolas Berggruen, billionaire and former owner of the department store chain Karstadt, is also involved in a whole string of offshore companies, all of which seem to be associated with investments in China. For the dazzling investor, the offshore business is clearly nothing special. Among others, his Karstadt investment allegedly also involved a tax haven structure, and it's also claimed that Berggruen's profits flow into a trust in the British Virgin Islands. Nicholas Berggruen had not responded to our enquiries about this by the time we went to press. His father, the art collector Heinz Berggruen, who died in 2007, was also no stranger to the offshore world; the Panamanian company register lists him as the director of two now inactive companies.

[ ]

In the parallel world of the rich and the super-rich, it may be the norm for accounts, shares, houses, yachts, and so on to be held by offshore companies that are, in part, spread across multiple continents and countries. Owning shell companies is, as we have already mentioned, in itself completely legal. It only becomes illegal when potential income is withheld from the financial authorities.

We can, however, certainly draw the conclusion that a two-tier system seems to have established itself internationally, whereby some people pay their taxes in the conventional way, while others, because they have the means to do so, decide for themselves when, how much and indeed whether they pay taxes at all.

It's a problem for every democracy if different classes form that no longer have much to do with one another. However, this problem is intensified if different rules seem to apply exclusively to the very wealthy.

Or no rules at all.

18

THE LOOTING MACHINE

According to the British author and *Financial Times* correspondent Tom Burgis, you ought to imagine what's happening in Africa like this: an invisible machine is working to plunder the continent. A looting machine. A coalition of corrupt dictators, unscrupulous large corporations and ruthless banks, all working hand in hand, united by their greed.

Mossack Fonseca is a key cog in this machine. With the law firm's help, transactions can go unnoticed. Our data reveals that autocrats and corrupt businesspeople are using Mossfon shell companies en masse in order to cover their tracks and to invest money abroad. An incredible amount of money.

Our colleague Will Fitzgibbon from the ICIJ writes to us from the Prometheus meeting in Johannesburg in September: 'Our colleagues here are enthusiastic about the possibilities that this data may offer in terms of clearing up at least a few of the countless affairs that have been shaking their African countries for years. For the first time, they will hopefully be in a position to take a look behind the scenes of multi-million and billion-dollar scandals and to shed some light on them.'

The ICIJ organized the meeting in Africa because only one African colleague, Justin Arenstein from South Africa, had been able to make it to our meeting in Munich. The others didn't have the money for it. That's another thing that becomes clearer to us each month we work on our investigation: the dream conditions under which we work. We're not threatened, arrested or shot dead, and we even earn good money for our work. What's more, if we want to go to Washington or Iceland, we simply book a flight.

It had long been clear to our partners from the ICIJ, who often work with colleagues in Africa, that there needed to be a separate meeting in Africa. That's why they organized a meeting in Johannesburg for the African Prometheus investigators. Will Fitzgibbon has a leading role here; he's been working on major ICIJ projects for a number of years, coordinating the African parts of the investigations. Recently, for example, his work involved investigating the questionable activities of Australian mining companies in Africa.

Will rented out a guesthouse in the centre of Johannesburg for the meeting. Fourteen journalists from eight different countries – South Africa, the US, Zimbabwe, Namibia, Botswana, Mali, Senegal and Tunisia – have the guesthouse to themselves for two days at the end of September. It's a research camp. Will Fitzgibbon gives them the lowdown on the project in much the same way as we did in Munich and Washington, explaining about the initial big stories, investigative approaches, graphic implementation and safety rules for communications.

It must have been a fantastic meeting. A couple of days after returning to the US, Will writes to us, telling us how when he explained the project, the room fell silent and everyone started searching through the data together. 'Silence out of anticipation and excitement.' The journalists became so absorbed in what they were doing that he had to force them to stop for coffee and lunch breaks. The urge to try to find links to Africa was so great that they simply wanted to carry on searching.

After a short time, our colleagues find their first hits. One by one, they find African politicians and their families. 'And the hits are quite literally from everywhere,' Will Fitzgibbon writes, 'from Sudan, Senegal, South Africa and Egypt.'

We're also enthusiastic. Our decision to share our leak with the world was based on the understanding that it was the only way we'd be able to shed light on all the important stories. Here in Germany, the African stories would slip through the cracks, hardly attracting any attention, just like our stories there. At the same time, we have the feeling that this investigation could be much more important for some African countries than it is for us. Here, shell companies create social injustice and help cover up crimes. In Africa, the clandestine dealings of dictators plunge entire nations into poverty. It's a completely different dimension.

[ ]

Africa is incredibly rich. Half the world's diamond deposits are found on African territory, along with a quarter of the world's gold reserves, 10 per cent of oil reserves and 9 per cent of gas reserves. And then there's uranium, mineral ores, and much more. The population gets virtually nothing from it: the money simply disappears, into the accounts of large multinational companies or the safes of the elite. Experts estimate that more than $50 billion flows out of Africa every year. $50 billion! On top of that, the African states avoid paying about $38 billion in taxes, because companies operating there divert their profits to tax havens, as revealed in 2013 by a group of experts led by Kofi Annan.

After the meeting in Johannesburg, we and our colleagues continue to find links to Africa on an almost daily basis. We find a company founded by Mossfon that the government of Gabon accuses of having evaded taxes worth $85 million, then we find the wife of a former president of Ghana in the data, and then a former Nigerian president of OPEC. The Mossfon data contains countless references to unresolved scandals and affairs in Africa. Below is a small list, which is by no means exhaustive:

- According to the Mossfon documents, a sister of Joseph Kabila, the controversial president of the **Democratic Republic of the Congo**, is a partner of Keratsu Holding Ltd, which in turn holds shares in various companies in Congo-Brazzaville.[1]

- According to the documents at our disposal, Teodoro Obiang, the son of the dictator of **Equatorial Guinea**, owns a company called Ebony Shine International Ltd. This company was established in the British Virgin Islands in 2006. A report of the United States Senate came to the conclusion that Obiang used it in order to buy himself a Gulfstream jet with presumably embezzled public funds.[2]

- Martina Joaquim Chissano, the daughter of the former president of **Mozambique**, has evidently been a shareholder of Prima Finance Development Ltd in the British Virgin Islands since 2013. Chissano, whose passport we find in the data, is also the director of the Prima Talent Group, a company that invests in oil and gas extraction in Mozambique.[3]

- Alongside a niece of Hastings Banda, the former president of Malawi, three former ministers from **Malawi** were also temporarily the directors of the offshore company Press Trust Overseas Ltd. According to the documents, the ministers in question were Aleke Banda, the former finance minister, Mapopa Chipeta, the former foreign minister, and Yusuf Mwawa, the former minister of education, science and technology. Mwawa was arrested in 2005 for allegedly using public funds to finance his wedding. He was later sentenced to five years' imprisonment.[4]

- According to the data, Bruno Itoua, the former energy minister of the **Republic of the Congo** and former head of the state-owned oil company SNPC, characterized as a sort of 'honorary son' of the Congolese president Denis Sassou Nguesso, temporarily had power of attorney for the Panamanian company Grafin Associated S.A.[5]

- The minister of petroleum of **Angola**, José Maria Botelho de Vasconcelos, appears in the data as the beneficiary of Medea Investments Ltd. The company was established in Niue in September 2001; at that time, he'd already been minister for two years.[6]

[john doe]: Any news? Also, are any African journalists involved?

[SZ]: Yes, several.

[john doe]: And?

[SZ]: They found Kabila's sister, the son of a dictator, countless scandals that have to do with oil or mining rights. And Kofi Annan's son.

[john doe]: Annan's son? This is a joke, right?

[SZ]: No.

[john doe]: Groan. Didn't know about that one either. This is very depressing.

Politicians and their families, that's the one side. The other side is large corporations from China and the West that readily pay bribes, and companies like Mossfon that ensure payments slip under the radar. These are transactions that are carried out in a parallel world. The public only hears about them on the very odd occasion. Let's take, for example, the Democratic Republic of the Congo (formerly known as Zaire): a poor, war-torn country. For thirty-two years, Zaire was ruled by the dictator Mobutu Sese Seko. After he was overthrown, numerous rebel groups tried to seize power. Because so many other African countries were involved in the conflict and supported one side or the other, experts spoke of an 'African world war'. Even though a peace agreement was signed in 2002, fights still flare up on a regular basis today.

In 2010 Joseph Kabila – who had been president of the country for a good fifteen years – gave his approval for two companies to drill for oil in the north east of his country; these companies were largely unknown within the industry and had only been registered a few months previously in the British Virgin Islands. The companies in question were Caprikat Ltd and Foxwhelp Ltd, both of which were established by Mossfon.

Now, it's common practice for the state to get the majority of the revenue generated from oil production. In Uganda, one of the Democratic Republic of the Congo's neighbours, for example, a company can only keep between 20 and 31.5 per cent of its revenue; the remainder goes to the state. In contrast, the South African news site News24 reported that the two Mossfon shell companies Caprikat and Foxwhelp can keep between 55 and 60 per cent. That sounds like an extremely unusual deal. A deal at the expense of the state.

Furthermore, it's alleged that the two companies only paid $6 million for the lucrative concessions, while other companies offered more than ten times that sum.[7]

Why did Kabila approve such a deal? Khulubuse Zuma, the nephew of the South African President Jacob Zuma, and Khulubuse Zuma's lawyer, signed the deal for Caprikat and Foxwhelp. The South African head of state had visited the Congo a few months before the transaction; according to News24, he'd engaged in private discussions with Kabila about oil. Coincidence?[8]

In any case, the deal was so shady that even Mossack Fonseca's ears pricked up.

In our data, we find an email from the summer of 2015. A Mossfon employee comes to the conclusion that there's a whole web of companies and foundations behind Caprikat and Foxwhelp, and if you were to disentangle it, you'd eventually find the owner, the investor Dan Gertler.[9] In 2012 Jean Pierre Muteba, head of a non-governmental organization that focuses on the consequences of mining in the Congo, told the *Guardian* that the Israeli billionaire had made his fortune by 'looting the Congo at the expense of its people'. In 2015 the *New York Times* called him a 'robber baron of our day'.

[ ]

Around this time, towards the end of 2015, we fly to Geneva, the city of secret money, to the place where the robber barons live. Only a few kilometres from the airport, down by Lake Geneva, the offices of dozens of offshore helpers we know only too well from the data are lined up: banks, lawyers and financial service providers, which use Mossfon to provide their clients with shell companies, foundations and numbered accounts. Based in the tax haven of Switzerland, they help smuggle money into other tax havens. It all takes place very discreetly; that goes without saying.

We spend hours wandering from one address we recognize from the data to the next, have a look at the branch of Deutsche Bank in Saint-Gervais Les Bergues, take a look at Mossfon's Geneva office on Rue Micheli-du-Crest, and marvel at the well-dressed men and women who get out of big Mercedes and BMWs with number plates from all over the world, and then – often after looking over their shoulders sheepishly – disappear into the marble entrance halls.

Sightseeing for offshore investigators.

In the late afternoon, we travel to Russin, a small village just a few minutes' train ride from Geneva. We're here to visit Jean Ziegler, citizen of the Republic and Canton of Geneva, sociologist, professor emeritus and former member of parliament. Ziegler appears at the door in his jogging bottoms; he didn't have time to change. 'Telephone conference with New York.' The octogenarian is a very busy man. At one time, he was a UN special rapporteur on the Right to Food, and he's now an adviser to the

UN Human Rights Council. For the past fifty years, he's been railing against the disparities between developed and developing countries. *We Let Them Starve* was the title of one of his most recent books. Subtitle: *Mass Destruction in The Third World*.

He's not the type to mince his words; he's the voice of the poor and a nightmare for the high and mighty.

He considers transnational private groups to be 'crusaders of neoliberalism', refers to the World Trade Organization, the International Monetary Fund and the World Bank as the 'three horsemen of the Apocalypse of organized hunger', views banks as 'receivers of the capitalist system' and his home country, Switzerland, as a type of 'Disneyland controlled by banks and bandits'.

Ziegler struggles to contain his anger about turbo-capitalism, to such an extent that he's always tied up in some sort of legal dispute because he's insulted one banker or another. His house, therefore, belongs to his wife, his car is leased, and his debts amount to several millions of Swiss francs. But it's all been worth it, Ziegler says. He has a strict sense of justice, and it starts with the terminology used. 'Don't call them tax havens,' he insists, 'it sounds too positive. They're scoundrel states!'

Ziegler invites us to a take a seat at the large oak table in his living room, pours us each a glass of red wine and then it's time for him to talk. About the scoundrel states...

In all likelihood, there are few offences – not to mention widespread tax evasion – that aren't in some way connected with offshore states. There's more criminal energy per square kilometre in the Bahamas and Panama than anywhere else in the world. More or less all transactions involving criminal money – whether criminal from the outset or used for criminal purposes – are carried out via financial business companies, trusts, institutions or foundations that are registered in offshore states. And the consequences are devastating: take, for example, the hundreds of thousands of deaths each year...

The hundreds of thousands of deaths. You need to explain that.

> *According to the UN, around thirty-two so-called low-intensity conflicts are currently raging around the world; these are conflicts that claim fewer than 10,000 lives each year. These are taking place in the Philippines, as well as Darfur, the Central African Republic, etc. etc. Each year, hundreds of thousands of people all over the world lose their lives in these conflicts. By enabling the purchase of weapons or the sale of blood diamonds, for example, offshore centres play an instrumental role in these conflicts.*

Politicians in the Virgin Islands, the Cook Islands and the Caymans would probably say that they aren't doing anything apart from allowing shell companies to set up there.

> *That isn't true. So-called tax havens and their service providers like Mossack Fonseca are nothing short of enemies of humanity.*

One thing that many offshore countries have in common is that they have virtually no resources. Business with shell companies is seen as their last resort.

> *Pah, you don't just go and say, 'My family's budget is too small, so I'm going to go and sell heroin in the neighbourhood, even though I know it's bad for the neighbours.'*

Ziegler talks himself into a rage; one hour passes, then two, then three. It's not long before we open the second bottle of wine. The conscience of the world, as his admirers refer to him, needs to speak. Tax havens, hedge funds, Mossack Fonseca, world hunger; for him, it's all one and the same. Everything is connected and mutually dependent. Ziegler sees the big picture. He tells us how he's spent too long seeing sleazy deals being negotiated in favour of the wealthy, seeing politicians willing to take bribes, exploiting their countries and stashing their illicit funds in the Bahamas, the Caymans or Panama with the help of offshore service providers.

Ziegler has seen what happens when African autocrats send their money abroad instead of investing it in schools and hospitals. He's seen how diseases caused by malnutrition eat away at the faces of African children, he's looked into the eyes of starving women and men and knows what hunger can lead to: emaciation, children with disabilities, death.

All of a sudden, our findings become something tangible; we become aware of the full impact of the operations of service providers like Mossfon. If the government of a country decides to lay the legal foundations for its existence as a tax haven, it's not just a private matter for that particular state. It's a problem for the whole world.

Ziegler believes that these 'scoundrel states' ought to be dried up. Business with companies registered there needs to stop. Why hasn't that already happened, a long time ago? Because the governments have been under pressure from banks, secret services, global corporations and the super-wealthy: the 'world dictatorship of globalized financial capital'.

As we leave, Ziegler hands us a copy of his latest book. It's entitled *Change the World!* The dedication inside it reads: 'With heartfelt, respectful friendship and solidarity'. He then shuts the door; a loud, likeable admonisher in a world that has remained strikingly silent about the offshore underworld for far too long.

[ ]

Back in Munich, we take another look at the data and find another billionaire with business interests in Africa: Beny Steinmetz. Until recently, Steinmetz owned a major share of the department store chain Karstadt. Steinmetz is one of the richest men in the world;

he uses his private jet to commute between Tel Aviv, London, Geneva and his many diamond companies. Our data trail leads us to Guinea, one of the poorest countries in the world.

In the hinterland of the West African state, in the middle of the jungle, is the Simandou mountain range. The summits of these mountains have names that sound strangely out of place, like Iron Maiden and Metallica. Naming the mountains after heavy metal bands is an allusion to the treasure lying dormant in the hills: iron ore.

In the late 1990s Guinea gave the Anglo-Australian company Rio Tinto permission to extract this ore. It was claimed to be the biggest untapped deposit in the world. The mining rights were extremely valuable, involving hundreds of millions of dollars. However, in 2008 the Guinean authorities suddenly withdrew the licence from Rio Tinto and issued it to a company that had made a fortune with diamonds, but hadn't had much experience in mining ores: Beny Steinmetz Group Resources, or BSGR. The story gets even stranger. According to media reports, the company didn't pay anything up front to the Guinean state for the mining rights. It had apparently declared that it was prepared to invest $165 million in the iron-ore field in the future.

'The paradox of plenty', referred to more ominously as 'the resource curse', is the term economists use to describe the phenomenon whereby poverty and corruption tend to prevail in countries like Guinea, which have an abundance of oil, gas or precious metals. The US economists Jeffrey Sachs and Andrew Warner investigated the connection a number of years ago and came to the conclusion that economic growth tends to be lower in countries with an abundance of natural resources than in those with fewer natural resources.

A year after Beny Steinmetz acquired the mining rights, his company BSGR sold half of the Simandou arm of his business empire to the Brazilian mining company Vale for an incredible $2.5 billion.

The annual budget of the Guinean government at that time was $1.2 billion, meaning that BSGR received twice as much as the government had available each year. It's important to note that this is the government of a country in which child mortality rates are so high that 104 in every 1,000 children don't reach their fifth year of life. In comparison, this figure is as low as four in every 1,000 in Germany. In the United Nations' Human Development Index, Guinea occupies position 179 of 187. That's the human impact of the resource curse.

The *Independent* referred to the BSGR–Vale deal as 'the corruption deal of the century'. And according to Transparency International, Guinea is one of the most corrupt countries in the world. The Guinean dictator Lansana Conté, under whose rule Steinmetz was awarded the mining rights, called his own ministers 'thieves'.

And that wasn't a joke.

Conté reportedly once remarked: 'If we had to shoot every Guinean who had stolen from Guinea there would be no one left to kill.' He evidently wasn't excluding himself.

In any case, the kleptocrat died just a few days after signing over the valuable Simandou concessions to BSGR. There was a military coup, and then another one. Ultimately, in the first somewhat democratic elections in the country's history, a man named Alpha Condé was elected. He'd left Guinea when it was still under French rule, studied law in Paris and lectured at the Sorbonne.

When he entered office, Alpha Condé pledged to be the Nelson Mandela of Guinea. One of his first official tasks was to review the Simandou deal, the fishiness of which had reached even the furthest-flung corners. The Sudanese billionaire Mo Ibrahim summed it up at an African economic conference at the time: 'Are the Guineans who did that deal idiots, or criminals, or both?'

The new president, whose advisers include Tony Blair and George Soros, hired American lawyers and risk analysts to find out how it had been possible for Steinmetz's company BSGR, for the most part inexperienced in terms of ore extraction, to win this contract.

The investigators soon found a man who was unusually well connected: the Frenchman Frédéric Cilins. Since 2000, he'd been a regular guest in Guinea, and always brought gifts for the officials with him: MP3 players, mobile phones, that type of thing. Nothing major in the West, but items that were sought after and difficult to get hold of in one of the poorest countries in the world. And that wasn't all; a select few also received diamond-encrusted models of Formula 1 cars.

In 2012 a committee engaged by Alpha Condé came to the conclusion that Frédéric Cilins was a 'secret front man' of Beny Steinmetz, and the investigators also came across irregularities in the BSGR-Simandou deal. They claimed that Frédéric Cilins had offered the former dictator Lansana Conté – the man who awarded the contract to Steinmetz shortly before he died – a golden, diamond-encrusted watch (which BSGR denies).[10]

BSGR does confirm that Frédéric Cilins worked for the company. But it claims that this had nothing to do with acquiring the mining rights for Simandou.

In 2012 the Guinean authorities discovered contracts that an offshore company called Pentler Holdings and BSGR had apparently concluded with Mamadie Touré, one of dictator Lansana Conté's four wives. In one of these contracts, a company called Matinda, owned by Mamadie Touré, agrees 'to do everything necessary in order to obtain the signature from the authorities for the mining area in question for the company BSG Resources Guinea'. Another document refers to $2.4 million that Matinda is to receive due to a 'cooperation contract' with Pentler Holdings. And then there's another contract terminating the cooperation of Touré, that is to say Matinda, with Pentler, and pledging Matinda a sum of $3.1 million for its share in the activities in Guinea.[11]

Mamadie Touré's brother was suddenly the vice president of BSGR Guinea, and BSGR was awarded the Simandou contract.[12]

When details about the contracts were revealed in 2012, Global Witness took special note. It was a perfect case for investigation by the non-governmental organization, which is committed to the fight against corruption, tax havens and the exploitation of entire countries, especially since it was backed by the American billionaire George Soros, one of the new president Alpha Condé's advisers. So the people at Global Witness commenced their investigations, and it wasn't long before they found something. Take, for example, the fact that BSGR had reported in a press release that the wife of the dictator had nothing to do with the Simandou deal. Consequently, Global Witness published a video from 2006 showing Frédéric Cilins and other BSGR representatives together with Mamadie Touré at an event focusing on the Simandou project. BSGR had also claimed that Mamadie Touré wasn't married to President Conté. In response to this, Global Witness published a copy of her passport. In it, it clearly states 'Epouse P.R.G.' Wife of the president of the Republic of Guinea.[13]

For more than three years, Global Witness has been focusing its attention on BSGR in this way. The man behind it all is Daniel Balint-Kurti. He was formerly based in Africa, where he worked as a journalist for *The Times* and the *Independent*. Now he works for Global Witness, questioning witnesses, procuring documents and ploughing through company registers all over the world. His aim: to prove that Beny Steinmetz ended up with the Simandou concession as a result of bribery. BSGR refers to it as a 'crude smear campaign'.

In 2013 BSGR initiated proceedings against Global Witness. Steinmetz's company wanted to know, among other things, who Balint-Kurti's sources are. The case was dropped.

We want to talk to Daniel Balint-Kurti. We want to find out more. We arrange to meet him in Munich; he has relatives in

Bavaria. We tell him that we're interested in the Simandou deal and the investigations he's been working on.

Balint-Kurti tells us how he ultimately discovered multiple companies that had been founded by Mossack Fonseca or that were among its clients: Pentler Holdings as well as Matinda in the British Virgin Islands. He likens the companies to a wall that he can't get past. 'The Simandou case is just one of many. Time and time again, Global Witness's investigations into corruption end with an individual shell company, or even a whole network.'

In this instance, we're now able to open a secret door and finally provide an insight into what was previously hidden.

We know that Pentler Holdings was founded in the British Virgin Islands in 2005. Shortly afterwards, the company concluded its first contracts with Mamadie Touré. However, according to Global Witness, BSGR claims to have nothing to do with Pentler.

Without our data, this story would end here. If you were to ask the authorities in the British Virgin Islands, you'd perhaps find out who the directors are. But that's all. So we go through the documents in the Pentler Holdings file and find out that the firm was founded under the authority of Onyx Financial Advisors Ltd, whose headquarters are in Switzerland.[14] According to a report in the *Financial Times* in 2013, Beny Steinmetz's company claims that Onyx, which according to internal Mossfon notes is now called Invicta Advisory, is 'wholly separate and fully independent of BSGR'. In late 2015 a spokesperson for BSGR tells us that 'Pentler is not associated with Onyx and was never owned by Onyx'.

However, Onyx – which once founded Pentler – and BSGR shared a floor in a small brick building at 7 Old Park Lane in London, not far from Buckingham Palace, until at least December 2015. At the time of going to press, the director of Onyx is one of the directors of BSGR.[15] Furthermore, we discover that a Mossfon employee met an Onyx employee in Geneva in June 2009. In the discussion, the Mossfon employee learns that the owners of the company are a 'French-Israeli family, operating in the trade of diamonds, oil and artworks'. Well: Beny Steinmetz was born in Israel, but also holds a French passport.

To put it diplomatically, that doesn't sound like 'fully independent'.[16]

Incidentally, Frédéric Cilins was arrested in the US in 2013. He had tried to convince Mamadie Touré, the wife of the since deceased dictator Lansana Conté, to destroy all documents relating to Pentler and BSGR. Over a chicken sandwich, Frédéric Cilins offered Touré money to destroy the documents. Frédéric Cilins therefore wanted to get rid of crucial evidence in one of Africa's biggest ever corruption investigations. Furthermore, Mamadie Touré was instructed to leave the US; he offered to pay for her flight. If BSGR survived the ongoing investigation by Guinea's mining committee and maintained its mining rights, she would get a further $5 million. The 'number one' had given it all his blessing. When asked who the number one was, he replied 'Beny'.[17]

What Frédéric Cilins didn't know was that Touré was wearing a microphone and recording the conversation. She'd made a deal with the FBI. Frédéric Cilins was arrested in Florida on 14 April 2013 and later admitted to having attempted to destroy evidence. However, he remained silent about who was pulling the strings. He was sentenced to two years' imprisonment.

The lawsuit documentation repeatedly mentions a 'Co-Conspirator 1'. According to investigations carried out by various media bodies, this relates to Beny Steinmetz. Since then, investigations into the Guinea deal have also been carried out in Switzerland and Guinea due to suspicion of corruption. The Onyx offices have been searched and Steinmetz has been questioned multiple times.[18]

In Guinea, Alpha Condé's government finally withdrew the Simandou concession from Beny Steinmetz's company in 2014. They claimed there was 'precise and consistent evidence' of 'corrupt practices' relating to the awarding of the concession. In addition to the Swiss, American and Guinean authorities, the British Serious Fraud Office has also carried out investigations. We learn that the Swiss investigators suspect that Steinmetz was directly involved in acts of corruption. They believe that Pentler was established by Onyx on the instructions of Steinmetz. According to the Swiss court documents we were able to consult, one Onyx employee almost exclusively took care of the administration of Steinmetz's companies and foundations. And what can we say: that's fully in line with what our data suggests.[19]

19

SECRET MEETINGS IN THE *KOMITÈROM*

We're in Lillehammer, at Lysgårdsbakken, the Olympic ski jumping hill. Below us lies the mountain valley of Gudbrandsdalen, where Norway's largest lake, Mjøsa, reaches one of its narrowest points. On its shore is Lillehammer, the city that hosted the 1994 Winter Olympics, in which German skier Markus Wasmeier sensationally won two gold medals. We can see the train tracks winding through the valley, the railway station where we arrived a day earlier and the friendly, albeit somewhat run-down hotel where we're staying.

The Radisson Hotel is built into the hillside a bit higher up. Here, from 8 to 11 October 2015, about 900 reporters from more than 100 different countries are currently meeting for the Global Investigative Journalism Conference. The conference takes place every other year and is held somewhere different each time. The programme includes workshop reports from prestigious colleagues and presentations from data specialists, undercover journalists and experts in press law. The conference has nothing to do with our Prometheus project, but some of our international partners are there too and we want to use the opportunity to speak to them in person.

Nine hundred investigative journalists. When we say that to friends and colleagues, the reaction is always the same: isn't the risk of an attack really high? If you assume that only one in every ten had made serious enemies through their work, the police would have ninety potential motives on their hands if a bomb were to go off. The conference visitors include many wealth reporters like us, who have occasionally been a thorn in the side of the Federal Intelligence Service, the US Secret Service, the General German Automobile Club (ADAC) or the German government. But many of the other visitors work in China, Russia, Ukraine, the Middle East or African states, where they face real, tangible threats. Some colleagues only work undercover, others operate under false names, or at least use a different name to publish articles. Roman Anin, our Russian colleague from the ICIJ with whom we're working on the Putin story, is asked at the podium whether he's afraid.

Anin shrugs his shoulders and says, 'If they want to kill me, they'll kill me.'

[ ]

For us, the conference isn't only exciting because the presentations are so interesting; it's also useful for our project. ICIJ Director Gerard Ryle, Prometheus project manager Marina Walker, head of data Mar Cabra, programmer Rigo Carvajal and everyone else who works at the ICIJ, plus at least thirty journalists who are investigating Prometheus with us, are all in Lillehammer. By now, there are already more than 100 groups and thousands of entries in our forum. But it's still best to discuss things in person, like here in Lillehammer. We keep retreating to hotel rooms or the small *Komitèrom*, which is where the heads of the International Olympic Committee gathered in 1994 to discuss matters of importance. You could call it the control room of the Olympic Games.

What is less ideal in the matter of secrecy is that some of our colleagues who are working with us on the Mossfon data bring up the project in overcrowded rooms and start talking about 'your crazy data' in front of others. We quickly steer the conversation in another direction or stare silently into space until the colleague gets the picture.

In Lillehammer, we show the ICIJ data specialists a new list of around 25,000 names along with information regarding transfers effected by Mossfon on behalf of its clients. Mar Cabra isn't sure what to make of it. On the one hand: yay, more material! On the other hand: there's already so much data, and everything is already so complicated...

We also explain that we ordered another new computer a couple of days before leaving for Lillehammer, the third one to date. The second one, our almost brand-new €6,000 supercomputer, couldn't cope with the sheer quantity of data, by now around 2.5 terabytes. Working with it had been extremely tedious; each individual search took minutes and it took even longer if you wanted to view the documents, assuming the computer didn't crash completely. Even though all the experts had told us that this computer would be powerful enough, it wasn't.

Of course, when we ordered the second computer, we knew than an even more expensive computer would have been even better suited to our needs, let's say a €17,000 computer. That's how much the version would have cost that the IT specialist recommended to us as a silver bullet. Suggesting that seemed no less absurd to us than suggesting building a floor on top of the SZ Tower just for us.

But our project had reached absurd dimensions, and it was simply no use: we couldn't work like that. We reluctantly made our way to the main editorial office, cautiously explained the present situation and proposed, somewhat more cautiously, that if we wanted to make the data searchable in the *Süddeutsche Zeitung*, we would need an even more expensive computer. If we wanted to rely on the ICIJ, we wouldn't need it... Our new proposal: a mega

PC with 128 gigabytes of RAM and five SSD hard drives with a total of 8.256 terabytes of memory. A server farm contained in the housing of a computer. Cost: €17,484.36.

Our chief editors decided: buy it.

When we tell ICIJ programmer Rigoberto Carvajal about this over dinner in Lillehammer, he can't believe it: '€17,000?! For *one* computer? You're crazy!' He laughs his head off and at the same time is completely fascinated, wanting to know every detail, every specification. We're almost embarrassed by the new computer, so we refer him to Vanessa Wormer, the data journalist who's been working in our small team since September; we recruited her from New York, where she'd completed a special course of study in data journalism at Columbia University. She writes programs that enable us to search the data more effectively, and takes care of the entire technical side of things. Since Vanessa's been working with us, we only concern ourselves with hard disk sizes, RAM or Excel formatting if it's absolutely necessary, and that's hardly ever the case. And that's very refreshing. Aside from that, Vanessa is a fantastic journalist and colleague who brings a great deal to our project.

Another new colleague has joined us for half a year: the freelance journalist Mauritius Much. He not only delves deeply into any case we present him with, above all relating to sports, but is also a competent Spanish speaker. This is by no means insignificant, as a considerable number of the emails and documents are written in Spanish.

Now there are four of us in the *Süddeutsche Zeitung*'s Prometheus team.

[ ]

Ensuring that the translation is spot on becomes increasingly important the closer we come to the publication date. Some of the tricks used by Mossfon employees only become apparent in the exact translation; for example, one of our favourite topics at present: dealing with the nominee beneficial owner. It's by far the most abstruse thing in the world of shell companies, which is not exactly lacking in terms of absurdity.

In the offshore industry, the beneficial owner is incontrovertibly at the end of the chain of cover-ups. Front men may well be deployed as directors, and other offshore companies may be registered as shareholders, but insofar as the beneficial owner, often referred to as the ultimate beneficial owner, is concerned, one thing is clear: they are the real owner of the company. These days, any relatively serious bank will only set up accounts for an offshore company if their ultimate beneficial owner is named. The bank then reviews this individual in order to verify who it's doing business with. The rule of having to name the person at the end of the chain is essential in order to prevent money laundering, the financing of terrorism and other criminal acts.

Mossack Fonseca's employees evidently seem to believe that this is a rule like many others. That is to say, another rule that can be applied flexibly.

Mossack Fonseca therefore repeatedly offers especially problematic clients the chance to switch off the banks' verification mechanism by offering the use of a nominee beneficial owner to appear in the place of the real ultimate beneficial owner.

Owner.

Nominee beneficial owner.

Real ultimate beneficial owner?

It sounds farcical. It's not only completely absurd, but also completely illegal. The high-ranking Mossack Fonseca manager Ramses Owens, until a few years ago director of the trust department, forms the same judgement when a colleague from the Mossfon office in Hong Kong asks him about it in May 2008. Ramses Owens tells him that the nominee beneficial owner service is 'these days' considered 'illegal', and goes on to explain how in Panama, an article in the criminal code prohibits the use of 'hidden beneficiaries' as well as lying about 'real ownership'.[1]

Only a year previously, Ramses Owens himself had offered precisely this service to a client, describing it as a 'delicate' service that Mossack Fonseca would, of course, treat with the 'utmost confidentiality'.

And a good six months later, *after* having described it as illegal, the very same Ramses Owens offers this service to another client. In January 2009 a US client gets in touch; Mossack Fonseca manages a hidden foreign account for her with HSBC. The client is panicky; she fears HSBC knows her name and suspects a Mossfon employee might have accidentally passed it on.

Ramses Owens attempts to pour oil on troubled waters. He writes to tell her that Mossfon can resolve the issue, offering her the natural person nominee service. He goes on to explain that this involves using someone as the beneficial owner, 'whose name is known to the bank'. However, Ramses Owens describes this service as 'very delicate', which means that it's also very expensive. The first year costs $30,000 and the second year costs $15,000. After all, it takes a lot of organization. 'We have to appoint the nominee owner, pay him, he has to sign a load of documents to cover us, we have to ensure that he can prove that he's capable, in economic terms, of possessing such a large amount of money, we need references, proof of residential address, and so on.' If the client were to accept the offer, Ramses Owens writes, she needs to be aware that it's a long-standing contract.[2]

We continue with our research and find out that the client accepted the offer. She paid around $60,000 for the service over the course of three years. The man acting for her as the real owner is like the Porsche among Mossfon's nominee directors. They like to recommend him in 'delicate' situations like this.

His name is Edmund W., and he's Ramón Fonseca's ex-father-in-law.

Mossack Fonseca usually brings Edmund W. into play as a natural person nominee, and reference is always made to his favourable attributes: he's an engineer, so he could theoretically have a lot of money, he's a British citizen who's been living in Panama for a long time and he rarely travels. The grandfather of Ramón Fonseca's children becomes, on paper, the owner of the client's company, and HSBC actually receives his passport and electricity bill from Mossfon, as if he were the ultimate owner.[3]

All of this is so clearly illegal that any discussion about it is essentially ridiculous. We're interested to know what Mossfon will say about it.

But Mossfon doesn't answer our question about whether they offer the natural person nominee service. The office sends a general statement, which doesn't relate to our allegation.

The most recent example of the natural person nominee service dates back to March 2014. A Mossfon employee offers this service to a Frenchman for a hefty $10,000 per year. The client probes into it, wanting to know if it would be possible to open a bank account in which he 'wouldn't appear at all' in the documentation.

Not a problem, the Mossfon employee explains, you could declare someone else as the 'ultimate beneficial owner'. This person's name would then be passed on to the bank, so the bank would carry out the due diligence on them, as the 'real owner'.[4]

We also use our time in Lillehammer to ask our partners if they have found obvious violations of the law, infringements of due diligence obligations, forgery of documents, assistance with money laundering, that type of thing, in the cases they are investigating. You can never have enough of those. In the nooks of the lobby, in hotel rooms or when taking a walk together, other Prometheus investigators tell us similar stories, time and time again.

[ ]

A few days after returning home, the source approaches us with a question that makes us nervous.

[john doe]: Ready for more data?
[SZ]: Seriously?
[john doe]: Very serious.
[SZ]: Okay. How much?
[john doe]: Less than 100GB this time. But still a lot.
[SZ]: Wow! It's crazy.

Even more data from Mossack Fonseca. We're already struggling to cope with what we've got. When we receive it, we put it to one side to start with. Our new supercomputer hasn't arrived yet and there are another few million documents from our current database that need to be converted into recognizable text so we can search them.

It's all too much.

But we still have a few months until we need to transform our investigations into a newspaper article.

20

AT THE MERCY OF MONSTERS

So far, we have identified criminals from the following groups among Mossack Fonseca's clients:

Drug lords.

Financial fraudsters.

Mafiosi.

Arms smugglers.

Tax evaders.

Sanction breakers.

Pretty much every type of fraudster.

And then there's the story of Andrew M. In the US in 2009, he was sentenced to eight years' imprisonment. His crime: he'd raped at least three Russian children. According to the investigators, he didn't just act out of inclination; he also had business motives. He had wanted to help set up an illegal child prostitution ring and to 'test' three girls. Andrew M. was allegedly one of the financial backers of this criminal organization and he helped to launder the profits from these crimes by smuggling them into a shell company.

Andrew M. is – with a different shell company – still a client of Mossack Fonseca today.[1]

Mossack Fonseca knows about M.'s crime, conviction and arrest; that much is clear from our documents. But despite that, Mossfon still keeps him as a client.

But first things first. The documents reveal that in 1995, Andrew M., who holds US as well as Russian citizenship, establishes two companies in the British Virgin Islands. He doesn't state a business purpose.

On the surface, M. lives a fairytale life: at the age of eighteen, he emigrated from Russia to the US with his father, was accepted by Columbia University in New York due to his special mathematical talent, and graduated with top marks. Then, within a few years, he makes a fortune selling special fire extinguishers and trading in German cars. In 2004 his firm is estimated to be worth more than $10 million. Andrew M. gets married, has three children and lives the American dream in a villa in Philadelphia.

But there's also a second life, a more sinister one. Investigation files and court documents allow us to reconstruct it. According to these sources, the website www.berenika.org goes online in 2002. It advertises something that its creators call a 'romantic studio'. In reality, it's a child prostitution ring. Hardly any attempts are made to try to cover it up; even the homepage features a naked girl with a rose in her hand. She looks young. Very young.

[ ]

The girls on berenika.org are presented as if they're products and offered according to size, weight and cup size. They are 'young and fresh' and are available for as little as $150 to $300 per hour. A whole night costs $500. On berenika.org, there's actually a pro forma declaration that all of the girls are over the age of eighteen. But if you're looking for underage girls, you'll soon know you've come to the right place. At the end, berenika.org's clients are guided to an inconspicuous apartment in Moscow. This is where the children are assaulted.

The American investigators come to the conclusion that Andrew M. was involved in the financing of this child prostitution ring. They write that M. invested 'in the expectation that he would get a share of the profits from the prostitution of adult and under-age women'. He apparently even translated the website into English in order to attract Western clients.[2]

At the end of 2003, M. travels to St Petersburg and picks up three girls from an orphanage on the outskirts of the city. They are thirteen and fourteen years old. M. promises to go on a sightseeing tour with them. Instead, he evidently forces them to have sex with him. 'I begged him not to do anything to me, I was still so little,' the English-language edition of the Russian newspaper *Pravda* later quoted one of the girls as saying. 'He gave me painkillers and started taking off my pyjamas.' Another girl made it quite clear that she didn't want to think about it and would rather just forget about what he had done to her.

Around the same time, Andrew M. sets up a foundation to help Russian victims of terrorism, especially children. He becomes the president of the foundation's Team USA. At evening functions, he meets the Russian ambassador to the US and has his photo taken in his role as benefactor at VIP parties with the Hollywood actress Heather Graham.

That's the illusion.

But the Berenika ring becomes the subject of Russian investiga-tions, and the investigators evidently tip off their US colleagues about Andrew M. When he returns from one of his trips in July 2004, police at Philadelphia Airport confiscate his laptop. In 2005, in the course of international investigations, four of his accomplices are sentenced to imprisonment in Russia. M. manages to escape, at least for the time being. Three years later the FBI manages to decode data that had been encoded on the laptop that was confiscated at the airport, and finds emails that link M. with berenika.org.

Later, the investigators discover Ifex Global Ltd, one of the two shell companies that Mossack Fonseca established in the British Virgin Islands in 1995. They want to know who's behind it and ask the Caribbean authorities for information. The local Financial Investigation Agency approaches Mossfon to ask for the names and addresses of the directors and shareholders of Ifex.

Mossack Fonseca tells the investigators that Ifex Global belongs to a man named D.G. and that Andrew M. is simply the director.

This is not true. In the internal Mossfon documents at our disposal, Andrew M. is clearly listed as the sole shareholder. Since 1995.

Furthermore, Mossfon explains that it doesn't have any information about other companies related to Ifex.

However, M. also registered a company called Maga Global Ltd at the same time as Ifex Global Ltd. Mossack Fonseca even filed one of Maga Global's business cards in its records. On it, Andrew M. is named as the deputy director.

Following Andrew M.'s arrest in the US in December 2008 and numerous prominent reports in the media about the multimillionaire who sexually abused and exploited children, Mossack Fonseca receives another letter from the authorities in the British Virgin Islands. This time, the investigators want to see all the documents relating to due diligence, that is to say the documents that show that Mossack Fonseca carefully and properly verified who it was doing business with.

However, Mossfon doesn't have anything like that, because it clearly hasn't been adequately verifying who it's been doing business with. For thirteen years.

When Andrew M. established his two companies in the British Virgin Islands in 1995, using the American company USA Corporation as an intermediary, he clearly wasn't even required to provide Mossfon with a copy of his passport.

For a company that boasts relentlessly about its strict rules and procedures, this doesn't look good. The employees at Mossfon start to get nervous, and rightly so. They try to gather together some tangible evidence and write to the American intermediary who initially commissioned the company Ifex on behalf of M. The intermediary replies that he has tried, and failed, to obtain the information from M.

Well, how would you be able to reach him quickly anyway? He's in prison, after all.

What the US corporation can offer: a certificate from Christiania Bank og Kreditkasse, a bank in Norway with which M.'s company had an account, and a driving licence that expired three (!) years previously. In January 2009 Mossfon sends both documents to the Financial Investigation Agency in the British Virgin Islands. Furthermore, Mossfon now confirms that M. is the owner of Ifex Global.[3]

A few days later, Andrew M. confesses before a regional court in Pennsylvania to having had sexual relations with three underage Russian girls. According to what we hear, a deal was made. M. admits to the rapes, and the charge for child trafficking is dropped. In September 2009 Andrew M. is finally sentenced to several years' imprisonment. The judges hold in his favour that he spared the three children from having to give testimony in court and instead came to an agreement with them out-of-court.

In the documentation of a civil procedure sought by M.'s victims in the US in 2009, a company by the name of Ifex Global also appears as the defendant company. According to the statement of claim, the costs incurred for the child prostitution ring had been recorded by Ifex Global as business expenses and the company had given the profits from the illegal activities the 'appearance of legitimacy'. Furthermore, the homepage www.berenika.org had been 'controlled' from M.'s private home or his business, that is to say Ifex Global. It's even suspected that money from company accounts was used to bribe Russian officials to let the Berenika operators do as they please.[4]

Admittedly, the court documents refer to an Ifex Global Inc., and not to the Mossfon company Ifex Global Ltd.

The only way to find out more details would be to review all the case files in full. However, apart from a few pages at our disposal, these are under lock and key; following his conviction, M.'s victims agreed to compensation payments out-of-court. This also means that the court documents aren't made publicly available.

[ ]

Although the media in the US and Russia report the millionaire's sentence in 2009, Mossack Fonseca clearly doesn't notice. It's not until spring 2014 – five years after his sentencing – that the law firm in Panama realizes that one of its clients is a convicted sex offender. The employees email newspaper articles around and class M. as a 'high-risk client'. Ultimately, the question arises as to whether Mossfon should inform the authorities in the British Virgin Islands.

The manager of Mossfon's compliance department makes the case against this, stating that Ifex Global wasn't ultimately 'involved in anything illegal'. In the end, the managing director decides not to inform the authorities: they don't see how the company profited from M's paedophilic acts.

Mossack Fonseca therefore keeps a convicted sex offender, that is to say the company of a convicted sex offender, as a client. This is a man who, according to the investigators, was involved in the financing of a criminal organization that organized the abuse of Russian children.

At the time of going to press, Ifex Global Ltd is actually still a regular, active company.

Andrew M. was released from prison in December 2015.

In the past, spokespeople for Jürgen Mossack regularly declared that Mossfon vigorously filtered out clients operating illegally – if they were aware of such activities.

21

THE RED NOBILITY

On 15 November 2011 a dead body is found in the Lucky Holiday Hotel, a three-star hotel in the hills of the metropolis of Chongqing in southern China. The corpse found in bungalow 1605 is quickly identified as British businessman Neil Heywood, and almost as quickly, the apparent cause of death is determined: heart failure as a result of alcohol consumption. The dead body is cremated without an autopsy.

However, Neil Heywood's family knew him as a teetotaler, as someone who never consumed alcohol. Why would he have drunk himself to death? What's more, Neil Heywood wasn't just any old person; he was a close friend of Bo Xilai and Gu Kailai. Bo Xilai, the son of one of the 'Eight Immortals', as the veterans of the revolution in China are known, was the party leader of Chongqing at that time. His wife Gu Kailai, the daughter of a general, worked as a lawyer.

The two of them have been the dream couple of Chinese politics for many years. Bo Xilai is one of the country's most popular politicians and his path already seems to have been marked out for him: right to the very top, to the forefront of the most populous country in the world. But then Heywood dies.

Heywood's ties with politics and a number of unanswered questions soon lead to rumours about what is behind the mysterious death. Chongqing's chief of police, who was reportedly in the know about the murder from the word go, secretly orders blood to be taken before the cremation. In the end, it's the chief of police who, as a result, is responsible for turning a suspected death due to alcohol into the biggest criminal case in recent Chinese history. Once it's established that Heywood was murdered in cold blood, an almost Shakespearian drama of love, power and money, set in the world of the Chinese elite, comes to an end.

In autumn 2011, when Heywood dies, everything still suggests that the following year Bo will become a member of the Politburo Standing Committee, the apex of political power in China. Bo had left his post as trade minister and moved to Chongqing in 2007. There, he changed the city on the Yangtze so dramatically that the whole of China was talking about him: the citizens have to sing party songs, he puts red flags up all over the city, celebrates Mao Zedong and prohibits the regional television company from broadcasting advertisements. In short, Bo Xilai returns the city to an era in which real Maoism was still the ideal in China, and capitalism the enemy.

At the same time, he launches the 'Smash the Black' campaign and cracks down on criminality and corruption. The party press celebrates him as the country's hottest anti-corruption fighter and as a talented economic developer; the whole country is soon talking about the 'Chongqing model'.

That's the façade. But even in the 1990s, when Bo Xilai is still the mayor of Dalian, a port city in the north east of China, there's an unspoken rule among businesspeople: if you want to succeed in Dalian, you have to give Bo's family a share. According to an article published in the *Spiegel* in 2012, Gu Kailai, Bo's wife, acted as 'something of a toll collector'. She collected the entrance money.

At that time, Neil Heywood is already a close friend of theirs. Heywood evidently sees to it that their son Bo Guagua attends an expensive private school in London before going on to university at

Oxford. At Harvard, where he studies for a master's degree, Bo Guagua drives around in a Porsche and lives in an apartment for which the monthly rent is equal to a quarter of his father's annual salary.

Heywood takes care of it. He's a man of the world, he wears linen jackets and drives a luxury car with the number plate '007'. Bo Guagua isn't all he takes care of either. He does business with friends and they earn millions, some of which they evidently park in offshore companies.

Until Heywood dies, in those unexplained circumstances. When Chongqing's chief of police, in fact a close friend and accomplice of Bo Xilai and his wife, confronts the politician with his findings, Bo doesn't want to hear about it. He yells at him, hits him and threatens to dismiss him.

The policeman panics and in February 2012 he seeks asylum in the US consulate 300 kilometres away in Chengdu, out of fear for his life. His version of events is as follows: Bo Xilai's wife killed the businessman, by first getting him drunk and then poisoning him. The policeman isn't granted asylum in the end and surrenders to the Chinese authorities a few days later.

His allegations hit China hard. A beloved politician, mixed up in murder and hidden money – unbelievable. The affair keeps China in suspense for weeks and the Communist Party finds itself in the biggest crisis of confidence since the Tiananmen Square massacre of 1989. As more information unfolds, star politician Bo Xilai starts to look worse and worse. In the end, the Communist Party even censors the words 'Bo Xilai' and 'truth' on the Internet.

Gu Kailai is ultimately given a 'conditional death sentence' for her crime. The judgment is later converted to life imprisonment. It is revealed that the married couple had a dark secret, for which Gu was prepared to kill. She murdered Heywood because he knew too much.

[ ]

We are spellbound when it transpires that part of this story can be retold, so to speak, through our data, meaning we are able to shed a bit more light on what happened. We see that in September 2000 Gu Kailai, together with a French architect, establishes Russell Properties S.A. in the British Virgin Islands. It's clear that the company's true ownership structure was meant to be concealed: there are nominee shareholders and nominee directors, which doesn't surprise us in the slightest, considering who we're dealing with.

It would have been her husband's political downfall if word had got out that Gu Kailai was investing millions abroad, especially since the money wasn't her own. Some of it came from a Chinese billionaire, who had become rich as part of Bo Xilai's entourage. He provided Gu and the architect with $3.2 million, which they then paid into an account held with a major British bank.

Gu's husband Bo Xilai knows the architect from his time in Dalian; the Frenchman had married into a prominent local family and designed prestigious buildings there. In the summer of 2001 Gu and the Frenchman bought a villa in the French Riviera through Russell Properties: situated above Cannes, 400 square metres, six bedrooms with grounds of 4,000 square metres. A palace – definitely too expensive for the wife of a Chinese politician. Furthermore, the law states that Chinese citizens are only allowed to take foreign currency up to approximately $50,000 abroad without requiring a special permit.

It's also important to point out that Gu's company, Russell Properties, didn't buy the Fontaine Saint Georges villa directly. Instead, another offshore company – Residences Fontaine Saint Georges S.A. – acted as the buyer. This company, in turn, belonged to Russell Properties. It doesn't get much more secretive than that.

However, the problem was clearly that Gu Kailai decided to involve Neil Heywood, their British family friend, in the deal. He was meant to manage the villa in Cannes and to help rent it out.

But Heywood blackmailed Gu. This was ultimately his death sentence.

Two weeks after she poisoned Heywood in the bungalow at the Luxury Holiday Hotel, Gu Kailai evidently tried to cover her tracks in the offshore world. In the Russell Properties S.A. data, held by Mossfon internally under reference number 6015818, we discover that the French architect was named as the sole director and shareholder of the company on 29 November 2011.

That would have actually got rid of the evidence, if only the Frenchman hadn't made a mistake. He gave an apartment block near the Olympic Stadium in Beijing as a correspondence address: a former address of Gu Kailai's law firm.

[ ]

The cadre of the Chinese Communist Party have, until now, been keen to use the term 'héxié shèhuì' to describe their country. It means that the People's Republic is a 'harmonious society'.

But the reality, as evidenced by the case of Bo Xilai, is different. Social tensions are increasing year on year. According to estimates from the World Bank, more than 300 million people in China have less than $2 a day at their disposal. According to *Forbes*, the 100 richest Chinese people, on the other hand, have accumulated fortunes worth more than $450 billion, which is an average of $4.5 billion each.

However, a considerable amount of that isn't located in the 'harmonious society'. Instead, it's in tax havens, mostly hidden behind inconspicuous company façades and the arbitrary names of hired nominee directors.

A while ago, we found Deng Jiagui in the secret documents: the brother-in-law of China's president Xi Jinping – the same Xi Jinping who's been presenting himself as a strong advocate of transparency for many years.[1]

We also discovered Li Xiaolin, the daughter of former prime minister Li Peng, known as the 'Butcher of Beijing' because of his role in the Tiananmen Square massacre. Li Xiaolin is one of the richest women in China today; without her father's connections, that probably wouldn't be the case.[2]

In China, politicians and their families aren't required to declare their assets. Citizens can only speculate about how much money is lying in offshore companies and how much tax the state is losing out on as a result. That's another reason why the stories about the president's brother-in-law Deng Jiagui and the former prime minister's daughter have the potential to be politically explosive. Critical reports about greedy politicians and their relatives who go around preaching humility while simultaneously lining their pockets are taboo in China; they jeopardize the already fragile cohesion in this society of extreme opposites. Experts estimate that since 2000, between $1 billion and $4 billion have disappeared from China by dubious means.

What little has been published about it in the past has been written by Western journalists. The news agency Bloomberg was the first, in 2012, to investigate the financial background of the family of Xi Jinping, the current president, after which it published a report claiming that Xi's relatives had accumulated millions by means of shareholdings and property deals. Bloomberg didn't suggest that Xi had made money this way himself, but state censorship immediately blocked access to this information online.

When the *Süddeutsche Zeitung* and the ICIJ reported on Chinese people in the Offshore Secrets data in early 2014, access to sueddeutsche.de from China was also blocked within a few hours and our account with Weibo, the Chinese version of Twitter, was deleted. The same thing happened to the *New York Times*, which reported that relatives of the president bought shares in a company owned by the richest person in China at an early stage and then went on to sell them, making a profit worth millions of dollars. The man who allegedly engineered this deal was Deng Jiagui, President Xi Jinping's brother-in-law. We are able to prove that this man owns three other shell companies that are not yet known to the public.

His family's offshore affairs won't bring down Xi Jinping, but it must be uncomfortable for him to be caught up in yet another revelation after the Bloomberg articles, the Offshore Secrets publications and the *New York Times* reports. After all, the *People's Daily*, the party organ of the Chinese Communist Party, contains slogans such as, 'Regardless of who you are, however big or small you may be, if you break the law, you'll be punished.'

Of course, we are not so naïve as to believe that this rule would apply to the elite the same way as it does to the common people. But it would be another instance where this contradiction would become evident.

[ ]

We are under no illusions: Chinese media will struggle to report it. The risks are too great. The *Süddeutsche Zeitung* and our project partners have more to fear in terms of bureaucratic revenge: reporters from the *New York Times* and Bloomberg were temporarily denied the standard visa. That's another reason why we're only reporting from Germany and why we decided not to involve *SZ*'s China correspondent in our investigations. He lives in the People's Republic with his children and family, and would like to remain there for a while yet.

Just when we are discussing all this, strange things start to happen. The *Süddeutsche Zeitung*'s IT department reports an unusually high volume of traffic on the newspaper's homepage. Does someone with automated access to the page intentionally want to overload the server and cause it to crash? This type of attack, known as a denial-of-service attack, is part of the standard repertoire of the Chinese and Russian secret services.

Perhaps it's a coincidence that these attacks suddenly start to increase dramatically at this time, when we just so happen to be investigating China and Russia. But who can be sure? It wouldn't be the first time that hackers have penetrated the editorial system of a major German weekly paper and deleted an article that was critical of China just before it was due to be published.

But regardless of how extensively the state carries out censorship, something of this magnitude can't be kept under wraps in the long-term. China's elite put so much money into tax havens that in 2011, a Chinese state bank reported that corrupt Chinese people were using shell companies like 'handbags'.

One of the biggest providers of these 'handbags' in China is, once again, Mossack Fonseca. This comes as no surprise. The Panamanian law firm has eight offices in mainland China; more than in any other country. It also has an office in Hong Kong. So in total, there are nine Mossfon offices on Chinese territory.

Because the demand is so high?

[ ]

However, trying to find good Chinese stories is much more difficult than in almost any other region in the world. Mossack Fonseca only refers to many Chinese names by their – ambiguous – transcription into Latin characters. Mandarin Chinese has over 400 syllables, which can be used in various pitches and combinations. In writing, only the Chinese characters create clarity. What's more, millions of Chinese people have very similar names. In fact, there are more people living in the People's Republic with the surname Wang than the total number of citizens in Germany. All of this means that it takes forever to check every single instance to see whether the name we find in the data also belongs to the person we're looking for. ID numbers have to be compared, dates of birth researched and business addresses located. It's not possible to verify everything definitively, and if we're only 99 per cent sure, we'll leave it.

Christoph Giesen from *SZ*'s economics team, who we worked with on Offshore Secrets, is also working in the small ICIJ China team. He speaks Chinese, travels there regularly and knows his stuff. We'd be lost without him. We find more and more Chinese people every day; there'll be thousands of them by the end. Here's a small list of names that the research group led by Christoph Giesen and Alexa Olesen, ICIJ's China specialist, have dug up:

- Wallace Yu Yiping, the husband of the niece of Deng Xiaoping, who ruled China for almost two decades. Wallace Yu Yiping is revealed as the director and sole shareholder of Galaxia Space Management, established in the British Virgin Islands.[3]
- Lee Shing Put, the son-in-law of Zhang Gaoli, the current vice premier of China and member of the Politburo. Lee Shing Put is a shareholder of the offshore companies Glory Top Investments Ltd and Zennon Capital Management Ltd.[4]
- Zeng Qinghuai, the brother of Zeng Qinghong, former vice premier of China. Critics have suspected Zeng Qinghong of corruption for a long time. A few years ago, his son bought a property in Sydney for more than $20 million. The source of that money has not yet been identified.[5]

All three men, Yu, Lee and Zeng, are so-called princelings (in Chinese: 'taizidang'): close relatives of China's powerful elite. They're political rivals, but one thing they have in common is their thirst for money.

[ ]

Some princelings made their billions in the private sector; others lead the country's banks or work in ministries. Some presumably set up secret companies in order to hide some of their fortunes, while others did so in order to invest in China secretly without anyone knowing who's really behind the business deals. We find eight of these princelings in the data; their relatives were or are members of the Politburo Standing Committee, China's most powerful body. All eight are entangled in offshore businesses.

It's important to point out that princelings are the first port of call for businesspeople who want to succeed in China. When bribes are paid in China, they don't usually go straight into the hands of a politician. That would be too conspicuous; too dangerous. It's safer, for example, to settle the invoices of a politician's son, sister-in-law or brother, or to finance an expensive apartment for them. In return, the investor can expect to be favoured in lucrative works contracts or suchlike. It's difficult to prove who has formed symbiotic relationships like this with whom. But the data gives us a tantalizing glimpse.

22

THE GAS PRINCESS AND
THE CHOCOLATE KING

The Cypriot middleman doesn't beat around the bush: he sends an email at the start of August 2014 stating that he wants to set up another offshore company with Mossack Fonseca. The shell company is to be called Prime Asset Partners Ltd and should be established in the British Virgin Islands. It all seems clear so far.

There's just one small twist: the middleman explains that the client and future shareholder is a 'person who's involved in politics'. The company, however, will have 'nothing to do with his political activities'.

An extremely subtle understatement.

The Cypriot middleman's client is Petro Poroshenko, the current president of Ukraine, a country at war.

Poroshenko, number fifty-five on our ever-growing list of links to heads of state, is one of the country's richest men. Depending on which list you consult, his fortune puts him in either sixth, seventh or eighth place.

He is known as the 'Chocolate King' because he made his fortune in chocolate, and the pralines his company produces are the market leader in Eastern Europe. His empire includes various media, car and seed businesses, as well as a shipyard. Poroshenko is regarded as a strong-willed and pragmatic leader. He has been involved in politics since the late 1990s, when Leonid Kuchma was still president. He is one of the founders of the Party of Regions, which later, under the leadership of Viktor Yanukovych, became a breeding ground for those who robbed the country and its state companies for their own benefit.

However, in 2004 Poroshenko sided with the Orange Revolution. When hundreds of thousands of Ukrainians took to the streets to protest against Yanukovych's manipulated victory in the presidential elections, Poroshenko's television station was the only one to report on the demonstrations. In the end, the demonstrators prevailed and the run-off elections were repeated; this time the winner was Viktor Yushchenko, who had been disfigured as a result of a poison attack. He was made president, Yulia Tymoshenko became prime minister and Chocolate King Petro Poroshenko became chair of the National Security and Defence Council, later serving as foreign minister and the minister of trade and economic development.

One thing that the protesters in Kiev's Maidan square demanded was that the 100 richest Ukrainians should no longer be involved in politics. They railed against the country's elite, against people like Yulia Tymoshenko and Petro Poroshenko. This is an elite that is immensely rich, while 80 per cent of Ukraine's 48 million residents are living below the poverty line, according to statistics from the United Nations. It was a demand that went unheard. In 2014 Petro Poroshenko stood for president against Yulia Tymoshenko, among others, and won. It seems likely that the promise he made in his election campaign played a role here; the oligarch who claims not to be an oligarch promised to sell his companies, declaring, 'As the president of Ukraine I will and want to only focus on the wellbeing of the nation.'

Big words. He hasn't stuck to them.

Over the past few years, Poroshenko has become even richer, while other oligarchs in Ukraine have lost huge amounts of money as a result of the crisis. Why did he fare so much better? Possibly because, in the summer of 2014, Poroshenko was also focusing intensely on his assets. Outside Ukraine, undercover.

Instead of bowing out of the economy, just two months after his election success, Poroshenko establishes Prime Asset Partners Ltd in the British Virgin Islands via the Cypriot middleman. Later, Poroshenko's middleman defines the company's objective as a 'holding for Cypriot and Ukrainian companies of the Roshen Group, one of the biggest European producers of confectionery'. The Chocolate King's empire. This was all carried out well out of the public eye. And that was how it was meant to stay: the emails mention that communication with Mossack Fonseca should take place via a 'secure email system'.

It is possible that Poroshenko wanted to group his companies in this offshore holding in order to sell them more easily. But it is also possible that he simply wanted to conceal the fact that he hadn't kept his electoral promise.[1]

[ ]

In any case, one thing that's more important to the people of Ukraine than whether or not Poroshenko intended to sell his companies is the question of morality. The Ukrainian president establishes his shell company in August 2014, of all times. This is during the height of the Ukrainian conflict, precisely when – from 10 August until 2 September – the Battle of Ilovaisk is raging in the south-eastern city, which is home to 15,000 people. For days on end around 7,000 soldiers, mainly members of the Ukrainian volunteer battalions, are trapped in the city, surrounded by pro-Russian troops, supported by Russian forces and tanks. The Ukrainian soldiers call for help but their appeals are in vain. The army, whose commander-in-chief is Poroshenko, fails to send any support.

After days of heavy fighting, both sides sign a ceasefire agreement. The Ukrainian units are told that they can leave the encircled city unscathed as long as they leave behind their weapons. When the Ukrainian soldiers pull out, they are suddenly shot at from tanks and mortars and up to 1,000 soldiers are killed. The Ukrainian government speaks of a 'massacre'.

And what does President Poroshenko do, after his promise to 'only focus on the wellbeing of the nation'? He registers a shell company.

While Ukrainian soldiers are losing their lives and the world is looking on at the conflict, Mossack Fonseca and Poroshenko's agent are discussing the details of the holding. Poroshenko finds his electricity bill and has it verified, his passport is certified and a director is chosen. Just one day before the end of the Battle of Ilovaisk on 2 September 2014, all the necessary formalities are completed.

It wouldn't be too presumptuous to assume that Poroshenko's offshore dealings will make the headlines in Ukraine. This is a country that stood out in the data; we find more high-ranking politicians from Ukraine, riddled with corruption and mismanagement, than virtually any other country. Aside from Poroshenko, the current president, we have also found links to two former prime ministers: Pavel Lazarenko is listed as the sole owner of an offshore company, and Yulia Tymoshenko is involved indirectly, via a company she was allegedly involved with.

It was Lazarenko who sent a fax to Mossfon in April 2005 claiming he'd just found out a few weeks previously that he owned Gateway Marketing Inc., a shell company that had been established by Mossack Fonseca. We also discover that the mayor of Odessa, Gennadiy Trukhanov, is the shareholder of a company registered in the British Virgin Islands. Furthermore, we find the son of the former prime minister Mykola Azarov and the family of a former member of parliament who was an assistant to over-thrown President Yanukovych, temporarily sanctioned by both Switzerland and the EU.[2]

[ ]

A current head of state and two former heads of government from a single country? We hesitate again for a moment: shouldn't this be making the headlines straight away? A while later, as we're sitting in front of the mass of documents relating to our hits in Ukraine, our thoughts instead turn to the question: will we be able to finish our investigations by spring, in time for the publication date we agreed on at the meeting in Munich?

For weeks, we have been torn in these two opposite directions. We can hardly wait for everything to finally be published. And at the same time, we could urgently do with more time. A lot more time. There's so much to investigate, so much to write. So many loose ends, so many unanswered questions, so many topics still left that we ought to, have to, and want to investigate in detail.

But there's only one solution: patience.

We don't know exactly how long we'll have to stay patient for. Since we decided to publish everything at the same time as our international partners in spring 2016, dozens of strong stories have come to the fore, resulting in more work than anticipated. What's more, we have fallen behind our deadlines in all technical areas; we haven't yet converted all our locally stored data into searchable text, even though a good 100,000 files are processed every week. The update that we received from our source in Lillehammer hasn't even been indexed yet.

Still, the decision about the project's name has since been made; this question had been unanswered since the meeting in Munich. It's going to be called the Panama Papers.

The hashtag on Twitter will be #panamapapers.

ICIJ Director Gerard Ryle came up with the suggestion. It's an allusion to the Pentagon Papers, the US Ministry of Defence's secret papers, published by the *New York Times* in 1971. The Pentagon Papers proved that US Presidents Harry S. Truman and Richard Nixon had lied about the Vietnam War. Thanks to the newspaper's revelations, the Americans found out that the Vietnam War, contrary to the claims made by Nixon and Truman, had been planned for a long time. Their claim that war had been intended as a way to save democracy in South Vietnam was revealed to be a pretext.

One of this project's many peculiarities is that the data includes someone who was also mixed up in the Watergate scandal. According to a witness, Gilbert Straub provided $50,000 to ensure the Watergate burglars remained silent. And according to the documentation, Mossfon did business with the Panamanian firm belonging to the very same Gilbert Straub in the 1980s.

Pentagon Papers.

Panama Papers.

It takes a bit of getting used to, but it works. Or have we long since lost the ability to see our monster project in any kind of objective way? In any case, it's devouring us: the online presence, logo, images, graphics, the eight-page special supplement in the print version of the *SZ* on the first and second days of publication, how the subsequent series of reports is going to pan out. We present our project to other teams at the *Süddeutsche Zeitung*, have frequent meetings with the legal department, transatlantic teleconferences with the ICIJ and meetings with our colleagues based abroad. And then there's our actual work, which involves investigating our cases, going through the many thousands of hits on our search lists according to relevance, checking documents, arranging meetings, posting in the international forum and catching up on the most recent cases that have been shared there.

Every single day we are thankful that the German team not only comprises us at the *SZ*, but also our colleagues from NRD and WDR.

And then there's this book, which is hard to juggle around our family lives. Our current division of work is as follows: for the first shift, one of us starts writing in the evening, after putting his children to bed. The other gets up at four in the morning and takes over until someone toddles in from his kids' bedroom just before seven. We can't keep this up in the long run, that much is clear to us. But the end is now in sight, so we put our lives on hold for a while, until we've worked through this mountain of data.

And at the same time, of course, the project is still a huge gift.

[ ]

When we take another look into the background of Pavel Lazarenko's curious company, which he apparently didn't realize existed for many years, it strikes us that this wasn't his only offshore company. His name also comes up in connection with a company called Bainfield, in which he held shares. However, Lazarenko's most interesting company is Bassington Ltd. It appears Yulia Tymoshenko was also involved with Bassington Ltd. and, at the same time, was involved in a massive case of suspected corruption and embezzlement.

Yulia Tymoshenko's rise to power starts in Dnipropetrovsk, a city in the south east of Ukraine that is evidently a type of biotope for political leaders. Leonid Brezhnev, the former leader of the USSR, Leonid Kuchma, the former Ukrainian prime minister and president, and Pavel Lazarenko were all born there. Local people speak of the 'Dnipropetrovsk mafia' and not just because of the concentration of big politicians the city has given birth to.

In this unpronounceable city, Tymoshenko lays the foundations for her later wealth, at a time when the end of 'actually existing socialism' is almost within reach. She makes money by renting out pirated copies of American films: *Rambo*, *Pretty Woman*, and allegedly pornographic films too. She soon earns her first million by doing so, according to reports. When the Soviet Union finally collapses, Tymoshenko, who according to the *Spiegel* is 'obsessed with money and power', goes into the oil business and in 1995 becomes the president of the company United Energy Systems of Ukraine. The young woman who grew up in a prefabricated apartment building makes a fortune. By the end of 1996 she's already controlling a large part of Ukraine's national economy. The *Wall Street Journal* reports that in the same financial year, her energy consortium paid just $11,000 in taxes. When questioned about this, a spokesperson for Tymoshenko said that this was 'untrue and not supported by any evidence'.

During that period, Yulia Tymoshenko is detained more than once. In 1995, for example, she gets held at Zaporizhia Airport with a large amount of cash on her; she has to spend several days in prison before being released. In 2001 she is imprisoned for forty-two days for gas smuggling and tax evasion. She is suspected of fraudulent conduct relating to the importation of gas from Russia during her time as president of United Energy Systems of Ukraine, but the case never reaches trial. In relation to this, Tymoshenko's spokesperson claimed that the governments of Leonid Kuchma and Viktor Yanukovych had attempted to 'politically and physically annihilate Yulia Tymoshenko'. For this reason, Ukrainian law enforcement authorities 'fabricated false criminal proceedings, the aim of which was to politically discredit Yulia Tymoshenko and to physically isolate her by illegally detaining and arresting her'.

At this time, the Mossack Fonseca company Bassington Ltd has already been active for quite some time. This is the company that investigators report Tymoshenko as having been involved with alongside her mentor Pavel Lazarenko. Lazarenko already has his best political period behind him; he'd been prime minister of Ukraine from 1996 to 1997, until he eventually stepped down, swept up in rumours of corruption. In 1998 he's detained when trying to enter Switzerland on allegations of money laundering. What's more, he allegedly embezzled several million dollars of state funds during his time as prime minister. He's let off with a warning and quickly leaves the country, only to be detained upon entering the US just a year later. He has to stand trial at a jury court in San Francisco. In the bill of indictment, Lazarenko, together with multiple accomplices, is accused of having siphoned off hundreds of millions of dollars 'through fraud, blackmail, bribery and embezzlement'. The US investigators name Yulia Tymoshenko as a 'not charged accomplice'.

This is by no means detrimental to her political success: with her hair dyed blonde and braided into a neat crown, she first becomes the heroine of the Orange Revolution in 2004, Ukraine's Joan of Arc, and then prime minister. Once from January until September 2005, and then again from December 2007 until March 2010.

Pavel Lazarenko sits in a US prison cell, while Yulia Tymoshenko rules Ukraine. In 2004 he's found guilty of money laundering and fraud. He is accused of smuggling $114 million, originating from corrupt sources, into the US. The judgment doesn't mention Tymoshenko. Some information about her possible involvement has come to light in another lawsuit that has been ongoing in the US since 2011, and at the same time about the role of Bassington Ltd, the company that was founded by Mossack Fonseca in 1996. A company from Massachusetts instituted proceedings against Bassington at the competent District Court in 2011, because the shell company owed it $18 million from a previous transaction with a company owned by Yulia Tymoshenko. The action states that Bassington was the parent company of Tymoshenko's United Energy Systems of Ukraine. It claims that Tymoshenko had bribed Lazarenko in connection with Bassington; she'd paid him half the revenue made from the illegal activities as a kick-back. Bassington had been 'a central element' in concealing Tymoshenko's company's assets and in 'concealing bribes paid to Lazarenko'. Ultimately, the district court ruled that Bassington owed the complainant $18.3 million. The court didn't elaborate on the accusation of bribery. When questioned, one of Yulia Tymoshenko's defence lawyers claimed that Tymoshenko and United Energy Systems of Ukraine had 'never had any relations' with Bassington Ltd. Furthermore, 'Neither Ms Tymoshenko nor the companies associated with her [...] had transferred any illegal money to Pavel Lazarenko or the companies associated with him.'

And with that, we're caught up in the battle of propaganda about the prerogative of interpretation of Yulia Tymoshenko. She divides opinion more than virtually any other Ukrainian politi-cian; some view her as the Ukrainian angel while others view her as a criminal oligarch.

After losing the presidential elections to Yanukovych in 2010, she was accused of having abused her position. Again, this related to transactions involving gas. A court in Kiev determined that in 2009, while she was prime minister, she negotiated a gas agree-ment with Putin, who'd inflicted serious economic damage on the country. She was sentenced to seven years' imprisonment. Her opponents celebrated the judgment as belated justice, whereas her supporters regard it as an act of revenge by an unjust regime.

From the outside, it's hard to judge the extent to which the stories put forward by either side are propaganda. However, it is clear that Ukraine has a huge problem when it comes to its politi-cians: a problem that is, in part, reflected in Mossack Fonseca's client lists.

[ ]

Incidentally, Mossack Fonseca's employees are aware that one of their clients is the current president of Ukraine. After all, the Cypriot middleman sent an email explaining that his client was 'involved in politics', and standard checks by Mossfon employees confirmed the client was the Ukrainian president. According to protocol, they request an explanation regarding the purpose of the company. Mossfon's advisers also demand further evidence regarding the source of the money and several other documents from Poroshenko's middleman. In the end, they get a type of clearance certificate for Poroshenko, issued by International Invest Bank. It states that Poroshenko has always kept his account 'properly and to our satisfaction'.

A more detailed look at this document reveals its background: Petro Poroshenko is a co-owner of International Invest Bank; he submitted a clearance certificate issued by his own bank.

23

THOSE GERMAN BANKS

And now to the German banks.

Specifically, to the more than twenty German banks that turn up in our data in various mostly rather dubious-sounding connections. More than 500 banks worldwide have used the services of Mossfon. Of the seven largest German banks, six provide access to or manage offshore companies – in most cases via subsidiaries in Switzerland or Luxembourg – or have done so in the past, namely:

Deutsche Bank.[1]

Commerzbank.[2]

DZ Bank.[3]

HypoVereinsbank.[4]

Landesbank Baden-Württemberg.[5]

BayernLB.[6]

If Dresdner Bank had not been taken over by Commerzbank in 2009, all seven of the largest banks would have been involved.

In other words, for years nearly all of the big German banks have been systematically helping their clients play their game of offshore hide-and-seek.

The chances are that, until the beginning of 2015, most of the German banks would have vehemently disputed this. And if it had come out, they would probably have tried to play it down, as Commerzbank did at the end of February 2015 after the raid on its offices by police and tax investigators, saying the cases were old ones dating back ten years or more, and no big deal. We have already proved this claim to be untrue, both in the newspaper and in this book. And, as we mentioned earlier, Commerzbank did reach a settlement with the public prosecutor's office, whereby the public prosecutor halted proceedings against the bank in return for a payment of €17 million.

Commerzbank is now the third bank to have had to pay fines running into millions in connection with offshore business – HypoVereinsbank and HSH Nordbank had both already settled with the public prosecutor's office, and also ended up having to stump up millions in fines.

These fines were levied after German investigators bought secret Mossack Fonseca documents from a whistle-blower that prove that banks and their employees aided and abetted tax evasion. The Mossfon data they purchased is only a fraction the size of the cache of data in our possession, and is considerably older, but there are overlaps. So we know that this precise combination of 'German banks plus Mossack Fonseca' led to criminal acts being committed. The German banks would hardly have agreed to payments running into millions if they had thought there was a chance of getting away unpunished. These payments make things a lot easier for us in legal terms.

Because of them, we are free to write here that German banks were evidently actively and systematically involved in helping clients evade tax. This went on for years, and quite a few of the shell companies they arranged for their clients are still up and running.

[ ]

That, however, is only one of the banks' three main strands of business. Besides organizing and managing offshore companies, more than ten German banks also earn money by holding accounts for anonymous shell companies, sometimes, in the case of certain institutions, without exercising due diligence. The third area involves banks' activities as 'correspondent banks'. This involves large banks enabling smaller institutions without the relevant foreign branches to transfer money from one country to another. There is nothing wrong with this in principle as long as all the rules are adhered to.

However, according to the documents in our possession, a number of German banks have been acting as correspondent bank for shady financial institutions that are strongly suspected of involvement in money laundering. This immediately opens up a whole new dimension, raising suspicions that in such cases banks are apparently willing to move money that has come from drug cartels, arms smugglers and terrorists.

The evidence we have before us of how German banks lost their moral compass at the end of the last century, if not earlier, is more extensive and more detailed than anything that has gone before. The supposedly secret email conversations between Mossack Fonseca employees and bank advisers make perfectly clear how together they went about it blatantly, on a large scale and without a scrap of guilt. For the most part, the only problem they ever saw in this was the risk of being found out.

Deutsche Bank, Germany's largest bank, presents a prime example of the unholy alliance between Mossack Fonseca and German financial institutions. It used to be one of the most prestigious companies in Germany, perhaps even in the world. Now, though, the bank has faced dozens of lawsuits worldwide, some of them still in progress, for money laundering, tax crimes and the manipulation of interest rates. The group figures on the books of Mossack Fonseca with a total of eleven different intermediary profiles, for example as Deutsche Bank Switzerland, Deutsche Bank Luxembourg and Deutsche Bank AG, but branches in Jersey, Guernsey, Mauritius, Beijing and Shanghai are also listed. All in all, the Deutsche Bank group has arranged or managed more than 400 offshore companies for its clients. In 2006 its Swiss arm, for example, paid around $160,000 just in annual fees for the more than 100 offshore companies that Mossfon had incorporated on its behalf.[7]

In May 2015 the author Stefan Willeke, writing in *Die Zeit*, posed the rhetorical question: should Deutsche Bank actually be viewed as a criminal organization? The answer is not the easy 'no' one might expect.

Mossack Fonseca saw Deutsche Bank as a difficult but extremely important client. In 2005, when the bank's Luxembourg branch first got talking to Mossfon, the partners in Jürgen Mossack's law firm went to great lengths to facilitate the relationship. When Deutsche Bank Luxembourg went as far as to ask for copies of the identity cards of the three partners prior to engaging in business, Jürgen Mossack not only agreed – he even 'just this once' allowed a copy of his German identity card to be sent.

And Deutsche Bank was granted other privileges too. Because it, 'like many other German banks, has a problem disclosing the names of the real owners of the offshore companies', writes one Mossfon employee, a special solution was found: anonymous bearer shares were issued as standard for the Deutsche Bank companies.[8] Nevertheless, most clients still wanted to be able to open their Swiss safe deposit box themselves. They therefore needed a power of attorney. This power of attorney would normally have to be signed by the Panamanian directors of their offshore company – who would then know the name of the end client. And that obviously caused concerns for Deutsche Bank. The solution: Mossack Fonseca sent blank powers of attorney signed by nominee directors to Deutsche Bank.[9] The bankers could then enter the names of the real owners themselves, and Mossack Fonseca never found out who received the power of attorney. Not only that, but Deutsche Bank, or at least at its Swiss branch, was also provided with blank, pre-signed account opening documents.

Both these practices are at odds with what Mossfon told us in February 2015: that the law firm had only sent blank documents very occasionally, and only for the sake of saving time, and that Mossfon had kept 'copies of the complete documents'. In other words, the opposite of the approach described above.

As we mentioned, Deutsche Bank even set up a dedicated website at www.dboffshore.com to promote its service. The site was taken down a few weeks after it was criticized in the Offshore Secrets reports by the *Süddeutsche Zeitung*, but we can still find archived screenshots.[10] These tell us that the offices in Jersey and Guernsey were opened back in 1972, the Deutsche Bank office in the Cayman Islands in 1983 and the Mauritius office in 1999. For a while, the site even bore the proud claim: 'Committed to offshore financial services for over 30 years.'

The client services that Deutsche Bank committed to provide were certainly not always illegal. But in some cases they were. While we were conducting our research, in November 2015, Deutsche Bank Switzerland, for example, had to pay $31 million in fines to the US authorities because between 2008 at the latest and 2013 it helped US citizens to circumvent their tax obligations. According to a report by the US Justice Department, 'Deutsche Bank Suisse offered a large number of services and allowed some practices which it knew could help American taxpayers to hide assets and income from the federal tax authority, which it did in fact do'.[11] One of our sources tells us that in Germany too, there are proceedings in progress against Deutsche Bank's Swiss branch.[12]

[ ]

Deutsche Bank's determination to accommodate its clients' wishes even quite recently is apparent from an example dated May 2014, when Deutsche Bank was thought to have long since given up this business: as part of its routine due diligence checks Mossack

Fonseca asked Deutsche Bank in Guernsey for the name of the real owner of an offshore company that was still active. The Deutsche Bank employee refused to cooperate and stated that she would first have to ask her client whether he agreed to it. In the end, Deutsche Bank stuck to its position that the name of the real owner could not be divulged, saying that in any case it was not just the company that was concerned here: there was also an associated foundation. Instead of disclosing the name, in autumn 2014 the Deutsche Bank employee announced that the client would no longer be doing business with Mossack Fonseca.[13]

[ ]

We could go on for pages about the offshore dealings of Deutsche Bank – a search on 'Deutsche Bank' produces more than 15,000 hits in our data. But although Deutsche Bank's involvement was the largest and most scandalous, it was not the only one engaging in these practices.

We have already talked about Commerzbank in detail in an earlier chapter. You will recall that it was the subject of a raid in February 2015, and for years it evidently helped to defraud the same state that, in 2008, gave the bank an €18 billion bailout.[14] It almost seems like a bad joke that it was Commerzbank that took over Dresdner Bank – one of the German banks that had arranged the most offshore companies through its Luxembourg operation.

One department at Dresdner Bank is worth a particular mention here: Dresdner Bank Latin America (DBLA), formerly known as Deutsch–Südamerikanische Bank. DBLA was in fact one of the first banks Jürgen Mossack did business with at the end of the 1970s, long before he went into partnership with Ramón Fonseca. At that time, his law firm still went by the name 'Jürgen Mossack Lawfirm'. Dresdner Bank Latin America was referred to internally as client number 17. Together Mossfon and DBLA helped hundreds of clients to acquire offshore companies, and these end clients included some of the most trusted associates of the Nicaraguan president Arnoldo 'Fat Man' Alemán, as well as Siemens managers, who restructured their slush funds with the help of one of the bank's advisers. At the end of 2004 UBS acquired the private client business of Dresdner Bank Latin America and relocated the majority of it to Hamburg, where the advisers carried on with their business – on the Latin America desk of the Swiss bank.

Absurd, maybe? Or perhaps not, since it meant the German bankers were then able to help their South American clients evade taxes in their home countries. This practice is apparently not prohibited in Germany, as Markus Meinzer of the Tax Justice Network explains: 'That is the crazy thing. The German government gives the impression that it is fighting tax fraud, but in truth there are banks operating perfectly legally out of Germany as accomplices to tax evaders all over the world.'

German bankers are only committing an offence under German law if they offer the same service to German clients.

Today UBS is secretly less enthusiastic about this acquisition and the associated risks, having discovered in the meantime that scores of its South American clients have been hoarding dirty money for years.

Apparently UBS has been trying for several years now, as part of its clean money strategy, to get rid of these clients or persuade them to adopt an honest approach in tax matters. But that, we hear, is not always easy.[15]

UBS Hamburg has an astonishing number of companies with Mossack Fonseca that were still active only recently: at the end of 2015 it had over seventy offshore companies up and running.[16]

[ ]

Mossfon's major German clients included – and in some cases still include – numerous government-funded banks such as Landesbank Baden-Württemberg, Landesbank Rheinland-Pfalz, HSH Nordbank and – you might say almost inevitably – the scandal-ridden BayernLB.

We can't help wondering what goes through the mind of one of these state bankers as he helps deprive the state of its due share.

Perhaps: 'Everyone's doing the same after all'?

Or: 'Nobody's going to notice'?

Whatever the case, hundreds of offshore companies were acquired and set up through the BayernLB subsidiary LBLux and the other Landesbank subsidiaries. Here, too, there seemed to be no sense of this posing a problem, at least not until the end of the last decade when word got around in banking circles that this business may come back to haunt them. And even then the banks reacted hesitantly. After a meeting with representatives of BayernLB's Luxembourg subsidiary in August 2010, Mossfon employees reported, for example, that the head of the asset management arm had said that it was under strict orders to no longer 'actively' offer clients shell companies in Panama or other tax havens. If, however, a client enquired about them, it would continue to provide assistance. And the existing offshore companies – there were more than ninety of them in Panama alone at that time – would be serviced as before.[17]

The big sell-off began not long afterwards. In 2011 HSH Nordbank sold its private client business in Luxembourg to Banque de Luxembourg, BayernLB followed suit in 2013 (also to Banque de Luxembourg) and LBBW sold its business in 2011 to DekaBank Luxembourg, another subsidiary of a German bank...

Briefly in passing: HSBC Germany is mentioned in connection with quite a number of companies, as are DZ Bank and the private BHF Bank, and even such peripheral banks as Deutsche Schiffsbank, which has since been taken over by Commerzbank, crop up in the data as managers, though in this case only as the intermediary for a single offshore company.[18]

But secretly, of all the banks that featured in our research, our favourite is the venerable Hamburg-based Berenberg Bank. When Mossack Fonseca recommends this bank to its clients, it rarely fails to point out that it is the oldest bank in Germany, or to be precise the oldest private bank: it was founded in 1590 and marked its 425th anniversary on its website with a kind of Berenberg quiz. The bank, which in times gone by even had a dedicated chef catering for its private clients at its Hamburg head office, trades on this image of tradition, and on Hamburg's fine reputation.

A number of tax investigators have told us the bank has recently started to appear on their radar, with the name cropping up in the voluntary disclosures of countless Germans.[19] According to our documents, the bank bought offshore companies from Mossack Fonseca for its clients, at least through its Luxembourg and Swiss offices. Probably not all that many, just a handful or so, but as things stand in autumn 2015 some of them are still active.[20] Much more fascinating, though, is the fact that Berenberg Bank is one of Mossack Fonseca's most trusted banks when it comes to providing bank accounts for offshore companies.

The second strand of the bank's business, in other words.

If you click through the folders in which Mossfon has filed the documents of particularly problematic clients, you can't help but notice how many of them have accounts with Berenberg's Swiss branch. We see from internal Mossfon emails that the bank was one of Mossack Fonseca's favourites. One emails states that its dealings with Berenberg had been 'very satisfactory'.

Quite a number of the accounts officially designated as belonging to firms with the usual fancy names are still are in fact being wholly managed by Mossfon itself. This means that a Mossfon employee can make transfers as an authorized third party – after consulting the real owner. However, it is unclear whether Berenberg Bank always knows who this real owner is.

And that's dangerous. After all, according to Lanny Breuer, who for years was head of the Criminal Division of the US Justice Department, it is a generally accepted fact that 'shell companies are the most popular vehicle for laundering dirty money and the proceeds of crime'. There are examples galore: for a long time Hezbollah financed its attacks in part through cigarette smuggling, which it transacted through several shell companies. The notorious arms dealer Viktor Bout concealed his business dealings through a dozen shell companies, Russian officials are proven to have been bribed through shell companies, Iranian sanctions circumvented, and so on.

Berenberg Bank isn't implicated in any of these. But if you take a closer look at the files where it is mentioned, you find accounts that have come up in our other investigations, such as those where Siemens kept its tainted funds.[21]

The provision of accounts for offshore companies would not have posed much of a problem if the 'Know Your Customer' rules had been followed. But we sometimes find that advisers patently had no knowledge whatsoever of the actual client. For instance, between February 2007 and October 2011 more than $60 million was transferred to a Deutsche Bank account in Hamburg held in the name of the shell company Val de Loire. The name Edmund W., former father-in-law of Ramón Fonseca, is stated as the company's shareholder, but in actual fact – as proven by a trust agreement we come across – Val de Loire belonged to someone else. However, the bank obviously knew nothing of this.[22] But since 1993 German banks are required by law to know the real owner – i.e. the beneficial owner – of all their accounts. If a German bank has the impression that a company like Val de Loire is feeding it false information in this regard, it is supposed to report it to the authorities. Edmund W. was officially employed as a financial controller at Mossfon and, according to our documents, received a very modest annual salary for this. This throws up all sorts of questions, and we put them to Deutsche Bank: did the bank ever conduct checks on Edmund W.? If so, with what outcome? Did it ever ask about the source of all these millions? Did it not occur to anyone to ask how on earth this Edmund W. was able to receive over $60 million in just four years?

Deutsche Bank stated that it could not give 'any information about possible or actual business relationships'.

We find time and again in our research that German banks – and we're now referring specifically not just to Deutsche Bank – were not too particular about the mandatory checks on their clients if their business stood to benefit. So in theory, behind every anonymous company there may be a corrupt politician siphoning money out of the country, an unscrupulous dictator paying for weapons for his army of child soldiers, or a terrorist group moving money in preparation for an attack.

A bank that does not know its clients willingly takes these risks on board.

24

A RAID BY THE VIKINGS OF FINANCE

'Today's the day,' ICIJ head of data Mar Cabra posts on our joint research forum on 29 October 2015: all the data that ICIJ has uploaded to its servers, everything we have received at that point, is now searchable. 8.2 million documents. Well over 2 terabytes.

Happy fishing, everyone.

At long last all the journalists are able to search all of the data rather than just part of it. By now, 'all the journalists' means more than 320 colleagues from over seventy countries and ninety media organizations. It is the largest journalistic collaboration in history.

Immediately all hell breaks loose on the forum. New hits are posted with each passing minute: a world-famous film director, a chess grand master and several ex-Formula 1 racing drivers. Just a few hours later our Swiss colleague Titus Plattner posts enthusiastically on the forum: 'What a difference! We originally found about 300 Swiss citizens in the data, but now we are up to more than 1,000 – many of them of great interest! The whole Swiss team is thrilled.'

And so are we.

The impact of having searchable data is greatest in relation to a country that was already prominently represented by its prime minister: Iceland. Our colleague Jóhannes Kr. Kristjánsson is working with us there on the research, and the next day he writes:

'I have been drinking coffee all night – to enable me to search.' He adds: 'In just twenty minutes I made some great finds in the data: Bjarni Benediktsson, finance minister and chairman of the Independence Party, Ólöf Nordal, newly elected vice-chair of the Independence Party.'[1]

What you need to know here is that the Independence Party is in government in Iceland and the vice-chair is simultaneously the serving interior minister. Her party is in coalition with the Progressive Party – whose party secretary also features in the data, as does the party leader – none other than the prime minister.

What a country. What an absurd state of affairs.

[ ]

In Reykjavik we meet our colleague Jóhannes Kristjánsson, argu-ably Iceland's best-known investigative journalist, with the most accolades to his name. He used to work in public radio in Iceland, and produced remarkable material on the causes of the banking crisis in his country. He has also conducted undercover research into drug abuse and exposed sex offenders. He is currently work-ing as a freelance journalist, focusing entirely on the Prometheus project. His story is bound to capture the attention of the masses in this country, whose political landscape was shattered by the banking crisis of 2008.

Prime Minister Sigmundur Gunnlaugsson, you will recall, cropped up early on in our investigations. If you remember, he and his wife, through the intermediary of the Luxembourg branch of Landsbanki, set up a company with Mossfon in the British Virgin Islands: Wintris Inc. They opened an account in its name with Credit Suisse in London. The only hitch with this: since the begin-ning of 2009 there has been a law in place in Iceland that requires parliamentarians to disclose their corporate shareholdings and assets. So Gunnlaugsson, who has been a member of parliament since April 2009, should have declared Wintris Inc., but failed to do so. At the end of 2009 he then 'sold' his stake to his wife: for one dollar.[2]

Just to recap: Iceland's prime minister features in the data, along with two of his ministers. That's a third of Iceland's cabinet. On top of that there are high-ranking officials of both governing parties, dozens of well-known business figures, and what feels like half of the country, says Jóhannes, who can hardly get his head around it all.

[ ]

As we take the long drive from the airport to the capital, Jóhannes explains to us how the revelations came at a significant time for the country. Here on this volcanic island in the Atlantic, it is the families who called the shots centuries ago, when the country earned its living from fishing and nothing else, who still pull the strings even today. The Icelanders have a name for this clique: 'The Octopus', because its members reached their tentacles into all sorts of places. Into the banks, the big corporations, the political parties. At the end of the 1990s this powerful elite effectively privatized the entire country. First the fishing fleets, then the banks. Iceland became one of the richest countries in the world. In Reykjavik, designer boutiques flourished, fancy restaurants were pricier than in London, and there were luxury 4x4s parked on every corner. According to a 2006 study, the 320,000 Icelanders were the happiest people in the world. 'Then came the wake-up call,' says Jóhannes.

For there were some less savoury aspects to the boom and privatization: the country's three largest banks – Kaupthing, Glitnir and Landsbanki – had been sold off to the 'octopuses' and their friends. Progressive Party supporters took over Kaupthing, while Landsbanki was handed over to the grandees of the Independence

Party, and Glitnir Bank was sold to a big retail chain mogul. Government and parliament took steps to relax the rules on mortgage lending, and suddenly you could take out property loans much more easily. A huge bubble developed.

When, in 2008, the signs started to suggest that this phase would not go on indefinitely, and it looked as if the big banks could be derailed, the octopuses went even further: they manipulated the banks' share prices. The principle was as simple as it was disastrous: the banks granted loans to shareholders who in turn used these loans to purchase shares in the same banks, which then caused an artificial hike in the share price. The result was that the book value of the top three banks grew to eight times the size of Iceland's GDP. Eight times!

It was the beginning of the end. In September 2008, in the wake of the financial markets crash triggered by the Lehman Brothers declaring bankruptcy, the banks were no longer able to repay their creditors and collapsed. The state had to stump up so much money in bailouts that Iceland itself faced insolvency. The people ran riot. A former state secretary for finance was later sentenced to several years in prison, as were the three former owners of Kaupthing – Ólafur Ólafsson, Hreiðar Már Sigurðsson and Sigurður Einarsson.

Jóhannes laughs. 'I came across all the Kaupthing people in your documents as well, but they're already locked up in prison.'

An unscrupulous elite had ruined one of the richest countries in the world in the space of just a few years – that is how most people here see it. And while ordinary Icelanders suffered as the cost of living went up, wages went down and mortgage debt soared, many of those who had brought about the crisis had long since moved their money out of the country.

'Financial Vikings' is the name the Icelanders still use for those risk-takers who, in their greed for ever more money, both miscalculated and enriched themselves at the same time. The Vikings were aided in this by the government at the time, which is still in power today, consisting of the Independence Party and the Progressive Party. Gunnlaugsson's party of progress.

[ ]

Wintris, the former offshore company of Prime Minister Sigmundur Gunnlaugsson, opened its account with the London branch of the Swiss bank Credit Suisse prior to the crisis, in March 2008 – in other words, at a time when it must have long been apparent to the financial Vikings with their inside view where Iceland was heading: into insolvency.

When we realized this, we went over every single document again. We talked to Jóhannes. We talked to experts. The big question was – and is: for what purpose did Iceland's prime minister need a company in the British Virgin Islands and an account with a Swiss bank? And above all: why didn't he properly declare them both?

Jóhannes found the answer: Wintris appears on the list of creditors of Kaupthing and Landsbanki. He later heard from a source that Wintris had also held Glitnir bonds. After the bank crash Wintris was owed the equivalent of several million euros for its Landsbanki and Kaupthing bonds alone.[3]

Either Gunnlaugsson and his wife bought the bonds of the three banks *before* the crisis hit, in which case he should have declared this publicly when he entered parliament in 2009.[4]

Or Gunnlaugsson – a graduate economist who spent time at Oxford University – and his wife bought the bonds *after* the collapse of the three banks, when they were worth only 3 to 5 per cent of their original value. That would mean they had speculated that bank prices would go up again before long.

Neither of the two possibilities casts Gunnlaugsson in a particularly good light. Especially as the fact he owned these bonds suddenly puts a whole new complexion on his political activity up to that point.

At this point there's something you need to know: when senior figures at Landsbanki realized that they were running out of money, they came up with a ruse to get hold of foreign currency. They set up an online subsidiary of Landsbanki, which they called Icesave. The subsidiary offered much higher interest rates than was the norm at the time, attracting savers from all over Europe, particularly the United Kingdom and the Netherlands, but also Germany. When Landsbanki went bankrupt, the hundreds of thousands of savers wanted their money back. But as Landsbanki had long ago run out of money, there were calls in Europe for the central bank, and hence every citizen of Iceland, to act as guarantor. The United Kingdom even used counter-terrorism legislation to freeze the assets of Landsbanki, the Central Bank of Iceland and the government. Iceland, everybody's darling until only recently, was placed on an equal footing with Al-Qaeda.

The centre-left coalition that took over the reins of power in 2009 in the aftermath of the crisis and attempted to bring order to the chaos left behind by its predecessors, the Independence Party and the Progressive Party, was understandably panic-stricken. The new government negotiated with the Dutch and the British and a proposal was eventually agreed on: Iceland would be granted new loans, and in return Dutch and British Icesave customers would get their savings back – guaranteed by the Icelandic government. This, it was hoped, would enable Iceland to rescue its reputation and avoid ruining its chances of EU accession.

But these plans met with opposition. The Icelanders – through their taxes – would have had to act as guarantors for the misadventures of the financial elite and would have been paying off the new loans for years to come. A political clash ensued. At this point a hitherto completely unknown grouping appeared on the scene and entered the political fray. It called itself 'InDefence' (short for 'In Defence of Iceland'), collected signatures online of those opposed to the planned deal and sent experts into parliament to speak out against the compromise. InDefence was composed of a mix of regular citizens – one of its leaders still works as a piano teacher today – and senior politicians.

One of its foremost speakers was none other than Sigmundur Gunnlaugsson, the newly elected chairman of the Progressive Party. The man who at the time was co-owner of the offshore company Wintris, and hence one of the creditors intent on getting their millions back from the banks.

However, according to sources in Iceland, he kept that nugget of information to himself, not even telling his fellow InDefence members.[5]

Three referendums were eventually held, and on each occasion the InDefence camp won. The government's proposed compromise was dropped from the agenda. This public victory marked the start of an ascent that took Gunnlaugsson all the way to the prime minister's office.

InDefence also proposed that all creditors should pay the government a 39 per cent stability tax if they wanted to withdraw their funds, which had been frozen by the government since 2008. In 2015, though, Gunnlaugsson's government agreed a different deal with the creditors, involving the payment of a 'stability contribution' which experts say will reduce the amount of money going into the state coffers by more than €2 billion. Even the fury of his former InDefence colleagues wasn't enough to change Gunnlaugsson's mind.

They won't be pleased to hear that the deal is extremely advantageous for the family of the premier: the approximately €2 billion that the government now loses out on goes to the creditors instead. And one of those creditors is the offshore company Wintris.

So in a way Gunnlaugsson was sitting on both sides of the negotiating table. A classic conflict of interest, which it wouldn't have been a bad idea to disclose.

[ ]

In summer 2015 Gunnlaugsson saw Iceland's tax authorities confronted with an interesting decision: an anonymous whistle-blower had offered Iceland's authorities a tax CD. The CD held secret data relating to shell companies owned by a number of Icelanders. Data which, according to our information, all came from Mossack Fonseca – though it was apparently much older and less detailed than the data in our possession.

The offer was made public, and there was a nationwide debate over whether or not the authorities should buy the data. What the Icelanders didn't know was that, according to our sources, the company that the prime minister had bought with his wife also featured on that CD. The head of the tax authority was in favour of buying the data. She had high hopes: after all, the CD was said to contain documents relating to between 300 and 500 shell compa-nies owned by Icelanders. Iceland's finance minister Bjarni Benediktsson – a member of one of the infamous Octopus families – was initially sceptical. He argued that 'giving an anonymous person a suitcase of money' for the data was 'completely unthinkable'.

But that is precisely what the head of the tax authority decided to do. The data was bought for the equivalent of around €200,000. And in a TV interview on the subject, asked whether he had held assets in tax havens or conducted transactions via tax havens at any time, the finance minister declared: 'No, I have never held assets in a tax haven or anything like that.'

When we go through this case with Jóhannes in Reykjavik, he points to his laptop: 'I've got the sentence on there, and I am going to have it scrolling right across the screen when we publish the story.'

On that night in October when Jóhannes sat drinking coffee after coffee while trawling through the cache of data that was finally fully searchable, Bjarni Benediktsson was one of the first names he entered. He found him. In 2006 the finance minister, along with two other business executives, was given power of attorney for the company Falson & Co. in the Seychelles – and an email from his bank adviser to Mossack Fonseca stated that the real owners were 'the same three names mentioned above'.[6]

According to our information, this firm, too, was on the CD purchased by the Icelandic authorities.

Is this the reason why Bjarni Benediktsson was initially sceptical about purchasing the data?[7]

Benediktsson is going to have to account for himself when Jóhannes publishes his stories in Iceland, if not before. Under the accepted rules of politics, as finance minister, no less, it will be hard for him to hold on to his position. This may also be the case for Ólöf Nordal, the serving interior minister, who according to Jóhannes had power of attorney for a company named Dooley Securities S.A.[8]

[ ]

The Panama Papers will place the government under extreme pressure to explain itself. 'The people of Iceland have gone through so much since the bank crisis that now they will have zero sympathy with an extremely rich prime minister and his extremely rich wife, who used an offshore company to secretly buy bank bonds,' Jóhannes explains.

He is in an absurd situation: he has the material that may force the prime minister of his country to step down, he has the story of the year ready and waiting, and has had since spring 2015 – yet he still has to wait, and keep on waiting, until we are all ready to publish in spring 2016.

What's more, he knows that a small chunk of data is already out there, in the hands of the revenue authorities. And Iceland is a very small country where everyone knows pretty much everyone else.

'I ask myself nearly every day: will the story keep?' he says.

A whole other problem for Jóhannes is that he has no idea where and how he will even be able to publish the story. He is a television journalist, and Iceland has three main television channels. But he has found senior figures from all three broadcasters and/or shareholders and/or close relatives of these in the data.

Jóhannes is uncomfortable about offering his story to one of the three broadcasters. Paradoxically, with each of his finds the scoop gets bigger – but so do his concerns about publication.

The newspapers are still an option, of course. It's just that *DV*, the tabloid known for its daring investigative stories, has just been taken over by a former politician from the Progressive Party – who would then have to publish reports about his friends. And the editor-in-chief of the leading daily newspaper, *Morgunblaðið*, is the former head of the central bank, Davið Oddsson, in other words one of the figures jointly responsible for the economic crisis.

Jóhannes is now considering simply publishing his research on a dedicated website. He has already acquired the name Reykjavik Media, and the web address Rme.is.

He laughs. 'But the name hardly matters. Everyone in Iceland will go on that website if we publish our stories there. Everyone will want to read it.'

And not just in Iceland.

25

DEAD-END TRAILS

It is now late autumn, and we are not the only ones becoming increasingly jittery. Obviously our source is too.

[john doe]: Is the plan still to come out with it in the spring? That's an awfully long time from now.
[SZ]: True. But it's also a huge amount of data. And if we rush it, we increase the risk that we make mistakes.
[john doe]: Sure, I just hate the idea of waiting that long.
[john doe]: Why not a little earlier? February?
[SZ]: We only have one shot. And everything has to fit. Each story is incredibly complicated for itself, Russia, Iceland, Siemens, the banks. . .
[SZ]: And if we go sooner, we would lose partners, and also impact.
[john doe]: Hmm. I wish the project would be more flexible.
[SZ]: So do we. But it's not. And we have come this far.

Every few days our little *SZ* team gathers in our 'war room' by the wall that, as of autumn 2015, shows nearly sixty trails pointing to heads of state and government, to discuss our latest findings.

Near the top of the list is the trail leading to the Kirchners, the two former Argentinian heads of state: Néstor Kirchner and his wife Cristina.

In fact, the documents relating to this case were the first that we got to examine in detail. We now have the documents for nearly all the companies concerned. But to cut a long story short, we have not found the 'smoking gun', the decisive proof of a connection to the Kirchners.

Our Argentinian colleagues at *La Nación* were also delighted at the prospect of exposing the secret business dealings of the woman who was their president at that time. But their investigations similarly failed to uncover proof of illegal goings-on, or of links to the presidential couple. We are now certain that the majority of these 123 firms are only linked to the Argentinian case by the fact that they have the same internal nominee directors as the handful of companies that do actually appear to belong to people linked to Kirchner. It seems that what Mossack Fonseca told us in February 2015 in response to our enquiry, namely that it 'has nothing to do with the "NML versus Argentina" case' may be true at least for the majority of the companies.

But whoever was responsible for structuring those other shell companies did a good job. We come up against three, four or even more impenetrable layers shielding the real owners from discovery. The trails end at anonymous companies in Switzerland and elsewhere.

These are the limits of our data: whatever the clients kept from Mossack Fonseca they also kept from us. The trail does not lead us to the owners, but to a blank wall.[1]

[ ]

Another promising trail that we followed early on was the one pointing in the direction of the former Libyan leader Muammar Gaddafi. We came across around a dozen companies that had already sparked the interest of Libya's investigators. Through these companies – according to a legal letter that we read – millions in public funds apparently flowed out of the country, including into the hidden accounts of a close associate of Gaddafi, a man named Ali Dabaiba.[2]

Not long after Muammar Gaddafi seized power from the Libyan king in 1969, Ali Dabaiba, a geography teacher by training, became mayor of the port city of Misrata. Dabaiba was very soon admitted into the autocrat's inner circle, the 'Companions of the Leader' as the clique was known in Libya. The Organization for Development of Administrative Centres (ODAC), the enormous state contracting agency headed by Dabaiba, placed contracts worth billions over the years, many of which, according to Libyan investigators, went to companies with links to the Dabaiba family. According to media reports, when auditors took a closer look at the contracts they found evidence of double bookkeeping. An adviser to Muammar Gaddafi later told Libyan investigators that discrepancies were noticed at ODAC from very early on but were not investigated further because Gaddafi and his sons 'were involved in the running of ODAC'.[3]

Straightforward enough so far. However, Dabaiba changed sides when Gaddafi's downfall drew near. He financed the Libyan rebels, placing millions at their disposal to defend his home city of Misrata. Overnight Dabaiba, Gaddafi loyalist, became Dabaiba, friend of the rebels. And that is what makes the affair so complicated.

For it is far from clear who actually holds power in Libya at present. The so-called Islamic State? The elected government based in Tobruk? Or the Islamist counter-government that has set itself up in Tripoli? And where does Dabaiba stand in this tangle of conflicting interests? Who is keen to haul him before a court, and who might want to prevent precisely that?

After the fall of Gaddafi, the new government froze the assets of 240 of the tyrant's former aides, including Ali Dabaiba. For a time, Libya even had Interpol hunting for Dabaiba, but Interpol's wanted alert disappeared as suddenly as it had appeared.[4] The transitional government also asked investigators to try to trace his assets, promising them a few per cent as a finder's reward if they managed to locate them.

We have in our possession more than a dozen digital folders containing hundreds of documents pertaining to shell companies that may be linked to this. Is it possible that we might hold the vital clue somewhere in our data, we wonder?

In a city in the Western hemisphere – we cannot be more specific – we meet someone who may be able to help us make some headway. The informant has to remain anonymous. His family is still living in Libya, while he himself has a regular job abroad. Only a few people are aware that he is working undercover to track down the assets of the Gaddafis and their associates – those people who, with Gaddafi's blessing, sucked Libya dry and hid their loot abroad.

The informant shows us a diagram on an A3 sheet of paper: it consists of a tangle of boxes and arrows in dozens of colours. Each little box represents a company (there are more than 100 in total), and every arrow symbolizes a link, a flow of money or a participating interest. There is a different colour for each country in which a company is based. Suffice to say, it is a very multi-coloured picture.

'Somewhere in here,' says the informant, 'are millions that in actual fact belong to the Libyan people.'

But where?

Some of the companies shown in the middle of the diagram are ones that are mentioned in our data.

[ ]

After our conversation with the informant, we go through our folders one at a time. We look for Gaddafi, his children, his close associates and for Ali Dabaiba. No luck. Looking at companies that the Libyan investigators think are owned by Dabaiba, we instead keep coming across the name Riad G., a British citizen who went to school in Libya and studied in London. His Facebook page shows that he is friends with Ali Dabaiba's brother.[5]

We call our informant to tell him about Riad G. – and get a clear answer: 'We believe that Ali Dabaiba was using G.!' Riad G. is thought to be some kind of front man for Dabaiba.

It is no more than a suspicion, though. We speak to Interpol. We want to know why Dabaiba was wanted in the first place, and why the request for his arrest, the 'Red Notice', later disappeared from the Internet again. Its answer is vague: all wanted notices, Interpol says, have been suspended in view of the current situation – meaning the civil war. 'The information cannot be released until further inquiries have been completed.'

Then we receive an email from an informant. 'Go to Geneva,' he writes. Riad G. is there right now. Someone saw him in a chocolate shop on Rue de Rive, right beside Lake Geneva.

However, the last flight from Munich to Geneva has already departed. We talk to a colleague from Switzerland's *SonntagsZeitung* who is working with us on the project, tell him what we know – and he is on the case. The very next morning he turns up at the Four Seasons hotel. At reception no one knows anything. They don't have a room booked in the name of Riad G. How about Auer Chocolatier? He is not there either. Where could he be?

Our colleague tries his luck at the Grand Hotel Kempinski, glamorously located directly on the shores of Lake Geneva. Behind its shiny façades it boasts, among other things, the largest suite in Europe with a living area of over 1,000 square metres and bullet-proof windows. At this time of year the moneyed aristocracy of the Gulf and the Maghreb gather here.

The receptionist has some trouble finding Mr G.'s room. 'Which room do you mean? He has a total of five rooms booked in his name.'

The man has come here on holiday with his extended family, but perhaps also with other purposes in mind. Our colleague puts all his eggs in one basket and telephones G., whose number we have been given by an informant. A hesitant voice answers the phone – Arabic accent, halting English – wanting to know who is calling, and above all: 'Where did you get this number?' He can't talk now, he says.

Finally, hours later, G. answers the telephone a second time, but puts off any meeting. He says he has urgent business to attend to the next day, then he wants to set aside a day to spend with his family.

In the end he never calls back and doesn't answer any more calls. He leaves Switzerland before our colleague can get a chance to speak to him for longer.

We see from our data that a company owned by Riad G. evidently part-owned a hotel in the Scottish Highlands for a time. Some time ago, Libyan investigators wrote to the British and Scottish authorities for assistance, saying Libyan state funds may be hidden in this same company. According to the commercial regis-ter, the company is run by two men who – and here's where it gets interesting – in 2008 both received contracts worth millions from ODAC – the same ODAC that Ali Dabaiba headed.[6]

However, at this point the trail goes cold. We find out both businessmen are under investigation. Yet both men remain at liberty. As for whether Riad G. really is the middleman for Dabaiba? We just can't say. The data doesn't tell us.[7]

[ ]

The Gaddafi and Kirchner cases are not the only ones of this kind. Again and again we have to give up on companies that give us cause for suspicion, sometimes backed up by all sorts of circum-stantial evidence, but just not enough of it.

The chances are that there are any number of clues hidden in the folders right under our noses that could eventually lead us to some extremely high-profile figures. We won't find them, though, because their advisers were careful enough not to give Mossack Fonseca any names.

It's frustrating.

Fortunately, though, not all our endeavours end in frustration.

For although we have no proof that Cristina Kirchner or Néstor Kirchner had anything to do with any of the 123 Nevada companies, we will instead be able to report on their successor in office. In early December 2015, Marina Walker writes to tell us that our colleagues at the Argentinian newspaper *La Nación* have found Mauricio Macri, Argentina's brand-new president, freshly elected in the run-off ballot, in our data. The conservative entrepreneur has not even taken up office, and already we have added him to our list in the 'war room'. We see from our data that Macri, along with two other close associates, arranged for a company to be set up in the Bahamas in 1998. It was known as Fleg Trading. At the time, Macri was chairman of the Argentinian football club Boca Juniors and a wealthy man. Later, in 2007, he was elected mayor of Buenos Aires. Now according to the Mossfon data, Fleg Trading was not wound up until 2008. However, the documents contained in the company records prove only that Macri was one of the directors of the company. The space for 'Owner' is blank in all the documents in our possession. Before the firm was shut down by the Bahamas authorities in 2008, Mossfon had asked umpteen times for details of the owners – but was never given the information.

When Macri was appointed mayor of Buenos Aires in 2007 he was required to disclose details of his bank accounts and corporate shareholdings. In his declaration, which an Argentinian colleague was able to access, there was no mention of a company in the

Bahamas. Under Argentinian legislation, providing false information is punishable by up to six years in prison.

Presented with our research, a spokesman for the president explained that Macri was 'occasionally' a director of the company. The company was part of the Macri family business. It was true that he had not declared Fleg Trading – but this was because he had never been a shareholder.

26

UNITED BY MARRIAGE, UNITED BY MONEY

There are not many photos showing Vladimir Putin with his family around him. The private life of the president is taboo in Russia. He keeps his two daughters firmly out of the public eye. So we were amazed when, in the course of our Internet research, we stumbled across a rather pixelated black and white photo showing a young, serious-looking Vladimir Putin. The snapshot was taken in 1985 in Leningrad, as St Petersburg was known during the Soviet era. Mikhail Gorbachev had just become general secretary and Vladimir Putin was still a minor, insignificant KGB officer. In the photo, he holds his baby daughter Maria in his arms, and standing next to him is his ex-wife Lyudmila; she has threaded her arm through his and looks happy.

Next to Lyudmila stands a young man with longish hair and a steady gaze. It is Sergei Roldugin, the godfather of Putin's daughter Maria. The mysterious cellist. During our research we found him to be at the centre of a web of anonymous offshore companies – but only once we had managed to peel away the various concealing layers in which Mossack Fonseca and the Swiss law firm we mentioned had shrouded it. Over the years, around $2 billion was channelled via this network with the aid of several banks, including some in the West, and quite a number of shell companies in Panama and the British Virgin Islands.

But Roldugin had told the *New York Times* that he didn't have millions to his name, that he was just a musician. Only a few months after this claim was made in an article on the strikingly rapid increase in the wealth of Putin's friends, several million was transferred to a Roldugin company account at the Swiss branch of a sanctioned Russian bank. Roldugin – and this is the curious thing about the story – is virtually unheard of in Russia. He is known mainly from films or biographies about the life of Vladimir Putin in which he is portrayed as a kind of sidekick, 'Putin's best friend', and makes admiring comments about the head of state.

[ ]

Putin and Roldugin met in the 1970s when they were both young men. Putin was like a brother to him, Roldugin later says in an interview. At night they would cruise the streets of St Petersburg, singing and getting into fistfights with other hooligans. Roldugin is also said to have introduced Putin to his wife-to-be, Lyudmila.

The bond between the two men evidently endures to this day, even though their paths in life could not have been more different. Shortly after the christening of his daughter Maria, Putin was posted to East Germany, and while there his second daughter Katerina was born. He only returned to St Petersburg after the fall of the Soviet Union. The KGB man became the mayor's assistant, then his deputy, before being appointed head of the domestic secret service, the FSB, then prime minister. In 2000 Putin became president. Sixteen years on he is more powerful than ever.

Roldugin was the principal cellist at the Mariinsky Theatre and rector of the St Petersburg Conservatory. As a musician he has won numerous accolades, and it is said he often plays at private soirées at Putin's house. He is also one of the very few people who can get away with divulging private insights to journalists. For example, Roldugin was able to disclose with impunity something that was not public knowledge up to that point: that the Russian president, who always likes to project the image of an eternally youthful muscle-man, has been a grandfather for a long time now and suffers from back trouble.

Godfather, long-standing friend, matchmaker, key source for the Putin biography, an insider on private matters and so on and so forth. All this suggests that Sergei Roldugin, if not the 'best friend', is at the very least a very important and trusted associate of the Russian president.

Now, it's fair to say that if Putin has really accumulated such fabulous riches as experts believe, he won't have put his name on them. The money would officially belong to people who don't come under public scrutiny, inconspicuous middlemen whom he nevertheless trusts implicitly.

People like Sergei Roldugin?

[ ]

The cellist, who had not replied to our enquiries by the time we went to press, popped up in our data in connection with five offshore companies: Roldugin was, at least for a time, the owner of the three shell companies International Media Overseas, Raytar and Sonnette – and these in turn have close links to the two companies Sunbarn and, most notably, Sandalwood Continental Ltd, which plays a particularly mysterious role within the network.

For Mossack Fonseca, the official contact for these firms was the Swiss law firm that we have already mentioned, and which also failed to respond to our enquiry. The law firm seems to act as a kind of gatekeeper to the Roldugin network. It may be the official contact for Mossack Fonseca, but individual offshore company documents reveal that, behind the scenes, it is Rossiya Bank employees who really pull the strings. Bank employee S. was authorized to sign documents for Roldugin's company

International Media Overseas, and others had similar powers for other firms in the network. Rossiya Bank is based in St Petersburg and was founded with Communist Party money at about the time Putin returned to the city from his posting to East Germany. Experts regard it as 'Putin's bank' and several of Putin's close friends own shares, including Roldugin. During the crisis in Ukraine, the US government placed the bank on its sanctions list in an attempt to penalize Putin's inner circle. He reacted promptly, ordering the state bank to support Rossiya Bank, and several state energy companies placed their money there.

[ ]

So we see that this Rossiya Bank is tied up in the same network as Roldugin's companies.

Rossiya Bank's role in the Roldugin network is apparent from an exchange of emails in 2009. A lawyer at Mossack Fonseca harboured concerns and decided to consult Jürgen Mossack and the Swiss partner Christoph Zollinger. A Rossiya Bank employee had told her that he wanted Mossfon to approve a $103 million credit line for the offshore company Sandalwood. The money was to come from a bank in Cyprus. We look at the attached forty-seven-page agreement, and the page that is meant to show details of the collateral is blank. That strikes us as extremely unusual for a transaction of this magnitude.

It was an agreement that must have looked suspicious even to Jürgen Mossack. It is probably money of dubious origin and equally dubious purpose, he writes in an internal email. It's a 'delicate' situation, he says.

A remarkable comment.

Despite Mossack's concerns the deal was not rejected.[1] Instead, Mossfon asked for a 'letter of indemnity' to be issued, an exemption from liability. If there turned out to be problems with the agreement, the client would be held responsible in the first instance, and not the offshore law firm. The $103 million credit line is one of many questionable transactions that have come to light in the Roldugin network. Money from Russian oligarchs evidently flowed into the network of shell companies as well. In 2013 alone, several shell companies linked to the brothers Boris and Arkady Rotenberg extended loans of around $200 million to an offshore company in the Roldugin network – and it is not apparent from the documents whether they were ever repaid. Shortly prior to that, one of Arkady Rotenberg's companies had been awarded the contract for the South Stream pipeline project, an undertaking worth billions, but which was suspended during the Ukrainian crisis. The Rotenbergs did not respond to our request for comment.

According to the data, around $1 billion was funnelled into the Roldugin network between 2009 and 2011 alone. A large portion of this evidently came from the Russian Commercial Bank (RCB) in Cyprus, at the time a wholly owned subsidiary of VTB Bank, which is largely in Russian state ownership. Where RCB got these sums of money from is not explained in our files. When we enquired, the bank said it could not comment on clients or transactions, but that it obeyed the law.

An industry insider told our colleagues at the *Guardian* that Putin and his inner circle apparently used RCB, at least during the 2000s, as a kind of personal credit card. The bank contests this, but according to the source, 'When one of Putin's favoured few or his wife needed money, whether for a shopping trip, a yacht or some other investment, RCB always stumped up the funds for them without question [. . .] RCB was a self-service store for the power elite.' This may explain why, during the euro crisis in 2013, the Russian government was so fiercely opposed to a 'haircut'. The plan was to use this approach to trim all deposits with Cypriot banks, including RCB. 'We were given to understand in no uncertain terms by those in the very highest positions of power in Russia that if we touched RCB the reaction would be unlike anything we had ever seen before,' the head of Cyprus's centrist party said later in a radio interview. RCB was largely exempted from the measure.

Experts who have reviewed the dubious loans found in the data see the unusual terms – with some loans, for example, there was virtually no interest to pay, or no sign of any repayment, or no requirement to furnish collateral – as a strong indicator that these were cash gifts rather than loans. 'It would appear that tax evasion, fraud and/or some other predicate act is underlying these transactions for purposes of money laundering,' says David Weber, a financial expert at the University of Maryland.

At the same time, the enormous loans are just one of the ways in which the offshore companies in Roldugin's network obtained money. Between May and June 2010, for example, the company Sunbarn receives payments running into millions for 'consulting services'. Sunbarn apparently advised another offshore company on 'investment and trade' in Russia, for which it was paid $30 million. There is much to suggest that what is going on here is an attempt to disguise flows of money intended for a completely different purpose. According to our research, the offshore company that paid for the advice was never known as an 'investor and trader' in Russia.

Money laundering experts view the term 'consulting services' as an easy smokescreen for massive movements of money.

Another pattern came to light early on in our research, which we called 'claiming failure fees'. It is extremely simple and at the same time an ideal way of shunting money from one place to another: one of the offshore companies in the network undertakes to buy corporate shares from another offshore company in Belize. However, the company 'fails' in its commitment to provide these shares – and has to pay almost $800,000 in 'compensation'. So there is a clear 'business transaction' and the transfer can be neatly labelled.

Roldugin's company International Media Overseas signs a particularly lucrative deal in February 2011: all rights to a $200 million loan are made over to it – for the price of one dollar. According to the agreement, which is among the Mossfon documents, the loan generates interest payments of $21,917 a day, which adds up to $8 million a year.

We also come across suspicious backdated equity transactions in this connection: according to these documents, companies from the Roldugin network buy shares in Russian companies for millions of dollars, which are then sold on again almost immediately – at a substantial profit. The people who stand to profit from these sales may be brilliant speculators. However, certain factors stand out that make us doubt this is the case. One example: on 5 June 2011 a Rossiya Bank employee asks Mossfon to ask the directors of Sandalwood to approve several share transactions. A normal procedure in itself: behind-the-scenes staff getting directors to sign contracts. But what's different in this case is that, according to the attached documents, the transactions appear to have already taken place five months previously, in January 2011.

[ ]

The dubious loans running into millions, the backdated share transactions, the consulting fees and compensation; all seem to be part of a colossal shadow system. A system in which vast amounts of money can be passed to opaque offshore companies in only a short space of time.

More often than not it is the Russian state that is the loser.

Now it's not really a good idea to milk the Russian state. Unless you happen to be one of those people who, thanks to their contacts, can get away with it.

Experts have long spoken of a kleptocracy when they talk about Russia under Putin. Indeed, Vladimir Putin's political ascent has been accompanied by massive corruption allegations from the outset, most of them since forgotten.

But now we see how, with the help of an old friend and close associate of Putin, hundreds of millions find their way, by devious routes, into an offshore pot of money.

To enable us to get a better understanding of the deals we have unearthed, we talk to a European investigator, one of the world's best-known trackers of money launderers and fraudsters. 'There are hundreds of ways of getting money out of a country like Russia,' he says, and the routes we had uncovered were among them. He says there is no way the Russian authorities were unaware of what was going on. In Russia the task of combatting money laundering is handled, he says, by an authority known as Rosfinmonitoring. Since its inception the authority has been headed by a Putin confidant and, unlike most other European authorities, operates more like a secret service than a police service. Rosfinmonitoring can read emails, tap phone conversations and access all of a person's bank details. 'Nothing escapes them,' the investigator adds with a combination of respect and envy.

[ ]

The small taskforce of Prometheus researchers covering Russia, which was set up at our meeting in Washington, is now having encrypted discussions almost daily about their research findings, puzzling loans, suspicious contracts and the latest projections of the amount of money siphoned off.

Our colleague Luke Harding from the *Guardian* puts it this way: we are on a quest for the 'Holy Grail of investigative journalism' – Putin's money. Things could quickly get dangerous for our Russian colleagues Roman Anin and Roman Shleynov in particular. In Russia it is often said that working as a journalist there is tantamount to suicide.

So if you are following the trail of Putin's money, what then?

We therefore decide together with ICIJ Project Manager Marina Walker to hold a work meeting on neutral ground, far from the Russian secret service. We want to talk to our Russian colleagues about what we have found so far and how we should proceed, without the fear of eavesdroppers.

[ ]

So, shortly before Christmas 2015 we travel to London. Our meeting place: Kings Place, 90 York Way, head office of the *Guardian*. We are meeting on one of the upper floors, where, at the end of a long corridor, there is a room that holds legendary status among investigative journalists: 'the bunker'.

The bare room, which can only be opened with one key and a special key card, is where the *Guardian* once analysed the secret documents leaked by the NSA whistle-blower Edward Snowden. Now there are up to ten editors here working on the Mossfon data that arrived at our offices in Munich several months previously.

The desks are tightly packed, the window to the corridor is obscured and the findings to date are all on Post-it notes on the walls, carefully sorted by category: celebrities, mercenaries, heads of state, sportspeople, politicians. When the Snowden documents were examined here, they even had two guards outside the door. That time word had already got out that the data was at the *Guardian*. We hope that's not the case this time.

[ ]

The group assembled in the bunker is a small one: besides us there is our Russian colleague Roman Anin, plus Luke Harding, who was once expelled from Russia for speculating about Putin's fortune in an article. Marina Walker, Gerard Ryle and Jake Bernstein from the ICIJ have made the journey, and we are also joined by BBC journalists and our colleagues Julia Stein from NDR and Petra Blum from WDR, who has been working her way through the Roldugin data for months.

Together we discuss what we have already found to date in the files: the brothers Arkady and Boris Rotenberg, for example.[2] Or the Russian oligarch and friend of Putin, Gennady Timchenko, who crops up in the data as a shareholder or authorized signatory of several shell companies.[3]

We also have a chuckle about Dmitry Peskov, Vladimir Putin's spokesman. Peskov recently came under fire because at his wedding to a well-known skier he wore a watch worth far more than he earns in a year. Then on top of that bloggers revealed that Peskov and his new bride spent a holiday on one of the world's most expensive sailing yachts. And now what do we see in the data? That until 2014 at least, his wife was the owner of a shell company named Carina Global Assets. In all, our data reveals connections to four Russian ministers and senior officials, four members of parliament and two governors. The son of Minister of Economic Development Alexey Ulyukaev, for example, was director of the offshore company Ronnieville Ltd. The nephew of Nikolai Patrushev, the former director of the secret service and current secretary of the powerful Security Council, crops up as a shareholder, on and off, in a company incorporated in the British Virgin Islands. Meanwhile, Deputy Interior Minister Alexander Makhonov appears to have controlled a whole network of shell companies via the shell company Nortwest Management.

They are all good stories, but it is the case of the cellist Roldugin that interests us most. We discover that he owned shares in Video International through offshore companies. Other companies managed by the same people at Rossiya Bank – in which Roldugin is a shareholder – and at the Swiss law firm who manage Roldugin's companies, hold and trade share options in the car manufacturer Lada and the truck and armoured vehicle manufacturer KamAZ. These share options leave a bitter aftertaste: it was mostly trucks from this manufacturer that were deployed in the war in Ukraine. The white Russian trucks that drove into eastern Ukraine, purportedly carrying relief supplies, were KamAZ trucks. KamAZ trucks were also spotted in Syria, where Russian ground troops have long been supporting the army of dictator Bashar al-Assad. Lada is also a supplier to the Russian army.

[ ]

So there we all sit on a grey December day in the bunker at the *Guardian* discussing the ownership of Russian banks, talking about those who are still close to Putin and those who have long since distanced themselves, when Roman Anin suddenly stuns us with one of his research findings.

In a positive way, that is.

Everyone jumps up and applauds. We shake our heads in disbelief. What has happened?

Shortly before, Reuters news agency had revealed that, in February 2013, unnoticed by the media, Putin's younger daughter Katerina had married a man in his mid-thirties named Kirill Shamalov. He is the son of Nikolai Shamalov, who is in turn a member of the legendary Ozero cooperative. Vladimir Putin had founded the cooperative in the 1990s with a number of friends who had recently acquired dachas on the banks of Lake Komsomolskoye, not far from St Petersburg. What began as simply an association of dacha owners soon evolved into a byword for cronyism. Ozero member Yury Kovalchuk, for example, is today the director and largest shareholder of Rossiya Bank, in which Nikolai Shamalov – whose son married Putin's daughter – also holds shares.

Putin's son-in-law became an even richer man within just a few months of the wedding, bumping up his stake in the petrochemicals giant SIBUR from just a few per cent to 21 per cent.

Even more interesting for us, though, is the location of the wedding: the Igora ski resort, an hour's drive north of St Petersburg, not far from the Ozero cooperative. Locals refer to the 'president's villa' as a lavish property and report that he often spends time here – although a different owner is entered in the land register. It is situated right next to the Igora resort.

In February 2013 the prominent newlyweds drove up here in a sleigh drawn by three white horses. Their guests received gifts of scarves embroidered with the letters K&K, the initials of the bride and groom, Katerina and Kirill.

Photography was banned and all guests had to hand over their mobile phones at the entrance. A massive security operation was in place. 'There were security guards on every corner. They wouldn't let anyone get close to the festivities,' was how an Igora resort employee described the scene to a Reuters journalist. There was plenty on offer for the wedding guests: ice skating, a laser show and a replica Russian village complete with actors and various kinds of folk dancing.

Now Roman Anin checked who the Igora resort currently belongs to. The owner of the site is a Russian firm called Ozon LLC, which was originally majority-owned by an impenetrable Cypriot offshore company and – via another intermediate company – 25 per cent owned by Putin confidant Yury Kovalchuk and his son. The company purchased the site around 2012. Kovalchuk is one of the members of the Ozero cooperative – so the resort that is part-owned by Kovalchuk is the venue for the wedding of the children of two other Ozero members: the daughter of Vladimir Putin and the son of Nikolai Shamalov. We just mention this to highlight the close ties between the members of the posse even today, nineteen years after Ozero was founded.

But it was for another reason that we in the 'bunker' at the *Guardian* were so pleased. We have long been familiar with the name Ozon LLC from our documents. At the end of 2009 Ozon LLC received a loan of around $5 million from Sandalwood, one of the offshore companies in the Roldugin network. Approximately two years later it received another loan for almost the same amount. According to our files the money was never repaid, and in 2013 Sandalwood was wound up.

Millions, apparently diverted and disguised via a shell company from the network, seem to have flowed via the offshore company that owned it into the resort where Putin's daughter got married, which is part-owned by one of Putin's friends in the cooperative. The whole operation was orchestrated by Rossiya Bank, which is owned by several Putin cronies. And it seems the front man for this network was Putin's best friend: Rossiya Bank co-owner Sergei Roldugin, godfather to Putin's other daughter.

So our months of research, starting out in Panama, end up leading us to Igora. To Vladimir Putin's closest family.

Incredible.

27

STAR, STAR, MEGA STAR

After the meeting in London it gets quieter on the forum and at our offices. Not much happens over Christmas and New Year, although we can't switch off completely. Obviously not, after all these new findings. But the unaccustomed peace and quiet gives us a chance to cast our eye over some of the old stories again. At this point we have well over 7,000 entries on the forum. Far too many to keep track of.

And although it may seem like it in this book, Mossack Fonseca's clients are not all shady characters. They also include famous directors and actresses, South American singers worshipped like gods in their own country, brilliant chess players and a whole string of owners and chairmen of top-flight football clubs.

Over the peaceful holiday period we click through hundreds of finds and read about dozens of ministers, famous dancers and the granddaughter of one of the best-known artists of classical modernism, about spies who had done arms deals with East Germany, and about the alleged lover of a European king.

There are still so many stories we could tell.

For legal reasons, however, we can only mention by name those we have researched in sufficient depth. And the number of these cases is limited by our time and energy – after all, sometimes we have to sleep too.

[ ]

It's the beginning of January 2016 and the Christmas holidays are barely over when the next really big case turns up.

Lionel Messi. The best footballer in the world. Maybe the best of all time.

The name of his Panamanian shell company sounds a little showy, but not entirely unfitting: Mega Star Enterprises. The company is run by five unknown nominee directors, but one of the names that crops up in the paperwork belongs to the mega-star of world football. His name appears in a document dating from June 2013 discovered by a Spanish colleague working on the Prometheus project.

In this document, an employee of a Uruguayan law firm notifies the offshore provider Mossack Fonseca that the ultimate beneficiaries of Mega Star Enterprises are Lionel Andrés Messi and his father, Jorge Horacio Messi.

That's all he needs. Lionel Messi is already facing questions over the way he has handled his finances. In October 2015 a Spanish examining magistrate decided that Messi and his father, who advises him, would be charged with tax evasion. The attorney's office is calling for a fine of €4.1 million, which is unlikely to be of great consequence to the multi-millionaire Lionel Messi. But above all it's calling for a nearly two-year jail sentence for the Barcelona playmaker. The start date for the trial has already been set for 31 May 2016.

It will be interesting to see how the Spanish authorities react to this new information. Mega Star Enterprises doesn't appear in the files already held by the state attorney's office, a spokesman for the authority confirms upon request. But it could fit the picture, because in the indictment Messi and his father are accused of having used shell companies, including for the alleged tax fraud involved in this case.

According to the indictment, Messi and his father used shell companies for the purposes of the tax fraud they have been charged with. From 2005, the Messis are said to have sold image rights, for very small sums, to offshore companies headquartered in Latin American tax havens such as Belize and Uruguay. As a result, advertising revenues of €10.1 million are said to have poured into these tax havens practically untaxed. What's more, the Messis are said to have withheld important information from the tax authorities to make sure they would not find out about the money channelled abroad. This allegedly enabled Messi to evade taxes of around €4.1 million between 2007 and 2009.

Mega Star Enterprises is incorporated on 8 February 2012 by an offshore provider in Panama, and the shares are issued as anonymous bearer shares. Agents of the abovementioned Uruguayan law firm act on Messi's behalf. Here is the first link to the charges in the indictment: according to these, nine days later the same law firm issues confirmation that Lionel Messi is the sole owner of the shell company Jenbril S.A. – which is at the centre of the existing tax evasion allegations. So Mega Star and Jenbril, which is mentioned in the indictment, are looked after behind the scenes by the same Uruguayan law firm.

The second point of connection emerges in summer 2013, when the investigations into Messi are made public. On 12 June 2013 the Spanish news agency EFE reports on the proceedings for the first time, and the international media follow suit. The very next day, Lionel Messi's Uruguayan lawyers send an email to Mossack Fonseca saying they want to change the offshore provider for Mega Star Enterprises; according to the email, this move has already been discussed on the phone. In future Mossack Fonseca is to manage the shell company.

Mossack Fonseca insists that it be issued with a letter of indemnity, under which Mossack Fonseca and the nominee directors it uses shall be compensated for any 'complaints, claims, actions, disputes, lawsuits, costs and expenses' related to Mega Star Enterprises. The document, which we have among our files, is dated 23 July 2013 and bears signatures in the names of Lionel Andrés Messi and Jorge Horacio Messi.

It is hard to say from the documents what role Mega Star played in the tangled web of companies owned by the Messis. In one document the general business purpose is given simply as 'Investments'. But so far no specific contracts or deals have been found among the leaked data. That, however, may be because the Messis seem to have had powers of attorney issued in relation to this company for themselves and other people involved – which would mean no documents whatsoever would need to go to Mossack Fonseca to be signed. At any rate, in a letter dated 23 June 2013, 'Horacio Jorge and Lionel Andrés Messi' assure Mossack Fonseca that, in the event of the termination of the business relationship with the Uruguayan law firm, they will help 'to revoke each and every one of the powers of attorney which the company has assigned to third parties'.

Anyone armed with one of these powers of attorney can sign contracts of any kind. They could open accounts, for example, or purchase real estate. Yet from the outside it is impossible to find out who actually owns the company since, as we mentioned, the shares are held anonymously.

The Spanish state attorney's office may well be very interested in finding out who was granted these powers of attorney – and for what purpose.

But whatever is written in the contracts of Mega Star Enterprises, Lionel Messi will hardly have to change his existing line of defence in the proceedings. The strategy of the FC Barcelona striker is clear – and similar to that of Franz Beckenbauer in the affair involving the German Football Association: 'I don't look at what I sign,' Messi told the examining magistrate, according to newspaper reports. 'If my father says I should sign, I do it with my eyes closed.' He also said: 'I sign what my father says I should sign. I don't look at it. I don't focus on it. I don't ask any questions.'

However, the strategy doesn't seem to have had the desired effect. The Spanish public prosecutor's office does believe that the initiative came from Messi's father – and the latter is willing to take all the blame – but the Ministry of Finance nevertheless decided that Lionel Messi himself should also be charged. Even the professional footballer must have found the transactions suspicious, argued the ministry spokesperson, for example when he received tax refunds for the years 2007 to 2009. According to the news agency AFP, the statement of reasons for the decision cites 'sufficient evidence to suggest that criminal actions were committed by both of the defendants'.

[ ]

We see from our data that Mega Star Enterprises undergoes a change of ownership on 1 December 2015. The bearer shares originally issued are superseded by ordinary shares, which are held by Lionel Messi's father. But the Uruguayan law firm has one more request in this regard: an agent asks Mossfon the next day to confirm that the shareholders of the companies it manages do not appear in the Panamanian public register of companies. If, says the agent, this happens as standard, could Mossfon please provide the lawyers with the necessary documents to prevent it.

At the time of going to press, Lionel Messi and Horacio Messi had not responded to the repeated joint enquiries of the ICIJ and the *Süddeutsche Zeitung*.[1] At the time of going to press, the Spanish trial had also not been concluded.

28

THE FOURTH MAN AND FIFA

The end of the FIFA crisis goes almost unnoticed from the outside. But FIFA itself and its new Swiss President, Gianni Infantino, make a point of proclaiming it. Speaking immediately after his election in the Hallenstadion in Zurich, he declares in the usual grandiose manner of FIFA presidents: 'We will restore the image of FIFA and the respect of FIFA. And everyone in the world will applaud us, and will applaud all of you for what we will do in FIFA in the future. We have to be proud of FIFA and everyone has to be proud of FIFA.'

Infantino's first word on stage, though, was: 'Whew!'

Our thoughts exactly: whew.

Because the name Gianni Infantino has been on our list since mid-2015, when we became aware of UEFA's deals in relation to Ecuadorian television rights, which had been bought from UEFA by the broadcasting rights agents Hugo Jinkis and his son, and then sold on for triple the price to the broadcaster Teleamazonas.

We seek the opinion of an insider involved in the FIFA investigations: he regards this contract with its margin of 1:3 as 'very suspicious'. Particularly if, as in this case, the rights were sold on in advance.

An expert in sports law also considers this model dubious.

According to the New York investigators, the Jinkises' business model consisted of bribing FIFA officials to give them access to cheap TV rights, which they could then sell on at a much higher price.[1] If these allegations are true, the method used was similar. With the key difference, though, that we haven't found any evidence of bribery at UEFA.

When we came across the contracts between UEFA and Cross Trading, we paid little attention at the time to the individuals acting on UEFA's behalf. On the two contracts between UEFA and Cross Trading, the names of a total of four officials are given as authorized signatories on the pages requiring signatures. Three of them were no longer in exposed positions at UEFA by 2015 or have since left the association.

But look who the fourth man is: Gianni Infantino. The current FIFA president.

This is explosive stuff.

But one thing at a time. The contract in which Infantino is named relates to Champions League rights for 2006 to 2009 for Ecuador. The second page of the contract is the signature page. The names of three people required to sign the contract are given here: for Cross Trading Hugo Jinkis, for UEFA the deputy general secretary of UEFA at that time, and Gianni Infantino, whose title is given as 'Director Legal Services'. We check this out and find that Infantino was indeed the director of UEFA's legal department at the time.

We learn from a sports rights expert that associations normally have contracts of this kind checked over by their legal department. When we try to ask UEFA whether this was also how it worked at UEFA at that time, we are initially thwarted by the association's ridiculously rigid press policy: that is an internal UEFA matter, we are told. Later UEFA tells us that its legal department does check every contract of that kind.

But why should the head of the legal department sign a contract for which he does not then have to assume responsibility? When we ask, UEFA explains that Infantino signed it because all contracts are signed by two directors who are authorized signatories. The contract involved small sums, a UEFA spokesman further explained, and Cross Trading acted as the authorized rights buying agent for Teleamazonas. Any deals concluded between Cross Trading and Teleamazonas were none of UEFA's business, he said. UEFA was only aware of the offer for $111,000. The fact is, it was Infantino's department that allowed the deal with the Jinkis duo to go ahead and helped the two men now indicted in the FIFA corruption case, Hugo and Mariano Jinkis, to get their hands on hundreds of thousands of US dollars. A deal about which UEFA had said, when Infantino was still its general secretary, that there had been 'no business relationship' with the Hugo Jinkis in question. The same Hugo Jinkis whose name is clearly legible three centimetres below Infantino's.

It is significant that the two Argentinians did not act anonymously. The Jinkises' company Cross Trading is well known in the industry, a subsidiary of their even better known company Full Play (which is also named in the FIFA indictment). And as chief of the UEFA legal department, Infantino ought to have known who he was doing business with. But that, it seems, was not the case: when probed about this, UEFA replied that it had not known who was behind Cross Trading.

Our colleague Catherine Boss of the Swiss newspaper *SonntagsZeitung* wanted in any case to ask Infantino whether, as a UEFA official, he'd had any business or other dealings with the accused sports rights brokers in the past. She put the question to him, mentioning names including Hugo Jinkis, Mariano Jinkis and Cross Trading.

FIFA replied that Gianni Infantino 'had not personally, in any of his positions at UEFA, had anything to do with any of the persons or organizations mentioned below, in a business connection or knowingly in any other connection'. FIFA subsequently stated that it had issued this response solely on the basis of information provided by UEFA. It's interesting that the statement about Infantino's involvement contains words like 'personally' and 'knowingly', even though FIFA asserts afterwards that this statement was based only on research by UEFA.

The way this situation developed seemed to us rather absurd. As UEFA general secretary Infantino was already an important person and his involvement in the affair was of interest. After all, back then, he was the second-most important man in UEFA after Michel Platini. Then Platini was banned because of dubious payments running into the millions and had to abandon his plan to get elected as the new FIFA president in Sepp Blatter's place. And suddenly we read that UEFA had settled on Infantino as its new candidate. In the early stages, though, he barely seemed to be in with a chance. Then in early 2016 more and more national associations declared they would be voting for him in February. In an interview with *Die Welt* ahead of the election he claimed to have 105 votes in the bag out of a total of 209. In the end he received 115.

And all of a sudden the strange story of UEFA and Ecuador takes on a new significance.

For football's world governing body this episode is also awkward because this election was supposed to draw a line under the biggest crisis it has faced since its inception 111 years ago, the FIFA corruption scandal.

[ ]

When describing FIFA, the British investigative journalist Andrew Jennings and our *SZ* colleague Thomas Kistner have often had occasion to use the term 'mafia'. Certainly, the last ten years have been marked by scandal after scandal. These concerned kickbacks involving the FIFA marketing partner ISL, questionable presidential elections, and possible bribery in relation to the award of the football World Cup tournaments. Sepp Blatter and his colleagues on the FIFA executive committee tried, after every scandal, to give the outward impression that from now on everything would be better. In retrospect these assurances seem laughable.

The FIFA ethics committee, ostensibly its last bastion of decency, has had its work cut out lately. Not only did it have to suspend its own boss Sepp Blatter, it also banned UEFA boss Michel Platini, FIFA Secretary General Jérôme Valcke and a long line of other senior officials including Jack Warner, Chuck Blazer, presidential candidate Chung Mong-joon and former FIFA Vice President Eugenio Figueredo.

The FIFA ethics committee has an almost impossible task on its hands: to clean up world football. The credibility of this committee depends chiefly, of course, on the personal integrity of its members – such as the German chairman of the committee's adjudicatory chamber, Hans-Joachim Eckert, a highly experienced criminal judge at Munich's district court. It would be reasonable to expect that all the other members of the two chambers had been similarly hand-picked, figures of moral authority in the embattled world governing body. But apparently you'd be wrong.

For in Eckert's own chamber we find someone who is himself bogged down in allegations, someone who already has the New York investigators on his tail. The man in question is Juan Pedro Damiani, an influential lawyer from Uruguay, and chairman of the Peñarol football club.

One of Juan Pedro Damiani's specialities is managing shell companies, of all things. His law firm is among the bigger clients of the offshore provider Mossack Fonseca. More than 400 companies have been or are currently managed by the law firm J.P. Damiani. That in itself is not ideal for someone who is now supposed to pass judgment on other people's ethics.

But there is more astonishing news to come: according to our documents, three of Damiani's long-standing clients are among the defendants in the FIFA scandal.

One of them is the former FIFA Vice President Eugenio Figueredo, who was arrested in Switzerland last year. The other two are the Argentinian TV rights agents Hugo Jinkis and his son Mariano Jinkis – who, according to our research, also worked with UEFA through their Mossfon company Cross Trading and who, according to the FIFA indictment, used shell companies to pay bribes.[2]

The pair had three shell companies incorporated by Mossack Fonseca, all with the same name, Cross Trading, but based in three different tax havens: the island of Niue in the South Pacific, the US federal state of Nevada and the Seychelles. The companies in Niue and Nevada were managed by Juan Pedro Damiani's law firm.

If you take the trouble to go through the FIFA indictment, you will find mentions of the name Cross Trading dotted all over the place. According to the charges, bribes were channelled through the accounts of the Cross Trading companies, such as a wire transfer of $5 million on 17 June 2013 to a Cross Trading account at Bank Hapoalim in Zurich. However, it's not clear from the indictment which of the three Cross Tradings held the bank account – and when asked, the US Justice Department declined to comment. The $5 million wire transfer is thought to have been part of a larger scheme whereby the chairmen of certain Latin American associations were given bribes worth millions to secure the broadcasting rights for football tournaments such as Copa América for Hugo and Mariano Jinkis and their business partners.

Mossack Fonseca's client advisers knew what kind of people they were dealing with. One of Mossfon's senior managers wrote that these were Argentinian end clients who expected 'a special confidentiality concept'.

And the man who guarded and organized this system of confidentiality, whom the Jinkises apparently needed for their deals with FIFA officials, was Juan Pedro Damiani. The Panama Papers prove that Damiani was involved from the time the first Cross Trading company was founded in Niue in 1998 until the Nevada firm was dissolved in 2015.

So for over fifteen years he has been doing deals with people who are believed by the prosecutors in the FIFA case to have bribed FIFA officials. And he is supposed to be in charge of cleaning up FIFA?[3]

Surely that's completely crazy – or is it just FIFA that's crazy?

Even if we give Damiani the benefit of the doubt and assume that he knew nothing of the bribery allegations against the Jinkises until the charges were brought by the New York investigators, he should have disclosed his involvement and stepped down from the ethics committee then at the latest. Especially as Hugo and Mariano Jinkis are not his only problem case.

Juan Pedro Damiani can be proven to have been working for Eugenio Figueredo, the arrested former FIFA vice president, since 2002. At the time Figueredo was the president of the Uruguayan football association. His name is linked to a whole host of offshore companies set up by Mossack Fonseca, most of them managed by Damiani's law firm.

Our documents show that as recently as February 2015, Damiani arranged a power of attorney for Figueredo's wife authorizing her to act on behalf of one of the companies.

Eugenio Figueredo's arrest on 27 May 2015 in Zurich comes as a shock to Damiani and Mossfon. The next day nervous emails fly back and forth between them. Mossfon gets its nominee directors to step down and has the power of attorney issued to Figueredo's wife revoked.

In June 2015 the head of the Mossfon compliance department writes an internal email wondering rather helplessly whether they can be sure that Figueredo's properties were not bought with money 'related to the FIFA affair' and asks: 'Do we have any evidence of this in the documents regarding the company?' In actual fact, the ex-official, who has now been extradited to Uruguay, not only admits when questioned to having pocketed bribes – he puts the amount at around $50,000 a month – but also discloses how he reinvested the money by combining his legal and illegal income, using it mainly to purchase real estate in Uruguay. And according to the Uruguayan weekly *Búsqueda*, which had access to his interrogation documents, he bought Panamanian companies for this purpose from Juan Pedro Damiani's law firm.[4]

In response to Mossfon's enquiry as to whether Figueredo's money could have come 'from the FIFA affair', the Damiani law firm sends a list of the assets that Figueredo holds in the Mossfon companies that are still active. These assets include a number of properties in Uruguay.[5] In January 2016 Damiani testified on the subject in court in Uruguay. He mentioned only three offshore companies (we can see seven) that he says he arranged for Figueredo. And he said his law firm had never received a fee from Figueredo. It had passed all information to the authorities and had never hidden goods.

The Uruguayan Damiani is not allowed to pass judgment on his fellow countryman Figueredo in the adjudicatory chamber of the FIFA ethics committee because judges have to abstain if they are from the same country as the persons they are judging. But: three of his clients were facing charges, and his colleagues from the FIFA ethics committees had to pass judgment on one of them – while Juan Pedro Damiani does what? Sits quietly and says nothing?

Asked about this by us and the ICIJ, a spokesman for Damiani stated that, in light of ongoing investigations, he was only able to provide limited information. He stated that Damiani had, however, notified the authorities and the FIFA ethics committee.

A spokesman for the FIFA ethics committee has confirmed this. However, he also stated that Damiani first notified the committee of his business relationship with Eugenio Figueredo on the evening of 18 March 2016, one day *after* we sent him a request for comment. Consequently the ethics committee launched a preliminary investigation the next day to clarify the circumstances. According to our information, the business relationship with Hugo and Mariano Jinkis was never mentioned.

Mossack Fonseca, the law firm, claims it has no evidence whatsoever that the companies managed by J.P. Damiani were involved in any kind of improprieties.

Juan Pedro Damiani, the ethics watchdog, is now himself under his colleagues' scrutiny.

Any shadow, no matter how small, that falls on members of the ethics committee is a problem for the committee, insiders tell us in confidence.

The FIFA ethics committee only makes sense to the outside world if it is seen as ethically unassailable. And only then can the committee implement dramatic decisions, internally as well as externally, such as the ban on its own President Sepp Blatter and the UEFA President Michel Platini in December 2015.

[ ]

And now we come full circle: on 27 December 2007 one Michel Platini, resident – the files tell us – in the small community of Genolier in French-speaking Switzerland, receives from Mossack Fonseca a permanent full power of attorney for the Panamanian company Balney Enterprises Corp. The power of attorney is set up by the Geneva-based private bank Baring Brothers Sturdza at the same time as the offshore company; in other words, it is in place right from the beginning. Many banks use this technique to avoid having to name the real owner of a company. This makes it likely that this Michel Platini is not only an authorized representative but also the owner of the company.

The files give no clue to the true owner of Balney Enterprises Corp., since all holdings are via an anonymous bearer share.

We soon establish that the Michel Platini in our files is the real Michel Platini: the community of Genolier is very close to Nyon and the UEFA headquarters are in Nyon. When Michel Platini became president of the European football association in 2007, one of his election promises was that he would move close to the headquarters and take an interest in the day-to-day business. The area around Genolier, in a pretty location on the shores of Lake Geneva, is popular with the rich and famous. Sean Connery and Phil Collins live there. The great Sir Peter Ustinov lived and died in Genolier itself. The Swiss tabloid *Blick* reported some time ago that Platini was planning to move to the Genolier complex 'Les terrasses du Léman'. This is the very address we find in the data in the full power of attorney.

The documents relating to Michel Platini don't actually show what deals the company enters into. That is partly due to the fact that it doesn't need any nominee directors to sign contracts. After all, Platini has full power of attorney, which means he can act almost unconditionally on behalf of the company. In other words, Platini can open an account, sign contracts, purchase property – anything. The present tense is correct here, as the company is still up and running, or at least it was at the end of 2015.

But why does Michel Platini need this kind of access to an offshore company?

The only firm clue is a letter received by Mossack Fonseca on 12 August 2015: a letter from the intermediary, the private bank Baring Brothers Sturdza. The subject line of the letter reads: 'Re: Account no. [authors' note: *account number deleted*] – BALNEY ENTERPRISES CORP'.

So the company has a bank account. We even know the number.

We contact Michel Platini's adviser and soon get an answer back: he says the Swiss authorities are fully aware of all Michel Platini's accounts and assets. Questioned further, the adviser states that the authorities have also been notified specifically of this account at Baring Brothers Sturdza – and that it was for personal reasons that Platini had opted to have an offshore company as the account holder. Furthermore, he had never used this account for FIFA or UEFA business.

We follow this up by asking how long the Swiss authorities have known about this account, whether Platini would be willing to send us proof of this, and whether there has ever been an investigation into the account.

These questions, says the adviser, should be put to the Swiss authorities and not to Michel Platini. But of course – and Platini's PR adviser must know this – Swiss authorities don't disclose information in response to these kinds of enquiries.

29

THE 99 PER CENT AND
THE FUTURE OF TAX HAVENS

The more than 2.6 terabytes of data from the servers of the Panamanian law firm Mossack Fonseca provide an insight into the offshore world that is more detailed, immediate and up to date than anyone could have previously imagined. Over the course of many months we have seen with our own eyes how Mossack Fonseca has a tailor-made solution for virtually anyone with something to hide. The right loophole can always be found in one or other of the tax havens: if the company in the Seychelles can't do it, then the Panamanian trust or the foundation in Bermuda probably can – or alternatively a combination of two, three or four of these elements. In our globalized world it seems there is hardly a single law that cannot be circumvented or have its impact lessened with the help of a few shell companies.

The British author Nicholas Shaxson sums this up rather neatly: 'Offshore is not only a place, an idea, a way of doing things, and a weapon of the financial industry. It is also a process: a race to the bottom to where the rules, laws and outward signs of democracy are worn away little by little.'[1] Used systematically, offshore offers an opportunity for an almost complete abdication of responsibility. It is very nearly impossible, we keep hearing in background discussions, for authorities to establish a chain of proof that holds up in court if the investigators come up against a network of shell companies strung out across five, ten or thirty tax havens.

This game of hide-and-seek has serious consequences, not only in cases where criminal activities are obviously being concealed. The legal constructs of the offshore world also create problems on a huge scale. In fact, an expert from the Tax Justice Network wrote in 2008 in a memorandum for the UK House of Commons Treasury Committee: 'Within the financial sector it would have been impossible for the current credit crunch to have happened if offshore had not existed.'

Not surprisingly, it was those who had caused the financial crisis who were the least affected by it. While billions were spent bailing out banks, and nearly all those responsible got away without being investigated, let alone charged, the victims, the people conned into taking out enormous loans, were abandoned often without a job, a house or any prospect of ever being able to live debt-free again. Those who had squirrelled their money away in an offshore trust, on the other hand, had no need to worry.

[ ]

There is another aspect that barely gets a mention in this book: the tax methods employed by multinational corporations like Amazon, Starbucks and Apple. Their boundless efforts, even now, to mini- mize their tax bills, are crucially dependent on offshore companies. The result of these manoeuvres is that the countries in which the companies operate and earn money and the people who live there lose out on billions in tax receipts – as became apparent from the recent Luxembourg Tax Files. Although President of the European Commission Jean-Claude Juncker, for years Luxembourg's prime minister, defends the country's actions as legal, an investigation found otherwise: the European Commission took the view that Luxembourg had granted the online bookseller Amazon illegal tax benefits. However, Mossack Fonseca does not tend to have links to the big corporations, which is why this topic is barely touched on here.

It's plain to see that a shocking number of players from the financial world are avoiding the scrutiny of the regulatory bodies in their countries with the help of shell companies. By doing this they are undermining democratic principles; when a society's rules, agreed on and supported by all, do not apply to those whose power and wealth allow them to circumvent them, they lose their meaning.

Why, then, should the others continue to accept these rules?

Why should the 99 per cent accept that their governments now have no more than a theoretical influence on the super-rich 1 per cent of society? An employee looking at his payslip sees what the state has taken from him and is powerless to do anything about it. But someone who has his dividends paid to a shell company in the British Virgin Islands can decide for himself whether or not to declare these earnings in the country in which he lives, whose amenities and protection he enjoys.

The feeling that, in the world of finance, 'the people at the top' can do whatever they want is more than just a feeling.

It's the reality.

The Danish sociologist Brooke Harrington, who trained for two years as an asset manager and immersed herself in this world, rightly warns of a 'neo-feudal concentration of wealth'. A small group of rich people, she says, are not only hiding their money and avoiding taxes, they are also evading the law.

The members of the international financial elite are effectively constructing their own legal system. If something isn't possible in one country, they simply do it in another jurisdiction. And Harrington sees offshore providers, companies like Mossack Fonseca, as playing a vital role as helpers and facilitators in this.

[ ]

The international world of finance is just one of the countless beneficiaries of the offshore industry. The financial industry does at least try to make sure its activities are carried out within the letter of the law, and is partly successful in this. But we, along with some 400 international colleagues, also came across countless criminals engaging in offshore activities. The Japanese mafia, the Italian mafia, the Russian mafia, drugs cartels, arms smugglers, people who finance terrorism. The suspected helpers of butchers like Assad and Gaddafi. Money laundering rings. As well as corruption cases by the dozen.

In short: the world of organized crime in all its many forms makes use of the offshore industry just as much as fraudsters and criminals acting individually, using it to erase its tracks and conceal its crimes.

That, too, is the reality.

The good news is that this reality is not irreversible.

The irresponsibility witnessed in the offshore centres of this world is the result of laws that can be changed.

The experts we met are largely in agreement in their assessment of the measures required. There are essentially two main requirements.

The first big step would be to introduce an effective system for the automatic global exchange of information about bank accounts. The British authorities would then automatically know about any accounts held by British citizens in, say, the Bahamas. This kind of exchange of information is still useless, though, if an account is held by an anonymous shell company. For if a UK citizen hides behind a shell company and holds the account in the company's name, then the UK authorities will never find out.

So what is needed, for numerous other reasons as well, is a globally transparent register of companies. It would have to list the real owners of companies and foundations – and providing false information would have to be made a criminal act punishable with tough sentences. That would be the second step.

That's how easy it would be to put an end to the tax havens.

It would mean that many of the services offered by Mossack Fonseca for the purpose of concealing the real owners of companies sold by the firm would be banned, including nominee shareholders, anonymous bearer shares and of course the hired 'real owners' who are in actual fact only front men. Nominee directors would be superfluous because the owners of companies would be known anyway.

Law firms such as Mossack Fonseca like to claim that only a small fraction of their clients harbour illegal intentions. It would be extremely interesting to see how many offshore companies would remain in business if the names of their owners were made public.

It is simply a matter of systematically implementing these two measures.

We hear again and again from the defenders of tax havens (mostly they cite something they call 'tax competition') that these reforms could never be implemented in practice. Certainly, this raises the question: why should the tax havens give in?

In fact the French author Gabriel Zucman, in his book *The Hidden Wealth of Nations: The Scourge of Tax Havens*, has worked through how the automatic exchange of information and the register of real owners could be implemented, using sanctions and enforcement if necessary.

Zucman argues that even countries like Luxembourg and Switzerland would change their mind the moment they found themselves facing drastic measures such as a trade boycott. For smaller countries even the threat of sanctions would likely be enough, and, if not, a series of small interim steps leading eventually to a trade boycott would encourage them in the right direction. 'No country can take a stand against the combined will of the United States and the big countries of the European Union,' writes Zucman.

In some cases the lobbyists for the tax dodgers and evaders hide their true intentions behind a veil of concern that some of the territories that are well known in this connection – the British Virgin Islands, Samoa, the Cook Islands – would have no future aside from their existence as a tax haven.

John Christensen from the Tax Justice Network, who himself comes from the tax haven of Jersey, is sick of that argument. 'We have a romanticized view of islands,' he says. 'Here, not far from London, some years ago a huge steel plant was closed down. A whole town was out of work. In that case anyone can answer with neoliberal detachment, "These things happen, that's the way of the market". Now just imagine for a moment that this town happened to be the only town on an island – would that make it worse?' He smiles. 'Or let's put it another way: if the inhabitants of one of these islands made their living from robbing cruise ships, would we still have sympathy then? Probably not. But these islands have been helping to rob whole societies for years! Perhaps we simply have to say: nowadays it is feasible to leave an island. And some islands have so little to offer that makes life there bearable that it is best to leave them uninhabited.'

Other objections to automatic data matching and transparent registers of the real owners of companies include the argument that the intrusion into people's private affairs would be huge. Really? These registers would record the names of the owners, their date of birth, a business address and the number of shares they hold. That's all that is needed. And if that's too much for some – well, no one is forcing them to use an offshore company.

Note, too, that tax secrecy is not in itself a universal human right. In parts of Scandinavia, such as Norway, tax records have been public for years. In Sweden there is not only a securities register listing the owners of all shares and bonds, but also, upwards of a certain income level, alphabetical lists of these wealthy citizens stating their salary, investment income and assets. Yet Swedes and Norwegians are not reputed to be envious people.

Anyone who argues against the register on the basis of the cost, amount of work and bureaucracy it would involve should be reminded of the billions that states are denied each year as a result of tax havens. The current situation is costing society incomparably more.

And anyone who argues these moves could expose the owners to public accusations has failed to understand that this is precisely about doing away with organized irresponsibility. The fear that mismanagement, unethical or illegal conduct could then be associated with actual individuals is not a legitimate excuse for companies to keep their true owners secret.

The other objection we hear is that tyrannical regimes could use information from these registers to pursue their adversaries. That is true in theory. But firstly this presents an almost naïve view of tyrannical regimes like Syria, as those in power there know very well who their political enemies are and where they keep their money. And secondly, in the data from our leak, as well as the data from Offshore Secrets and the HSBC Files, it's extremely rare to come across the hidden assets of opposition politicians. But we have hundreds of examples of corrupt officials and the allies of rogue regimes hiding away their millions.

[ ]

So if there are ways of ending what goes on in the tax havens, the question we should be asking is not, as we put it earlier: why should society put up with it?

But rather: why does society put up with it?

More specifically: why do our politicians put up with it? Why don't the big nations simply take more radical action to stop it?

After all, this is not just about fairness. In some cases, outrageous crimes are also involved.

Because it is the big nations, specifically, that have a lot to lose – and they would end up having to threaten themselves with sanctions.

The USA has its own mainland tax havens like Nevada, Wyoming and Delaware, and Mossack Fonseca even has its own branches in the first two of these. A US draft bill to combat the abuse of offshore havens, which the then Senator Barack Obama tabled in the Senate in 2007, has still not been passed. The United Kingdom has some of the most prominent tax havens in its jurisdiction, such as its overseas territories and the Channel Islands. Mossfon has incorporated more than 100,000 companies in the British Virgin Islands alone.

And Germany?

Although it likes to present itself as generally open to reforms, Germany in fact ranks as one of those impeding progress in Europe. Again and again we hear that whenever there is an attempt to demand greater transparency, whether through the EU or other bodies, German representatives operate behind the scenes to try to prevent precisely that. The power of the financial lobby, even eight years after the global financial crisis, is undiminished. There is also billions in foreign money held in German banks – much of it almost certainly untaxed.

That's because German banks are only liable to prosecution for tax evasion if they do it within Germany. Tax evasion in Brazil or New Zealand, on the other hand, does not come under German law.

Moreover there are also anonymous companies in Germany, as bearer shares are permitted there. With these, whoever has the shares in their physical possession is deemed the owner of a company.

For Germany too, a public register of the real owners and part owners of all companies without exception would be something new. Certainly it is something that has been called for and debated for a long time. Organizations including Attac, the Tax Justice Network and Transparency International Deutschland are among its public advocates. Detlev von Larcher from Attac, for example, said shortly after we published details of the Offshore Secrets in spring 2013: 'We have to put an end to anonymous companies. Shell companies serve no economic purpose and are used solely by kleptocrats, tax evaders and money launderers. If Germany stands in the way of this, all its strong words condemning shadow financial centres are nothing but hypocrisy.'

The absurd thing is that a register of companies showing the real owners was basically decided on long ago. The participating countries agreed on it at the G8 summit in Northern Ireland in 2013. It just wasn't systematically implemented. The United Kingdom wants to start with the mainland, excluding the notorious British overseas territories. Other countries have said they would set up a register of this kind, but that only government authorities would be able to access it. It is important, however, that a directory of this kind is also accessible to academics and non-governmental organizations – experts with the time and will to peruse it, something the state has never had.

[ ]

For Mossack Fonseca, an international clampdown on tax havens would amount to a threat to its business. However, once the Panama Papers are published this clampdown is likely to be the least of its problems.

Law enforcement agencies in many of the countries in which our ICIJ colleagues publish are bound to take an interest in Mossfon. German investigators are already on its tail. The security services will be taking note as well. They are likely to be very interested in flows of money and transactions designed to obscure – after all, we have identified numerous clients from countries known to be used as conduits of terror funding.

The state investigators will have a field day: employees of the Mossack Fonseca group have often displayed conduct that is questionable or even illegal or criminal.

Mossack Fonseca is insistent that due diligence – the duty it has to check who it is doing business with – is the law firm's number one priority. But we have numerous examples of how exception after exception is approved, for example whenever a valued client doesn't wish to disclose the name of the true owner.

But Mossack Fonseca, with its lax business policy, is evidently not an isolated case: in 2012 a team of American and Australian researchers wrote to around 3,700 offshore providers in 182 countries asking to set up a company. Half of the providers did not perform the required ID checks, and nearly a quarter did not even ask to see identification documents. The researchers dropped hints in their letters that the aim of their request was to conceal corruption or even finance terrorism. The reactions were shocking, with many providers deliberately ignoring all the warning signs. One of the supposed clients presented himself in such a way that you couldn't help suspecting him of financing terrorism. One provider replied: 'It sounds as if you want to establish a company anonymously for the state, is that correct? We can do that for a surcharge of $25. If we only incorporate one company for you and no more than that we don't need any documents at all from you.'[2]

Our perspective on things has also changed, not just because of the leaked files and the evidence of wrongdoing they contain, but also as a result of stories told to us by Daniel Balint-Kurti of Global Witness, among others. He investigated covert deals in Burundi, which, in the usual way, involved amounts running into many millions being smuggled out of the country. A country, says Daniel, in which the people are so poor that many families have to take turns to eat: the adults eat one day and the children the next.

These people are the victims of the offshore industry. Commercial lawyers sitting in European corporate head offices put a lot of thought into how they can use offshore companies to ensure their African subsidiaries pay as little tax as possible in those countries, and because of this the governments of those countries lack the money they need for schools, clothing and food. According to a study by the Tax Justice Network, Africa loses out on twice as much money through tax evasion as it receives in development aid.

But it's not only the poor who are made to suffer. Terrorism, drug smuggling and illegal arms trading, for example, are crimes that concern us all and that are almost impossible to combat due in part to the concealment tactics of the offshore industry. The European Union alone loses out on a thousand billion euros a year due to tax fraud and tax evasion.

The ones who pay the price for the tax haven model are the citizens of all the countries whose tax receipts are reduced due to the activities of shell companies, or whose public funds are funnelled out of the country and stashed away in the Caribbean. And the populations of all the countries whose heads of state embezzle money and hide it away in private accounts.

To end on a more optimistic note: the international community *will* take action. Whether the reforms by the EU, the UN or the Organisation for Economic Co-operation and Development (OECD) will go far enough is highly doubtful – chances are they won't in the first instance – but further steps will follow. Public pressure, which is bound to increase as a result of the Panama Papers, will see to that – a phenomenon we already observed at the time of the Offshore Secrets and Luxembourg Tax Files.

But there is one more thing.

No one, anywhere, who conducts secret transactions and leaves a digital trace is safe any more. Whatever they do, wherever they do it. Anyone who acquires an anonymous shell company should know that, in this digital age, secrecy is an illusion.

Somewhere there will always be employees who have had enough of watching these goings-on. Somewhere there will always be activists who find holes in databases. Somewhere there will always be engineers who occasionally help themselves to a few gigabytes of data.

This leak is not the first leak. Nevertheless, it does perhaps mark the start of something.

The start of the end of the tax havens.

30

THE COLD HEART OF
THE OFFSHORE WORLD

Panama City. The view is phenomenal even from a distance: dozens of skyscrapers, some taller than others, lined up on the shores of the Pacific, testament to a wealth earned partly from the big business of secret money. *Bienvenidos a Panama*. Welcome to Panama.

Our aeroplane is on its approach to the airport. Below us, just off the coast, we see container ships waiting to enter the Panama Canal, on the horizon is the jungle, and between them the financial district in which Mossack Fonseca also has its head office: the law firm whose activities have occupied us for more than a year now. We have now read several thousand pages of internal documents from the law firm, know its clients and staff, know which ones have a relaxed attitude to the law and also which ones are regularly over-ruled when they voice concerns. Here, clearly, is where the Panama Papers project that we set in motion will have its greatest repercussions. Now, with only a few weeks to go before we start publishing our findings, we are about to head into the lion's den. Provided we can do it without being noticed, we want to get our own first-hand view of Mossfon, its staff and the tax haven of Panama.

The flight is a good opportunity to take a breather and let what has actually happened to us sink in. That an anonymous source contacted us, of all people, with the question: 'Interested in data?' – and that it then developed into the world's largest investigative project to date. That we now have some 400 journalists from more than eighty countries working on the files, that we have found clues leading to dozens of heads of state in the records, and traces of scandals in pretty much every country in the world, trails leading to FIFA and its president, to UEFA and its president, various mafia organizations, Hezbollah, Al-Qaeda, the Ukrainian president, the prime minister of Iceland (who was recently named Iceland's 'Businessman of the Year' – along with the same finance minister we also found in the data) – and to Vladimir Putin.

But now we are also glad that we will soon be going public, as the project is consuming us and sapping our strength. We have been helping the ICIJ to organize things, and helping journalists all over the world with their research. At the *Süddeutsche Zeitung* we have seven people just in our investigative team working on the Panama Papers and nothing else: besides the two of us there's the data expert Vanessa Wormer, freelance journalist Mauritius Much and our *SZ* colleagues Katrin Langhans, Hannes Munzinger and Gianna Niewel. Then there's the team, growing by the day, that will bring the stories to life on digital and online platforms and in print. There's going to be a special *SZ* website (www.panamapapers.de); for weeks we have had an illustrator working exclusively on our project; there's going to be a 'Making Of' film and so on. The whole of *SZ* is involved; colleagues on umpteen desks are working on the stories with us. In the last few weeks we have spent countless days just planning how the layout, the illustrations, the graphics will look.

There have also been hours of discussions with the editors-in-chief and our lawyers. We have talked through who we can name and who we can't. Where we might have to tone down our wording, and where we can afford to be more aggressive. At night we have less and less time to sleep, and at the weekends less and less time for our families. We have long stopped counting how many coffees and cans of Red Bull we get through each day. There is just so much still to do.

The thought that it will all soon be over keeps us motivated, as does the sense of suspense, growing daily, over how it will all turn out. And whether we'll be able to keep everything under wraps until the publication date – which to be honest we don't really believe. Too many people are involved now.

[ ]

Just a few weeks ago we received a piece of news that caused huge excitement among the whole Prometheus team: the Brazilian police had temporarily detained several Mossfon employees for suspected involvement in 'Operation Car Wash', a big, if not the biggest corruption scandal to hit Latin America. Essentially it's alleged that the Brazilian governing party and its allies made money out of overpriced contracts between the partly state-owned oil corporation Petrobras and several construction companies. In all, several billion US dollars are said to have vanished into the shadows. Even former President Lula da Silva is suspected of being involved.

The investigations have been going on since 2014, but new dirty tricks keep coming to light. To keep track of it all, Brazilian public prosecutors have numbered the various stages of their investigations and given them catchy codenames.

Now, in Phase 22 – codenamed 'Triplo X' – the investigators have Mossfon in their sights. An arrested Mossfon employee is accused of having hidden documents from the police and subsequently destroyed them. These are thought to have been due diligence documents, in other words the papers that show how serious – or probably how lax in Mossfon's case – the law firm was about checking out its clients, and what steps it took to make sure it only took on clean clients. The Brazilian public prosecutor Carlos Fernando dos Santos Lima said not long ago at a press conference that although investigations were still ongoing, this much was already clear: there was proof that Mossfon was a 'huge money laundering operation'.

Mossack Fonseca responded by issuing a press release insisting that all Mossfon offices are committed to the 'highest standards of due diligence' and work in compliance with all the international laws and regulations. What's more, it said, Mossack Fonseca Brazil is independent of Mossack Fonseca & Co. Panama. The law firm, it said, had nothing to do with Operation Car Wash. It was the same old story: everything is fine, the law firm obeys the law and if something has gone wrong then it's the fault of offices that aren't directly linked to Mossfon. We can't wait to see what's left of this line of argument when the Panama Papers research findings are published in over eighty countries.

Our Brazilian partners are particularly nervous right now. They are afraid that the arrest and the search of Mossfon's Brazilian office could destroy all their work over the last few months, and that laboriously researched details could now come to light before we publish our findings worldwide. Marina Walker, the ICIJ project manager, has the job of both warning and reassuring. She has to reassure colleagues that the story will keep – after all, it's clear not even the Brazilian police have as much information as we do. At the same time she has to warn everyone to stick to the agreed timings – we don't want anyone to panic and publish early.

[ ]

We too have been approached on several occasions by colleagues from other German media organizations asking what this project is that we are working on. That worries us, of course. On the other hand it also stands to reason that something of this kind cannot be kept entirely secret. After all, we have hundreds of colleagues working on the project worldwide. If each of them were to spill the beans to one other person, that would already be nearly 1,000 people who would know about it. What's more, a quick look at the newspaper is all it takes to realize the Brothers Obermay/ier haven't published anything for several months now.

We, meanwhile, try to maintain as relaxed an attitude as possible. Some colleagues are aware that we are working on something big, but they obviously have no idea what exactly. So when, at a recent evening event a colleague from a news magazine said to us with a wink that it must be really stressful for us at the moment, we didn't hesitate to answer: yes it is. The children are really hard work at the moment. One of them has just started kindergarten, and the other is just learning to ride a balance bike.

[ ]

It was 5°C when we boarded the plane in Munich. Now, stepping out of the plane at the Aeropuerto Internacional de Tocumen, it is 35°C, with 60 per cent humidity. What a contrast. It's strange – we have never been to Panama before, and yet already, after just a few metres, we spot some familiar sights: the Tocumen Royal Saloon, for example. We know from our data that this VIP lounge is where Mossfon staff like to meet with important clients who are passing through. That will happen to us a lot during the course of our stay: we see things and meet people that we've never seen before, yet we already know them inside out from the data.

Our project partners at *La Prensa* newspaper have arranged for us to have a driver for the duration of our stay in Panama. A taciturn man, a bear of a man. Our own driver – that's a new experience for us. With the patience of a saint he manoeuvres us through the rush hour. We are heading for the high-rise buildings in the distance, the Distrito Financiero. We drive past slums – evidence that there are still many people in Panama who don't have enough money for three meals a day. And just a few hundred metres from the miserable shacks, flashy façades tower up, gleaming in the sunshine. High rises in every conceivable shape and size. The Trump Tower, for example, resembles a giant sail, while other skyscrapers are reminiscent of rockets, torches or juice cartons with an indentation that looks like it's been made by a giant performing a karate chop. Every month new tower blocks appear. Ever taller, ever stranger. This, too, is Panama. The most conspicuous to date is the 243-metre Tornillo – also known as Revolution Tower – a building that looks like a screw twisted around its own axis.

The Mossack Fonseca building, on the other hand, which has the Tornillo reflected in its façade, looks almost like something from another age: it's only three storeys high, is located in a side street, and has a doctor's surgery on the ground floor. The two security guards eye every passer-by suspiciously. They look at us sceptically as we drive slowly by in the car, taking photos unobtrusively with our phone camera. Could the dark-haired lady who has just parked her Toyota in the company car park be Leticia Montoya, the queen of offshore, the woman who, on paper, is the director of thousands of companies? Could it be Jürgen Mossack himself sitting in the black SUV that is just turning in to the Mossfon basement car park? It's hugely tempting just to get out of the car, march into the building and confront the Mossfon people with our findings.

But we have to hold on for a few more days, until the letters containing all our allegations come out. We'll already have left the country by then. For safety's sake.

[ ]

We drive to *La Prensa*. The paper's offices are located in an industrial area in the north east of Panama City, next door to a DIY store and a car dealership. It's a newspaper in the old style: from its offices on the first floor you look down on the print shop where the next day's edition is just being produced. The whole building smells of printing ink.

This is Rita Vásquez's domain. The deputy editor-in-chief of *La Prensa* receives us in her office: a bare, windowless room. We already know Rita from our project meeting in Munich. This is a woman with a very interesting background, who herself once worked in the offshore industry, in the British Virgin Islands, and she knows a lot of the Mossfon staff in person. Now she calls her team together: her husband Scott Bronstein, talented researcher Ereida Prieto-Barreiro, and Rolando Rodríguez, a top investigative journalist in Panama who has already uncovered quite a number of scandals. They tell us about their findings to date: the trails leading to influential Panamanian companies, to major scandals from the past, to a former president. 'This story is going to explode with the force of an atomic bomb,' says Scott. In terms of the attention it is set to generate in the national and foreign media, he sees the Panama Papers as being on a par with the US invasion of the country in 1989.

Back then, the eyes of the whole world were on Panama.

For *La Prensa*, the Panama Papers is quite an ambitious project. The newspaper only has a circulation of around 40,000 – with a mainly upper-class readership from the same tier of society as the Panameños they are finding almost daily in the data.

So it's no wonder the project is top secret. So far not even ten people at the *La Prensa* editorial offices are in the know. The risk of something getting out is too great. In Panama everyone knows everyone else. In fact, we hear at least one Mossfon employee used to work at *La Prensa*. Rita and her colleagues see her regularly at barbecues and on the golf course.

Above all, though, Panama is a country prone to violence. If you ask too many questions you put yourself in danger. For example, Rita's colleagues are currently conducting research into a Panamanian company involved in an enormous scandal – the

Mossfon data provides whole new insights. The authorities are on the case as well. However, one of the investigators has disappeared without trace, assumed dead. Another public official involved in the case was stabbed on his way to a meeting.

La Prensa, too, is expecting the worst. Some time ago the editorial team bought a set of bulletproof vests. Once the material is published, all the journalists involved are meant to wear them. When they go outside, they will need to be accompanied by a bodyguard. The bodyguard we had assumed to be our driver. As it turns out, Rita has been looking after our safety too.

[·]

Our bodyguard, who really doesn't leave our side the whole time we're there, chauffeurs us to Altos del Golf, the exclusive residential area where Panama's autocratic leader Manuel Noriega once lived. There are expensive-looking 4x4s and limousines in front of the houses, cameras pointing down at visitors from all sides, and barbed wire and electric fences to protect the owners from unwelcome visitors. Two former presidents of Panama live here, protected by numerous security guards, and Mossfon co-owner Jürgen Mossack is also said to live here.

[ ]

This trip, for us, is like a crash course in offshore studies. We take a zigzag route through Panama City, this tropical version of Manhattan, drive through the old town, Casco Viejo, the financial district, and the commuter town Costa del Este. We meet government advisers, public officials, money laundering experts, former investigators and representatives of the Panamanian law society. We follow their arguments, listen as some say that this whole tax haven business is just idle talk fuelled by the envy of other countries, foremost among them the USA, which merely wants to divert people's attention from the fact that it has its very own tax havens in the form of Delaware and Nevada. We hear excited talk about the fact that, just a few days previously, Panama was finally taken off the OECD's grey list – and discuss why the country is still blacklisted by the EU. We listen to the critics who tell us that it's obvious, surely, that Panama's wealth is at least partly attributable to the fact that so many advisers knowingly do business with all kinds of dubious clients, with drug dealers, fraudsters and sanctions violators.

With every conversation it becomes clearer to us how divided Panama is, how the battle lines are drawn between the tax haven apologists and the champions of transparency. But above all we start to realize the extent of the legal problems that are brewing for Mossfon and its owners, considering its years of doing business with sanctioned parties, the fact that the law firm is obviously not able to name the beneficial owners of all the companies it manages, and its use of nominee beneficial owners.

The matter of the nominee directors in particular sticks in our mind: Carlos Barsallo, chairman of the ethics committee of the Panamanian Bar Association, tells us that these nominee directors can be held accountable for any statutory violations by the companies they are in charge of – at least on paper – and that they could face the threat of claims for compensation running into millions.

We wonder whether the nominee directors we found in the Mossfon files are aware of this. People like Leticia Montoya, the queen of offshore, who has been the director of more than 25,000 companies, including companies that managed secret accounts, and firms that also crop up in the investigations into the FIFA scandal. If Montoya were taken to court over the activities of just one company it would probably ruin her; as we have seen, her earnings are paltry. So why does she do it? Why does she take that risk? We want to ask her. We know her address from the files.

[ ]

We leave the glamorous world of Panama City. We cross the Panama Canal and travel for forty minutes inland, to Vacamonte. The wind blows plastic bags across the street. Rubbish burns next to a kiosk. It stinks. There are rows of single-storey houses, some looking more like a ruin than a shelter. The young men we ask for directions eye us suspiciously. We are starting to understand why Rita didn't want to let us drive here unless we brought someone from *La Prensa* as well as our bodyguard.

Vacamonte is a no-go area, and even our *La Prensa* colleagues have never been here before. Here is where the queen of offshore lives.

After half an hour of driving around, we finally find Leticia Montoya's house: a decent-looking bungalow for the neighbour-hood. A Japanese-made car is parked under a car port, with children's toys lying next to it. A grumpy-looking older gentleman opens the door. He says that no, his wife is not there, and asks us what we want to talk to her about.

Well, how shall we put it: we want to talk about her offshore companies. How she manages to run thousands of companies. And whether she realizes what scandal-ridden companies are among them.

It's a strange conversation. Somehow, Montoya's husband doesn't seem very clued up about his wife's work. At some point he pulls out his mobile phone and dictates her number, suggesting that we give her a call.

She doesn't answer. But she now has the number of our *La Prensa* colleague on her display.

[ ]

On the way back we talk for a long time about the strange phenomenon of the nominee directors. They serve a useful purpose for
people who have something to hide, and for companies like
Mossack Fonseca they are big business. But what about the nominee directors themselves? They are the exploited underclass of the
offshore world – there's really no other way of putting it.

A little while later our *La Prensa* colleague's mobile phone rings.
Leticia Montoya is on the line. She's furious. Why did her idiot
husband give us her number in the first place, she yells down the
phone.

Of course, she says, she is the director of thousands of companies.

But how does she manage to perform her duties when she has such
a mass of offshore companies – thousands of them – to look after?

She is remarkably open: 'I have no idea what the companies are
for, who they were sold to, or what exactly they do.'

For anything else, she says, we will have to contact the registered
agent – in this case, as we already know: Mossack Fonseca.

Then she hangs up.[1]

[ ]

Next we set out to find Ramses Owens. He worked as a lawyer for
Mossfon until 2010, more specifically for MF Trust, one of the
departments that work directly with the end clients themselves.
We know him from hundreds of emails, a lot of them decorated
with smileys, hence our nickname for him: Smiley Man. It was
Ramses Owens who offered Mossfon clients the 'nominee beneficial owner' or 'natural person nominee' service mentioned earlier
in this book and sent them the relevant documentation, in other
words offering them the services of a real person who, in dealings
with banks and others, passes himself off as the owner of the
company in place of the actual owner, thereby making a mockery
of anti-money laundering measures. For how is a bank, for

example, supposed to check whether its client is a criminal if it thinks it is checking the client's details but in fact is only checking the details of some front man – not realizing that he is merely standing in for someone else?

Owens now works just a few hundred metres from the Mossfon office at his own law firm. He set it up with a friend from his student days. They were the two best law students in their year, Owens announces, almost as soon as we've introduced ourselves. Modesty isn't his thing. He takes us through his chambers, raves about the private chef who cooks for him and his colleagues every day, tells us about the high standards his law firm is committed to. On a table in his office he shows us all the magazines and newspapers that have written about him.

Owens is a man who likes the limelight. He immediately agrees to an interview, and has no objection to us filming it. 'I have nothing to hide,' he says. It's important, he says, for the industry to be candid towards journalists. After all, its good reputation is at stake, he says. And it has suffered badly since the US magazine *Vice* reported on Mossfon – and him – in December 2014. The whole thing, Owens is convinced, was a stitch-up by Jewish Republicans.

We can't help grinning. *Vice* only wrote about all the rumours that were circulating. We, on the other hand, will soon be supplying proof. What, we wonder, will he say then? A conspiracy by the CIA and the Freemasons?

In any event, Owens is unstoppable. He enthuses about compliance and due diligence, rules of transparency, measures designed to prevent shady characters from taking advantage of the services on offer. Potential clients are turned away if it's clear they are trying to set up shell companies in order to dodge taxes. After all, he said, law firms that incorporate shell companies have to adhere to the rules. And so on.

The words seem absurd coming from someone like Ramses Owens, whom we find in our data in all kinds of highly problematic connections. And he even goes one better. Mossfon, he says, is a model of prestige and integrity.

We change the subject: we'd like to talk about nominee beneficial owners, we say (in other words, the service Owens offered clients during his time at Mossfon).

We might have expected him to beat about the bush or hide behind empty phrases, as lawyers like to do when things get hairy.

But Owens says something astonishing: that the practice, in his view, amounts to money laundering.

The beneficial owner needs to be disclosed, he says. Anyone who doesn't do that and has someone else pretend to be the real owner is acting illegally. Owens picks up a book lying on his desk: the Código Penal, the Panamanian penal code. In here, says Owens meaningfully, it is written that the use of nominee beneficial owners is punishable with a lengthy prison sentence.

We are flabbergasted.

So even after more than a year of studying the inner workings of Mossack Fonseca, there are still things that can leave us completely astounded. And the best thing is: we filmed Owens's words – we've got them recorded.[2]

[ ]

Our last drive through Panama City. We pass Jürgen Mossack's house, the financial district and the Mossack Fonseca building one last time. Then we drive to Tocumen Airport, where Mossfon people like to meet clients who have just flown in, in an exclusive lounge.

We take a last look at Panama from the air.

We won't be coming back.

EPILOGUE

Shortly after 7.30pm, Sunday, 3 April 2016. There is just under half an hour to go until the Panama Papers are finally published – at 8pm, the results of our research will be made public on the *Süddeutsche Zeitung* website. In fact, the web pages featuring our stories are already 'live' and online, at least unofficially. The elaborate website created by our colleagues from 'digital' has to be tested under real conditions. We're not particularly happy about that, of course, but our colleagues confidently dispel all our objections. No one will accidentally stumble upon our Panama reports in the half hour before the official publication time. You would have to know about our project and enter the exact web address to find it. In other words, you would have to deliberately search for it. So we spend the last few minutes testing this and that, reading through the English translations once more and preparing the first tweets so that we can get started at 8pm on the dot.

Our stories for the first day of publication have been ready for a long time. All the legal checks have been carried out, all the revisions are complete and all the images prepared. The first newspapers have been printed and loaded onto the trucks on their way to our readers.

Everything is ready. Only fifteen minutes to go.

It goes without saying that we are all very nervous. We have been working on this for over a year and no one knows what will happen next. How will other media institutions take up the story? How will the general population respond? Or will the story fail to attract the attention it deserves, dismissed as 'just another leak'?

A colleague calls unexpectedly: 'Edward Snowden has just tweeted us!'

We look at each other, baffled. 7.48pm. Edward Snowden?

We go on Twitter, and indeed, Edward Snowden has tweeted this message to his 2 million followers: 'Biggest leak in the history of data journalism just went live, and it's about corruption.' Snowden also provides a link to the *Süddeutsche Zeitung* website and the English version of our article on Iceland and the shell companies owned by Prime Minister Sigmundur Gunnlaugsson and two other cabinet members.

Snowden is spreading the word about our investigation. That's not a bad sign. A little later we are also retweeted by WikiLeaks. And then the clocks strike 8pm.

Madness breaks out.

Before long, #panamapapers is the top Twitter topic, generating hundreds of thousands of tweets. Globally. By the following day, the Panama Papers will be *the* topic of hot discussion on every continent. It's on the front pages of newspapers in Thailand, South Korea, Canada, South America, Africa and Australia, and of course in Europe, as we knew it would be. In the USA, the story dominates the front pages of the *Washington Post*, the *Wall Street Journal*, the *Financial Times* and the *New York Times* for days, even though as yet none of these papers was involved in the collaborative project. All the major news channels are reporting on the story. The Panama Papers is the main story wherever we turn.

Bob Woodward, one of the most important investigative journalists in the world and the man who brought down President Richard Nixon by exposing the Watergate scandal, calls our project 'a triumph of journalism'. The *New York Times* suggests the story may even have changed the face of journalism forever.

[ ]

Within a few weeks of publication it's clear that the story has not only attracted far more attention among the media and the public than we expected, it has also triggered a far more consequential response from the political sphere.

Barack Obama makes a statement on the Panama Papers and declares tax evasion to be a serious and pressing problem which he wants to tackle. The G20 countries respond with a new catalogue of measures, while the EU parliament even sets up a dedicated committee of enquiry.

A long list of more concrete measures has also been carried out. Raids and searches take place in several countries. The authorities search UEFA's offices and its marketing agency in Switzerland, Amedeo Modigliani's *Seated Man with a Cane* is seized at the Geneva Freeport, and officials search the Mossack Fonseca offices in El Salvador and Peru.

Then, finally, police raid the Mossack Fonseca headquarters in Panama. Investigators work through the night, spending twenty-seven hours working their way through the building floor by floor, collecting what appears to be a huge volume of data. The authorities later find piles of shredded documents in another Mossfon building in Panama City.

As a result of the Panama Papers, investigations are launched in several countries into the business activities of hundreds of individuals – not only fraudsters, drug lords and private individuals, but also Mossfon owners Jürgen Mossack and Ramón Fonseca. The banking regulator in New York orders thirteen banks – among them Deutsche Bank, ABN AMRO and Société Générale – to hand over all their data on business dealings with Mossack Fonseca. At the same time, several acting heads of government also come under pressure – in Iceland, Argentina, Malta, Pakistan and the United Kingdom.

But let's take things one step at a time.

[ ]

The Icelandic prime minister Sigmundur Gunnlaugsson's involvement in the scandal had already become known three weeks before the publication of the Panama Papers as a result of a memorable interview conducted by Swedish journalists and our Icelandic colleague Jóhannes Kristjánsson. After a couple of innocuous questions – asking for Gunnlaugsson's views on shell companies, the Icelandic banking crisis and ethics in the offshore world – the prime minister was presented with an unwelcome surprise:

'What about you, Mr Prime Minister, do you or did you have any connection yourself to an offshore company?'

'Myself? No . . .'

Gunnlaugsson clearly has no idea what to say and begins to stammer.

Yes, he then says, he has worked with businesses that have connections to offshore companies. But he has always declared everything to the tax authorities. What kind of strange questions are these?

'I can confirm I have never hidden any of my assets.'

Follow-up question: 'So you have never had any connection to an offshore company?'

'As I said, I have always declared my assets.'

Then comes the critical question: 'What can you tell me about a company called Wintris?'

Silence. Prime Minister Gunnlaugsson stutters.

'Well, it's a company, if I recall correctly, which is associated with one of the companies that I was on the board of.'

Silence.

'And it had an account, which as I have mentioned, has been on the tax account since it was established.'

For Gunnlaugsson, the penny begins to drop. At this point, our Icelandic colleague Jóhannes, who had until then remained in the background, steps forward.

'Why haven't you said that you have connections with Wintris?'

Gunnlaugsson starts to lose his cool.

'As I've said, that's all been declared in my tax return since the beginning.'

Why didn't he disclose the company in the parliament's register of interests?

Because it was a 'special case'.

'Is this company owned by you?'

'My wife sold a part of the company to her family. A bank was then appointed to take care of it and they made some arrangements, the result of which was this company.'

'What holdings does the company own?'

Gunnlauggson stands up, breaks off the interview and leaves the room.

Even before the interview is made public, the prime minister's wife writes a Facebook post saying that Wintris was always owned by her and her alone. Meanwhile, her husband gives a newspaper and radio interview – but it's all in vain.

On 3 April our colleague Jóhannes Kristjánsson broadcasts the interview on television. The programme gets an audience share of more than 50 per cent and is watched online thousands of times within just a few hours. One commentator calls it the 'greatest breach of trust in the history of the Icelandic parliament'. Rumours are already circulating on the evening of the broadcast that Gunnlaugsson will resign and there are mass demonstrations in Iceland on the following day. Thousands of people gather in the square outside the Althing, Iceland's parliament. They press against the crowd barriers, beating against them with bicycle helmets and saucepan lids. Bananas, drinks cans and rolls of toilet paper are hurled against the façade of the parliament building.

More than 20,000 people march on the streets to demand their prime minister's resignation – a huge number for a country with a population of only 330,000. Imagine 7 million Germans demonstrating against Angela Merkel or 4.5 million Brits marching against David Cameron.

An undignified spectacle then begins, with Gunnlaugsson announcing that he will not stand down, then saying a day later that he will resign – only to retract his resignation shortly afterwards. In the end, he announces that he is temporarily handing over power.

And with that, Sigmundur Gunnlaugsson becomes the first head of government forced to resign his position as a consequence of the data leaked to us more than a year earlier by our source – now known to the world as 'John Doe'.

[ ]

Our British colleagues discover Blairmore Holdings at a very early stage in their investigations. It's an investment fund established in Panama in 1982 by Ian Cameron, the father of British Prime Minister David Cameron. For us, this was just one case among many. Of course, it is sensational that, of all people, the father of the man who was keen to be seen leading the charge against tax havens set up obscure company structures in exactly those countries. But can a son be charged with his father's crimes? We felt not.

What we hadn't considered, however, was that David Cameron himself could have profited from this very fund – or that he would choose an unfortunate communication strategy to boot. On day one of the global Panama Papers revelations, Cameron's spokesperson dismisses questions about the fund, saying that it is 'a private matter'. On day two, Cameron himself makes a personal statement

– an announcement that initially appears to be clear enough: 'I have no shares, no offshore trusts, no offshore funds, nothing like that. And so that, I think, is a very clear description.' The prime minister's office also publishes a written statement on the same day: 'To be clear, the prime minister, his wife and their children do not benefit from any offshore funds. The prime minister owns no shares.' On day three, Cameron's PR specialists eventually attempt to provide more clarity: 'There are no offshore funds/trusts which the prime minister, Mrs Cameron or their children will benefit from in future.'

By now, Cameron has denied benefitting personally from offshore companies in the present and future tenses. But what about the past?

He eventually answers this question in a TV interview with ITV News: 'We owned 5,000 units in Blairmore Investment Trust, which we sold in January 2010.' Cameron admits having profited from his father's offshore fund. Thousands of protesters demand his resignation in a number of demonstrations in London following this admission. Several months later one of his closest aides, Sir Craig Oliver, recalls in his memoirs that he thought the Panama Papers would cost Cameron his job. He somehow survived the scandal intact, only to run into Brexit.

[ ]

At almost exactly the same time as the protesters hit the streets of Reykjavik and London, thousands of demonstrators in Malta gather outside the prime minister's office to call on Joseph Muscat, the social-democratic head of government, to stand down. The banners carry the word '*Barra*!', Maltese for 'Out!' There is soon talk of a 'second Iceland' – a second island state whose government has been plunged into crisis by the revelations of the Panama Papers.

Two of Prime Minister Muscat's allies – Energy and Health Minister Konrad Mizzi and Chief of Staff Keith Schembri – have evidently concealed money from Maltese tax authorities using a network of companies in Panama and trusts in New Zealand. Both confirm that they owned the companies and trusts. However, they claim they did not know that they should have declared these to the Maltese authorities. On 28 April, Mizzi steps down from his position to become a minister without portfolio.

[ ]

The Panama Papers also got Argentinian president Mauricio Macri, elected in November 2015, into hot water. According to our documents, he was the director of a shell company called Fleg Trading Ltd for a period of time. It was also revealed that he signed over his share in a hydroelectric power company to an offshore company owned by his father just a few weeks before the revelations. Three months after he took office.

And as if that was not enough, a number of Macri's allies also appear in the Panama Papers or have been linked to offshore companies over the course of the revelations. Among them is Néstor Grindetti, Macri's former finance minister for the city of Buenos Aires; the two men travelled to Panama together in 2013, officially to arrange an urban development loan. Another name that comes up is Daniel Angelici, who – with Macri's support – was elected president of Boca Juniors football club. The list also includes Macri's Human Rights Commissioner Claudio Avruj, Director of the Federal Intelligence Agency Gustavo Arribas, several of Macri's brothers, and his cousin Jorge, mayor of the municipality of Vicente López on the outskirts of the capital, Buenos Aires.

When the story broke, the left-leaning daily newspaper *Página/12* featured on the cover a photo of Macri, his head bowed, with the headline '*Panamacri*'. Argentina's public prosecutor has launched an investigation after a member of the opposition reported Macri to the authorities. The national anti-corruption office also intends to investigate the case.

[ ]

In Pakistan, meanwhile, Prime Minister Nawaz Sharif came under fire following revelations about shell companies owned by his children, and news that they held London property worth millions of pounds. When Sharif left Pakistan in mid-April 2016 to undergo medical treatment in London, as the official explanation would have it, rumours immediately began to circulate that he would not return until the investigation into the matter was concluded. In November, the police dissolved a huge demonstration against Sharif's Panama Papers business, using teargas and barricades. A few days later, the Supreme Court finally ordered a commission to probe the Panama Papers leaks and the involvement of Sharif's family.

In Spain, Minister for Industry José Manuel Soria resigned after trying for days to talk his way out of his entanglement in offshore businesses. He even claimed that the person named in the Panama Papers was not him, but merely his namesake.

In Denmark, directors from the country's three largest banks – Nordea, Danske Bank and Jyske Bank – were called upon to answer questions before a parliamentary commission; a number of Finnish political parties and the country's most powerful union closed their accounts with Nordea; senior bankers in Austria and the Netherlands were forced to resign. So too the head of the Chilean branch of Transparency International, whose name came up in the Panama Papers in connection with at least five shell companies.

At FIFA, Juan Pedro Damiani, founding member of the ethics committee, handed in his resignation after it was revealed in the Panama Papers that he had done business with three of the accused FIFA officials.

As of November 2016, according to the ICIJ, 6,520 individuals and companies were under investigation worldwide due to the Panama Papers. 110 million US dollars had already been recovered – and this was in just four countries (Colombia, Mexico, Slovenia and Uruguay). Nearly 100 countries had launched their own investigations, inquiries and audits.

[ ]

The Panama Papers has also had some negative consequences.

The term 'Panama Papers' was censored in China within a few hours of the story's initial publication. One lawyer was arrested for sharing a comic photo montage showing the current leader of the Communist Party and two former leaders – Xi Jinping, Deng Xiaoping and Jiang Zemin – wading through the Panama Canal.

In Hong Kong, Keung Kwok-yuen, the executive chief editor of the *Ming Pao* newspaper, was dismissed hours after the Panama Papers revelations were made public. The official reason given for the sacking was that the paper had to cut costs.

Our newspaper colleagues in Panama had to print the first issues about the Panama Papers at a secret location for fear that someone would use violence to stop their work. They needed the protection of a bodyguard until late autumn 2016, and they still fear repercussions.

One of our Venezuelan colleagues was dismissed by her employer, the pro-regime newspaper *Últimas Noticias*. She had kept her involvement in the Panama Papers project a secret from the paper, fearing that her bosses might give the parties under investigation advance warning of the enquiry. The website of our Tunisian partner – the online magazine *Inkyfada* – was attacked by hackers after it reported on the offshore connections of a former adviser to the president.

In Ecuador, President Rafael Correa tweeted the names of the journalists involved in the Panama Papers investigation. The message was clear: he wanted to put them under pressure. A few days later it was revealed that Correa's name also appears in the Panama Papers, in connection with a company whose activities had still not been fully clarified as this edition of the book went to press.

Our Turkish colleagues from *Cumhuriyet* – whom we had invited to join our international team some weeks after we first published – received a death threat after they investigated the role of businessmen close to President Recep Tayyip Erdoğan. 'Don't make this man a killer,' one of the businessmen breathed down the phone. Several months later, more than ten reporters from *Cumhuriyet* were jailed, probably unrelated to the Panama Papers, in the aftermath of the unsuccessful coup d'état in Turkey.

[ ]

Of all the stories, we were most worried about the consequences that would emerge following the revelations regarding Putin's best friend, Sergei Roldugin. For reasons of safety, this was the case in which we waited for the longest period of time before confronting the parties involved. After all, one of those parties was Vladimir Putin himself. It would be impossible to predict how he would respond. Our Russian colleagues feared for their lives.

It was the strangest feeling to be sending dozens of questions to Putin's personal press secretary, Dmitry Peskov, a few days before publication – the same Peskov, incidentally, whose wife we found listed in the data as being a temporary owner of a shell company. We did not expect an answer.

On Easter Monday, Peskov appeared before the Russian media and stated that the Kremlin had received a 'list of questions prepared in an interrogation-type manner'. These, he claimed, were part of an 'information attack' on the president and his family. Allegations were being made regarding a multitude of offshore companies

– companies Putin knew nothing about. Peskov suspected that it was not only journalists behind this 'attack', but also 'representatives of special services and other organizations'.

For the press secretary of the Russian president to respond publicly to a journalist's questions with a demonstration of anger like this is by no means an everyday occurrence. To be more precise, it has never happened before.

The consequences for two of our Russian colleagues were severe. Their photos were shown on Russian television, and the pair branded as agents disseminating propaganda on behalf of the American government. Attempts were made to blackmail the chief editor of *Novaya Gazeta* to prevent him from publishing the story. He published the story nevertheless and is now facing a tax audit – a standard reprisal in Russia. Our Russian colleague Roman Anin wrote to us a few days later: 'We don't regret anything and we're ready to face the consequences.' A few days later he and the others left the country after hearing rumours that the government might go after them.

Just two weeks after the revelations, Vladimir Putin made his annual appearance on the TV programme *Direct Line* to answer questions submitted by the people.

He made use of this appearance to launch an attack on us: 'Who makes them, these provocations? We know that there are some staff from official American institutions there. Where did the article first appear? I asked Peskov, my press secretary, yesterday: in the *Süddeutsche Zeitung*, which is part of a media holding, and that media holding is owned by an American financial corporation: Goldman Sachs.'

This statement is incorrect. The *Süddeutsche Zeitung* is not owned by Goldman Sachs, neither directly nor indirectly. It is a subsidiary wholly owned by the Süddeutscher Verlag, of which company 18.75 per cent is owned by a Munich publishing family and 81.25 per cent by Südwestdeutsche Medienholding – and the latter company is also not owned by the American investment bank. The Kremlin later had to apologize for misrepresenting the facts.

One crucial statement was almost drowned out by the hullaba-loo, namely Putin's acknowledgement on the *Direct Line* programme that the information in the Panama Papers was accu-rate. 'The information is correct,' he confirmed. A few days later, he declined a request by the *Süddeutsche Zeitung* for an interview.

Several weeks after the dust had settled, our Russian colleagues felt they could return to their home country.

[ ]

In all honesty, we had not expected much from our revelations. We hoped to attract the interest of our readers and we expected trite demands from politicians across the globe. But real change? Genuine progress in the battle against the shady world of offshore business? Not really.

'Panama is the last major holdout that continues to allow funds to be hidden offshore from tax and law enforcement authorities,' wrote Angel Gurría, secretary-general of the OECD, just a few hours after our stories were first published.

A few days later, Panama's President Juan Carlos Varela announced that bearer shares would be abolished. Furthermore, Panama would participate in the global exchange of tax and financial data. Ninety-seven countries had already signed up to the agreement, among them the British Virgin Islands, Luxembourg, Switzerland and the Channel Islands. But is change really possible in Panama? Mossack Fonseca is only one of many Panamanian law firms that are involved in the offshore business. And nearly all of them have ties to the Panamanian government. For instance, the minister of the presidency owns a law firm that provides offshore services. And Panama's economy minister once worked for Morgan y Morgan, a law firm also in the business of shell companies. One of its partners happens to be President Varela's deputy foreign minister. It is not without reason that critics have spoken of Panama's 'offshore cabinet'.

[ ]

Just a few days after the Panama Papers broke, President Varela appointed an allegedly independent commission to review the country's financial and legal practices. The appointed chairman was top economist and Nobel Laureate Joseph Stiglitz. It seemed like a step in the right direction.

Not even close.

Weeks later, Stiglitz and his colleague, the Swiss anti-corruption specialist Mark Pieth, resigned from the commission. They said they found the government unwilling to back an open investigation. 'I thought the government was more committed, but obviously they're not,' Stiglitz said. 'It's amazing how they tried to undermine us.' Stiglitz and Pieth said they got a letter from the government backing off from its commitment to making the committee's findings public. 'We can only infer that the government is facing pressure from those who are making profits from the current non-transparent financial system in Panama,' Stiglitz said.

[ ]

In October 2016, President Varela travelled to Germany. His apparent task: damage control. Varela kicked off his PR tour in Berlin at a meeting with Angela Merkel. The Chancellery rolled out the red carpet for Varela. He was received with the guard of honour and all the trimmings of a state visit. The press conference was garnished with speakers' podiums, national flags, and a striking absence of criticism. Not surprisingly, Merkel voiced her hope that German companies would get business from Panama. And she would like to see an agreement come to fruition on the exchange of tax-related data between Panama and Germany. Such an agreement would make it easier to track down tax evaders and money launderers. Merkel made an effort not to have Varela portrayed as the president of tax tricksters. 'The good thing is,' she said, 'that we already have a previous agreement.' She didn't mention the bad thing, which is that the agreement had never entered into force.

Varela's journey to Germany was part of a PR blitz by the Panamanian government. Documents published in the United States by the Department of Justice appear to show that the tour was being managed by Bellwether, a PR firm specializing in damage control. More specifically, Mike Holtzman, a PR professional known for handling sensitive situations, was on the case. Holtzman supported the Chinese government's bid for the Olympic Games. Syrian dictator Bashar al-Assad has also called on Holtzman's services in the past.

In Munich, where Varela spoke to business VIPs at Bavaria's Ministry of the Economy, we had a showdown with Varela. He greeted us, then his press secretary went straight on the offensive. He claimed that branding Panama in such a manner was unfair and politically motivated. Since the story broke, the Panamanian view has been that the Panama Papers are a conspiracy against their tiny country.

Varela began in Spanish, but then switched to English to avoid being misunderstood. The atmosphere was tense, but his tone calm and objective. In the past, under his predecessor Ricardo Martinelli or the autocrat Manuel Noriega, there were dubious dealings, said Varela. 'But all that is over.' The canal and tourism: that is Panama's future. Not money from dodgy sources. Varela asserted that he himself has focused on cleaning up since he was elected president in 2014. When we asked about his friend and ex-advisor, the Mossfon owner Ramón Fonseca, he said that investigations take time. Varela's friend had repeatedly maintained his innocence. We asked the president if he also saw it this way. Varela's answer: 'If he had really always acted correctly, he wouldn't have any problems now.' The firm is finished, said Varela. And his friend Fonseca? 'He will have to take responsibility for his actions – and ultimately face the judge.'

At first, Varela's response sounded good. It really seemed as though he and his government had got the message. Panama was saying: We learnt our lesson. A few weeks later, he would claim publicly that Panama was over the scandal. So easy.

[ ]

In November 2016, Joseph Stiglitz and Mark Pieth published their own alternative Panama Papers report, 'Overcoming the Shadow Economy'. The twenty-five-page report argues that it is not only offshore countries like Panama or the British Virgin Islands who need to rethink their attitude and legislation. The US and the European Union 'have an obligation to force financial centres to comply with global transparency standards'. The US and EU have shown they have the tools to stem the flow of dirty money in the fight against terrorism, but have failed to use these same tools as forcefully in the fight against financial corruption and tax dodging. 'Secrecy has to be attacked globally – offshore and onshore,' Stiglitz and Pieth write. 'There can be no places to hide.'

It is a high aim – and a necessary fight. However, we believe that the most effective action in the battle against tax havens would be to establish a global register revealing the true owners of shell companies. That, as former UK Chancellor George Osborne eloquently put it, would be 'a hammer blow against those that would illegally evade taxes and hide their wealth in the dark corners of the financial system'. But the only thing we have seen used so far in the battle against tax havens is a pair of kid gloves.

Finally, Mossack Fonseca, the firm at the centre of this book, has experienced some fallout. Just weeks after the first article appeared, they had to close one of their offices, and others followed. As of November 2016, nine Mossack Fonseca offices, in the British dependencies of Jersey, the Isle of Man and Gibraltar, Peru, São Paolo in Brazil, the Netherlands, New Zealand, Lugano in Switzerland, and Nevada, have shuttered, according to media reports and corporate registries. In the same month, the Mossack Fonseca office in the British Virgin Islands (BVI) was fined 440,000 US dollars for 'contravention of numerous sections of the Anti-Money Laundering and Terrorist Financing Code of Practice and BVI Regulatory Code'. We even heard rumours that Mossfon planned to close down their BVI office – by far their most important office, which has founded more than 100,000 companies. A vast number of clients have fled Mossack Fonseca and transferred their offshore companies to competitors, and several employees have left voluntarily. Some have erased their former employer from their curriculum vitae.

Europol, Europe's law enforcement agency, revealed in November 2016 that it had found 3,469 probable matches to organized crime, tax fraud and other criminal activities from the public Panama Papers database provided by the ICIJ, compared against information in its own files. Out of those matches, 116 related to Europol's project on Islamic terrorism, codenamed Hydra. 'The main point here is that we can link companies from the Panama Papers leak not only with economic crimes like money laundering,' said Europol's head of financial intelligence, Simon Riondet, 'but also with terrorism, Russian OCGs [Organized Crime Groups], drug trafficking, human trafficking, illegal immigration, [and] cybercrime.'

In February 2017, as this edition was going to press, it was reported that Ramón Fonseca and Jürgen Mossack had been arrested in Panama allegedly on charges of money-laundering, and had been refused bail.

The debate triggered by the Panama Papers will continue for a long while yet – and it illustrates that a very different world is an achievable possibility. .

Where there's a will …

THE REVOLUTION WILL BE DIGITIZED

A statement by John Doe, 6 May 2016

Income inequality is one of the defining issues of our time. It
affects all of us, the world over. The debate over its sudden accel-
eration has raged for years, with politicians, academics and activists
alike helpless to stop its steady growth despite countless speeches,
statistical analyses, a few meagre protests and the occasional docu-
mentary. Still, questions remain: why? And why now?

The Panama Papers provide a compelling answer to these questions: massive, pervasive corruption. And it's not a coincidence that
the answer comes from a law firm. More than just a cog in the
machine of 'wealth management', Mossack Fonseca used its influence to write and bend laws worldwide to favour the interests of
criminals over a period of decades. In the case of the island of
Niue, the firm essentially ran a tax haven from start to finish.
Ramón Fonseca and Jürgen Mossack would have us believe that
their firm's shell companies, sometimes called 'special purpose
vehicles', are just like cars. But used car salesmen don't write laws.
And the only 'special purpose' of the vehicles they produced was
too often fraud, on a grand scale.

Shell companies are often associated with the crime of tax
evasion, but the Panama Papers show beyond a shadow of a doubt
that although shell companies are not illegal by definition, they are
used to carry out a wide array of serious crimes that go beyond

evading taxes. I decided to expose Mossack Fonseca because I thought its founders, employees and clients should have to answer for their roles in these crimes, only some of which have come to light thus far. It will take years, possibly decades, for the full extent of the firm's sordid acts to become known.

In the meantime, a new global debate has started, which is encouraging. Unlike the polite rhetoric of yesteryear that carefully omitted any suggestion of wrongdoing by the elite, this debate focuses directly on what matters.

In that regard, I have a few thoughts.

For the record, I do not work for any government or intelligence agency, directly or as a contractor, and I never have. My viewpoint is entirely my own, as was my decision to share the documents with the *Süddeutsche Zeitung* and the International Consortium of Investigative Journalists (ICIJ), not for any specific political purpose, but simply because I understood enough about their contents to realize the scale of the injustices they described.

The prevailing media narrative thus far has focused on the scandal of what is legal and allowed in this system. What is allowed is indeed scandalous and must be changed. But we must not lose sight of another important fact: the law firm, its founders and employees actually did knowingly violate myriad laws worldwide, repeatedly. Publicly they plead ignorance, but the documents show detailed knowledge and deliberate wrongdoing. At the very least we already know that Jürgen Mossack personally perjured himself before a federal court in Nevada, and we also know that his information technology staff attempted to cover up the underlying lies. They should all be prosecuted accordingly with no special treatment.

In the end, thousands of prosecutions could stem from the Panama Papers, if only law enforcement could access and evaluate the actual documents. The ICIJ and its partner publications have rightly stated that they will not provide them to law enforcement agencies. I, however, would be willing to cooperate with law enforcement to the extent that I am able.

That being said, I have watched as one after another, whistle-blowers and activists in the United States and Europe have had their lives destroyed by the circumstances they find themselves in after shining a light on obvious wrongdoing. Edward Snowden is stranded in Moscow, exiled by the Obama administration's decision to prosecute him under the Espionage Act. For his revelations about the NSA, he deserves a hero's welcome and a substantial prize, not banishment. Bradley Birkenfeld was awarded millions for his information concerning Swiss bank UBS – and was still given a prison sentence by the Justice Department. Antoine Deltour is presently on trial for providing journalists with information about how Luxembourg granted secret 'sweetheart' tax deals to multinational corporations, effectively stealing billions in tax revenues from its neighbour countries. And there are plenty more examples.

Legitimate whistle-blowers who expose unquestionable wrong-doing, whether insiders or outsiders, deserve immunity from government retribution, full stop. Until governments codify legal protections for whistle-blowers into law, enforcement agencies will simply have to depend on their own resources or ongoing global media coverage for documents.

In the meantime, I call on the European Commission, the British Parliament, the United States Congress and all nations to take swift action not only to protect whistle-blowers, but to put an end to the global abuse of corporate registers. In the European Union, every member state's corporate register should be freely accessible, with detailed data plainly available on ultimate beneficial owners. The United Kingdom can be proud of its domestic initiatives thus far, but it still has a vital role to play by ending financial secrecy on its various island territories, which are unquestionably the cornerstone of institutional corruption worldwide.

And the United States can clearly no longer trust its fifty states to make sound decisions about their own corporate data. It is long past time for Congress to step in and force transparency by setting standards for disclosure and public access.

And while it's one thing to extol the virtues of government transparency at summits and in soundbites, it's quite another to actually implement it. It is an open secret that in the United States, elected representatives spend the majority of their time fundraising. Tax evasion cannot possibly be fixed while elected officials are pleading for money from the very elites who have the strongest incentives to avoid taxes relative to any other segment of the population. These unsavoury political practices have come full circle and they are irreconcilable. Reform of America's broken campaign finance system cannot wait.

Of course, those are hardly the only issues that need fixing. Prime Minister John Key of New Zealand has been curiously quiet about his country's role in enabling the financial fraud mecca that is the Cook Islands. In Britain, the Tories have been shameless about concealing their own practices involving offshore companies, while Jennifer Shasky Calvery, the director of the Financial Crimes Enforcement Network at the US Department of the Treasury, just announced her resignation to work instead for HSBC, one of the most notorious banks on the planet (not coincidentally headquartered in London). And so the familiar swish of America's revolving door echoes amid deafening global silence from thousands of yet-to-be-discovered ultimate beneficial owners who are likely praying that her replacement is equally spineless. In the face of political cowardice, it's tempting to yield to defeatism, to argue that the status quo remains fundamentally unchanged, while the Panama Papers are, if nothing else, a glaring symptom of our society's progressively diseased and decaying moral fabric.

But the issue is finally on the table, and that change takes time is no surprise. For fifty years, executive, legislative and judicial branches around the globe have utterly failed to address the metastasizing tax havens spotting Earth's surface. Even today, Panama says it wants to be known for more than papers, but its government has conveniently examined only one of the horses on its offshore merry-go-round.

Banks, financial regulators and tax authorities have failed. Decisions have been made that have spared the wealthy while focusing instead on reining in middle- and low-income citizens.

Hopelessly backward and inefficient courts have failed. Judges have too often acquiesced to the arguments of the rich, whose lawyers – and not just Mossack Fonseca – are well trained in honouring the letter of the law, while simultaneously doing everything in their power to desecrate its spirit. The media has failed. Many news networks are cartoonish parodies of their former selves, individual billionaires appear to have taken up newspaper ownership as a hobby, limiting coverage of serious matters concerning the wealthy, and serious investigative journalists lack funding. The impact is real: in addition to the *Süddeutsche Zeitung* and the ICIJ, and despite explicit claims to the contrary, several major media outlets did have editors review documents from the Panama Papers. They chose not to cover them. The sad truth is that among the most prominent and capable media organizations in the world there was not a single one interested in reporting on the story. Even WikiLeaks didn't answer its tip line repeatedly.

But most of all, the legal profession has failed. Democratic governance depends upon responsible individuals throughout the entire system who understand and uphold the law, not who understand and exploit it. On average, lawyers have become so deeply corrupt that it is imperative for major changes in the profession to take place, far beyond the meek proposals already on the table. To start, the term 'legal ethics', upon which codes of conduct and licensure are nominally based, has become an oxymoron. Mossack Fonseca did not work in a vacuum – despite repeated fines and documented regulatory violations, it found allies and clients at major law firms in virtually every nation. If the industry's shattered economics were not already evidence enough, there is now no denying that lawyers can no longer be permitted to regulate one another. It simply doesn't work. Those able to pay the most can always find a lawyer to serve their ends, whether that lawyer is at Mossack Fonseca or another firm of which we remain unaware. What about the rest of society?

The collective impact of these failures has been a complete erosion of ethical standards, ultimately leading to a novel system we still call capitalism, but which is tantamount to economic slavery. In this system – our system – the slaves are unaware both of their status and of their masters, who exist in a world apart where the intangible shackles are carefully hidden among reams of unreachable legalese. The horrific magnitude of detriment to the world should shock us all awake. But when it takes a whistle-blower to sound the alarm, it is cause for even greater concern. It signals that democracy's checks and balances have all failed, that the breakdown is systemic, and that severe instability could be just around the corner. So now is the time for real action, and that starts with asking questions.

Historians can easily recount how issues involving taxation and imbalances of power have led to revolutions in ages past. Then, military might was necessary to subjugate peoples, whereas now, curtailing information access is just as effective, or more so, since the act is often invisible. Yet we live in a time of inexpensive, limitless digital storage and fast Internet connections that transcend national boundaries. It doesn't take much to connect the dots: from start to finish, inception to global media distribution, the next revolution will be digitized.

Or perhaps it has already begun.

ACKNOWLEDGEMENTS

First and foremost we would like to thank our source, the person who leaked to us the 2.6 terabytes of internal data that formed the basis for this research. He/she took a very big risk in passing on the material – it was his/her courage that made the world's largest cross-border journalistic collaboration to date possible. Without the source we would not have discovered how Iceland's elite deceived an entire nation, how Vladimir Putin's circle of friends are evidently shunting millions from one place to another and how gunrunners, drug dealers, mafiosi and secret services disguise their flows of money – all of it clearly with the help of Mossack Fonseca.

Our thanks also to the publishing house Kiepenheuer & Witsch for publishing this legally risky book. Thank you for having faith in us! And thank you to Kiepenheuer & Witsch for providing us with the services of the excellent lawyer Sven Krüger for this project. We are well aware that this is not something to be taken for granted. Of course we owe an even bigger debt of gratitude to Martin Breitfeld, for the many telephone calls, helpful comments and words of encouragement – but above all for his speedy copy-editing. This book was finished literally at the last minute. Without his patience and calm, especially towards the end, this would never have worked out.

Our thanks also to the *Süddeutsche Zeitung*. Without its fantastic editorial team this book could never have been written. We would like to take this opportunity to thank, in particular: Wolfgang Krach and Kurt Kister, who assisted from the outset and through-out the months of research; Hans Leyendecker, who encouraged us at every stage; Vanessa Wormer, who tamed the data; Mauritius Much, who battled his way through hundreds of pages of contracts; as well as Klaus Ott, Bastian Brinkmann, Christoph Giesen, Gianna Niewel, Katrin Langhans, Elena Adam, Hannes Munzinger – and not least our colleagues in the text archive, who, over the months, dealt patiently with our requests, some of them very complicated.

We would also especially like to thank our ICIJ colleagues, the data specialists Mar Cabra, Matthew Caruana Galizia and Rigoberto Carvajal, as well as Gerard Ryle and Marina Walker for their judicious coordination: they kept their cool, even when the publication date was changed at relatively short notice.

Our thanks go to the 400 or so journalists from more than eighty countries, without whom this investigation would not have been the same. We would particularly like to mention Oliver Zihlmann, Titus Plattner and Catherine Boss for their research in Switzerland, Roman Anin and Roman Shleynov, who put their lives on the line in the course of their investigations in Russia – may they always have a guardian angel watching over them. We are grateful to Jóhannes Kr. Kristjánsson for the many conversations that gave us a whole new perspective on Iceland. Our thanks go also to Jake Bernstein for his assistance with the Modigliani research. We would also like to thank Vlad Lavrov for his help on Ukraine – we are well aware that this research was a tricky balanc-ing act for him, since the owner of *Kyiv Post*, in other words the owner of the newspaper Vlad works for, also shows up in the Panama Papers. Massive thanks also to Monica Almeida, who worked on the UEFA story in Ecuador and managed to make the breakthrough. This book is also the result of a big collaboration with Norddeutscher Rundfunk and Westdeutscher Rundfunk, which analysed the Panama Papers in conjunction with the

Süddeutsche Zeitung. Without the fantastic joint effort by the editorial teams it would have been hard to bring this project to fruition in the way we have done.

This book incorporates a lot of research done by our colleagues. Specifically we would like to thank Julia Stein, without whose organizational skills this project would have struggled, Jan Strozyk, whose good instincts helped us make headway on many stories, especially the Siemens case, and not least Petra Blum, who spent months digging out details of the Roldugin network and its dealings. Thanks also to John Goetz, Toni Kempmann and Reiko Pinkert, who spent weeks analysing documents.

[ ]

We are grateful to our families for their patience and infinite understanding. We have asked a lot of them in the last few months – we know that.

GLOSSARY

Offshore provider: There are dozens of companies worldwide that specialize in selling shell companies. They provide new companies and old, mostly based in one of the various tax havens, as well as foundations of all kinds. Many offshore providers are law firms. Mossack Fonseca is among the largest of these.

Registered agent: In most tax havens you cannot simply set up a shell company yourself – you need to use an authorized service provider, a 'registered agent' such as Mossack Fonseca. This agent checks whether the intended company name is still available, takes care of the paperwork required by the local authorities, then looks after the payment of the annual fees. Normally the official address of the shell company is the same as that of the registered agent. That is why so many companies registered in Panama have the address Calle 54 Este – that is the address of Mossack Fonseca.

Intermediary: In most cases, a registered agent like Mossack Fonseca would not be approached directly by a private individual, but by an asset manager or a bank acting on behalf of its clients.

End client: Mossack Fonseca likes to maintain that it does not do business with 'end clients'. It says it only enters into contracts with banks, asset managers and lawyers, i.e. intermediaries. That is not the whole truth of the matter, however. Mossfon works directly with end clients in many cases, even taking care of their banking transactions.

Shell company: A shell company, or letterbox company, is a company that has no employees at its official registered office – which is normally at the address of the registered agent – but only a letterbox. This often produces an absurd situation in which thousands of firms have their registered office in a single building in a tax haven. In the US tax haven of Delaware, for example, over 200,000 companies are thought to be registered at 1209 North Orange Street.

Shelf company: A shelf company is a 'second-hand' shell company. Offshore providers sometimes set up companies that they keep in reserve so that they can be sold to clients who need a shell company that does not look as if it has only just been established.

Bearer share: A bearer share is a company share that is not registered in a person's name but belongs to the 'bearer'. There is no public record of the real owner. Whoever has the document in their possession is the official owner of the share in the company. Transactions can be performed quickly and easily using bearer shares, but they also present opportunities for criminal undertakings. Money laundering, for example, can be accomplished quite easily.

Beneficial owner: The beneficial owner, also often referred to as the ultimate beneficial owner, is the real owner of a company – the person who receives the 'benefit'. A different person may be named as a partner on paper, but this might be purely for show, which is why he or she is referred to as a nominee shareholder.

Nominee shareholder: A nominee shareholder acts as if he/she were the shareholder. A nominee shareholder can be a person, but also a company – in each case company shares are held in the manner of a trustee. This hides the beneficial owner.

Nominee beneficial owner: A nominee beneficial owner pretends to be the ultimate beneficial owner (UBO). If, for example, a bank asks for the name of a UBO in order to fulfil its due diligence obligations, the owner of a company may provide it with the name of a nominee owner. This person then claims to be the owner of the company, which means background checks are conducted only on him/her. The real UBO remains hidden. There is a catch to this: the practice counts as a criminal act in many places.

Real ultimate beneficial owner: In the offshore world, the real ultimate beneficial owner is the owner of a company who hides behind a front man who himself claims to be the ultimate beneficial owner. The term 'real ultimate beneficial owner' was coined to distinguish the nominee UBO from the real UBO.

Nominee director: A nominee director is a front man or front woman who is paid to act as the director of a particular company. In reality, nominee directors only do this on paper. All decisions are made by the real owner. If, say, there are contracts to be signed, the real owner asks the nominee director to sign them, but the nominee director has no further involvement.

Holding company: A holding company is a company that has no other purpose than to hold equity stakes in other companies. If a holding company has its registered office in a tax haven, the profits of the subsidiary companies can quite easily be transferred to the holding company in order to save on taxes. Holding companies also often have a sophisticated multi-layered structure designed to hide the identity of the owner.

Letter of indemnity: A letter of indemnity is an exemption from liability. If a client turned out to be conducting illegal business through the shell company, this letter ensures that only the client would be liable in the event of any claims for damages.

NOTES

Prologue
1 See Chapter 12, particularly for Hans-Joachim K.'s reaction.

1 Start
1 See Chapters 15 and 30 for further information, particularly regarding Leticia Montoya.
2 At the time of going to press, Mossfon had not responded to a request for comment.

2 Vladimir Putin's mysterious friend
1 At the time of going to press, Mossfon had not responded to a request for comment.

3 The shadow of the past
1 At the time of going to press, neither Mossfon nor Jürgen Mossack had responded to a request for comment.
2 After having been confronted with the research for this book, Ramón Fonseca announced in March 2016 that he was taking a leave of absence from both these posts.
3 At the time of going to press, Ramón Fonseca had not responded to a request for comment.
4 As of March 2016.
5 See Chapter 24 for Gunnlaugsson's reaction.
6 See Chapter 24.
7 At the time of going to press, Arnoldo 'Fat Man' Alémán had not responded to a request for comment.

4 Commerzbank and its lies

1 At the time of going to press, Burson-Marsteller had not commented on these allegations.

2 See Chapter 13, especially for Mossack Fonseca's response to our enquiries.

3 It is not clear whether Burson-Marsteller is still working for Mossfon in 2016.

4 See Chapter 23, in particular for statements by Commerzbank.

5 See Chapter 23, in particular for statements by the banks mentioned.

6 See Chapter 23, in particular for statements by the banks mentioned.

7 See Chapter 23, in particular for statements by the banks mentioned.

8 See Chapter 24, in particular for Gunnlaugsson's reaction.

5 Mossack Fonseca's role in the Syrian war

1 At the time of going to press, Hafez Makhlouf had not responded to a request for comment.

2 At the time of going to press, neither Iyad nor Ihab Makhlouf had responded to a request for comment.

3 See Chapter 16, in particular for Zollinger's reaction. After a request for further information, HSBC referred us to an earlier statement saying that it complied 'worldwide' 'with all applicable sanctions laws and regulations'.

4 At the time of going to press, Jürgen Mossack had not responded to a request for comment.

5 At the time of going to press, John Bredenkamp had not responded to a request for comment.

6 At the time of going to press, Jean-Claude N'Da Ametchi had not responded to a request for comment.

7 Muller Conrad Rautenbach's lawyer emphasized that his client had now been removed from both sanctions lists. This decision by the EU and the US also covered all companies associated with Rautenbach.

8 In response to our enquiries, Savo Stjepanovic explained that he had first heard of his having been placed on a US sanctions list in the media. He had already requested that his name be deleted from the list. He had established the firm run by Mossfon in order to be able to sell mobile phone apps via the Google Play store, as this was not possible for Slovenian companies.

9 A spokeswoman for Anatoly Ternavsky said that she considered the sanctions to be politically motivated. The company managed by Mossfon was still active as of spring 2016.

10 A law firm mandated by Gennady Timchenko explained that its client 'is aware of no circumstances regarding him and/or the companies mentioned [*by us, the Authors*] that might justify a breach of sanctions by a US citizen'. According to Timchenko's lawyers, Mossack Fonseca seemed 'not to have the necessary ties to the United States of America to break the sanctions'.

11 In response to our enquiries, Marllory Dadiana Chacón Rossell and her lawyer did not wish to comment on the matter.

12 At the time of going to press, Rami Makhlouf had not responded to our enquiries about Drex Technologies S.A.

13 At the time of going to press, Kuo Oil Pte. Ltd had not responded to a request for comment.

14 In response to our enquiries, a lawyer representing Kassim Tajideen stated that his client was neither a member nor a supporter of Hezbollah.

15 At the time of going to press, Petropars Ltd had not responded to a request for comment.

16 At the time of going to press, John Bredenkamp had not responded to a request for comment.

17 See Chapter 22, in particular for Yulia Tymoshenko's statement.

18 See Chapter 22, in particular for the lack of response from Pavel Lazarenko.

19 In response to our enquiries, a law firm representing Suleiman Marouf stated that the earlier sanctions against its client were based on 'false and unsubstantiated allegations'.

20 At the time of going to press, the law firm representing Suleiman Marouf had not responded to our further enquiries about Marouf's suspected activities on Asma al-Assad's behalf.

21 At the time of going to press, neither Maxima Middle East Trading Co. nor Ahmad Barqawi had responded to a request for comment.

22 At the time of going to press, Pangates International Corporation Ltd had not responded to a request for comment.

23 At the time of going to press, Mossack Fonseca had not responded to a request for comment.

6 From the Waffen-SS to the CIA and Panama

1 See Chapter 25, in particular for the lack of response from Dabaiba.

7 The football factory

1 For Figueredo's response, see Chapter 28.
2 We were unable to reach Hugo and Mariano Jinkis to ask for their response to this allegation.
3 We were unable to reach Hugo and Mariano Jinkis to ask for their response to this allegation.

8 On fishing, finding and fine art

1 At the time of going to press, Helly Nahmad had not responded to a request for comment.

9 A view of the White House

1 At the time of going to press, Alaa Mubarak had not responded to a request for comment.
2 See Chapter 5 for Mossfon statements concerning dealing with sanctioned persons.

10 Sparks fly

1 At the time of going to press, neither Prime Minister Nawaz Sharif nor his daughter had responded to a request for comment.
2 At the time of going to press, Prime Minister Nawaz Sharif had not responded to a request for comment.
3 See also Chapter 24, particularly regarding Prime Minister Gunnlaugsson's response.
4 See also Chapter 5.
5 When contacted by the ICIJ, Ayad Allawi confirmed that he is the 'only director and shareholder' of Foxwood Estates Ltd, Moonlight Estates Ltd and IMF Holdings Inc. He also claimed that IMF Holdings had been established in order to hold property, and that any taxes due had been paid on time.
6 See also Chapter 21, particularly regarding Deng Jiagui's failure to respond.
7 See also Chapter 21, particularly regarding Li Xiaolin's failure to respond.
8 Rostec, of which Sergey Chemezov is CEO, confirmed that Chemezov's son is the beneficiary of a company. Rostec did not give the name of the company.
9 At the time of going to press, Boris and Arkady Rotenberg had not responded to a request for comment.

11 Fear and trepidation

1 At the time of going to press, neither Ilham Aliyev nor his family had responded to a request for comment.

12 The Siemens millions

1 When we questioned him about this, K. did not answer.
2 When we questioned him about this, K. did not answer.
3 At the time of going to press, Jürgen Mossack had not responded to a request for comment.
4 When we questioned him about this, K. did not answer. L.L. denies that any of the events we describe here took place.
5 K. denies the meeting took place.
6 L.L. explained on the phone that he has never received money from Gillard Management. He says he hasn't even heard of the company.
7 K. denies ever transferring this money.
8 'RPS' did not respond to our query.

13 'Regarding my meeting with Harry Potter...'

1 At the time of going to press, neither Jürgen Mossack nor Ramón Fonseca had responded to a request for comment.
2 At the time of going to press, Mossfon had not responded to a request for comment.
3 A lawyer initially responded to our query by requesting more time to answer. Then, a week later, he simply said that the Siemens director had no knowledge of these transactions. He finally wrote, saying that his client could give 'no information' in answer to our queries.
4 At the time of going to press, Mossfon had not responded to a request for comment.
5 At the time of going to press, Mossfon had not responded to a request for comment.

14 A secret meeting with Alpine views

1 At the time of going to press, Boris and Arkady Rotenberg had not responded to a request for comment.
2 A lawyer appointed by Usmanov explained that his client's 'most important operating companies' are registered in Russia. Foreign companies are used 'on a very limited basis' and 'in strict compliance with the law'.

3 When questioned by the OCCRP, the company Rostec (of which Sergey Chemezov is CEO) confirmed the connection between Chemezov's son and Svyazdorinvest and stated that the problem had been resolved internally.

15 Mossfon Holdings

1 At the time of going to press, neither Jürgen Mossack nor Mossfon had responded to a request for comment.
2 When asked, Christoph Zollinger denied having been a shareholder of Tornbell Associates.
3 Later, Montoya clearly earned significantly more. At the end of 2015, we find a current document that states that she earns $10,800 per year. The imbalance compared to the revenue that Mossfon makes from her only changes marginally as a result.
4 At the time of going to press, Jürgen Mossack had not responded to a request for comment.
5 At the time of going to press, Jürgen Mossack had not responded to a request for comment.
6 At the time of going to press, Peter Mossack had not responded to new enquiries.

16 Spirit of Panama

1 All ownership structures stated here reflect the status in mid-2015, as shown in the data.

17 The world is not enough

1 At the time of going to press, Baldernach had not responded to a request for comment.
2 Quote taken from: Nicholas Shaxson, *Treasure Islands* (Vintage Books: London), 2012.
3 At the time of going to press, Sanford I. Weill had not responded to a request for comment.
4 At the time of going to press, Al Nahyan had not responded to a request for comment.
5 When asked, Helmut Linssen confirmed that the companies Longdown Properties Corp. (Bahamas) and Longdown Properties Corp. (Panama) had

belonged to him. He stated that he was unfamiliar with Mossack Fonseca and that his business partner had been HSBC Trinkaus.

18 The looting machine

1 At the time of going to press, Kabila's sister had not responded to a request for comment.

2 At the time of going to press, Teodoro Obiang had not responded to a request for comment.

3 At the time of going to press, we had not been able to reach Martina Chissano for her comments.

4 At the time of going to press, we had not been able to reach Hastings Banda's niece, Mapopa Chipeta or Yusuf Mwawa for their comments.

5 When questioned by *Le Monde*, Bruno Itoua replied that he does not comment on financial matters.

6 At the time of going to press, José Maria Botelho de Vasconcelos had not responded to a request for comment.

7 When questioned, a PR agency explained that Caprikat and Foxwhelp are fully owned by the Fleurette Group. When the contract was concluded, Caprikat and Foxwhelp did in fact pay a total of $6 million to the Democratic Republic of the Congo. In addition, $2.5 million was provided for the exploration permit. According to the information provided, approximately 60 per cent of oil revenues went to the state.

8 At the time of going to press, neither Jacob Zuma, Khulubuse Zuma nor Joseph Kabila had responded to a request for comment.

9 When questioned, a spokesperson confirmed that Caprikat and Foxwhelp are fully owned by the Fleurette Group, which in turn is held as a 'discretionary trust to the family of Dan Gertler'.

10 When questioned, Frédéric Cilins did not wish to comment on this matter. BSGR said that Cilins hadn't 'bribed anyone on the order of BSGR'.

11 When questioned, a spokesperson from BSGR explained that he had never heard of a company by the name of Matinda.

12 At the time of going to press, BSGR had not responded to a request for comment.

13 When questioned, a spokesperson for BSGR explained that there was 'strong evidence' that Touré wasn't the fourth wife of Conté; he didn't elaborate on the matter.

14 When questioned, a spokesperson for BSGR disputed this.

15 When questioned, a spokesperson for BSGR disputed this.

16 When questioned, BSGR repeated that Onyx was independent of BSGR. At the time of going to press, Onyx had not responded to a request for comment.

17 A spokesperson for BSGR explained that Cilins had not acted on behalf of either BSGR or Beny Steinmetz himself. At the time of going to press, Beny Steinmetz had not responded to a request for comment.

18 A spokesperson for BSGR commented that they did not know anything else about this.

19 At the time of going to press, Onyx had not responded to a request for comment.

19 Secret meetings in the *Komitèrom*

1 For further information on this, in particular with regard to the response by Ramses Owens, see Chapter 30.

2 For further information about Ramses Owens and his response to the accusations, see Chapter 30.

3 At the time of going to press, Edmund W. had not responded to a request for comment.

4 At the time of going to press, Mossack Fonseca had not responded to a request for comment regarding this particular case.

20 At the mercy of monsters

1 As of March 2016.

2 When questioned, Andrew M. explained that he had never been involved with the operation of Berenika, invested any money in it or had any share in its profits.

3 Andrew M. responded to corresponding enquiries. He didn't want to speak publicly about the company Ifex Global, but sent his response from an email address that ended @ifex.us.

4 When questioned, Andrew M. explained that the allegation that he'd been part of the Berenika ring was 'completely and utterly false' and based on a 'tall story' concocted by the Russian authorities. According to Andrew M., the aim of it all was to ruin his reputation, as he was a critic of Putin. He added that he had never invested in the child prostitution ring, nor had he profited from it financially. He didn't explicitly deny having had sex with minors.

21 The red nobility

1 At the time of going to press, neither Deng Jiagui nor Xi Jinping had responded to a request for comment.

2 At the time of going to press, Li Xiaolin had not responded to a request for comment.

3 At the time of going to press, Wallace Yu Yiping had not responded to a request for comment.

4 At the time of going to press, Lee Shing Put had not responded to a request for comment.

5 At the time of going to press, Zeng Qinghuai had not responded to a request for comment.

22 The Gas Princess and the Chocolate King

1 In fact, his adviser has since announced that the rates are currently too low and the president hasn't yet sold his companies because he didn't want to squander the money. When questioned, the president's press office explained that Prime Assets Partners Ltd is 'part of the process' of transferring Petro Poroshenko's money into a trust. Recently, Poroshenko made public 'all information regarding his assets, expenditure and income'.

2 At the time of going to press, neither Gennadiy Trukhanov nor the son of Mykola Azarov had responded to a request for comment.

23 Those German banks

1 Deutsche Bank, when asked to comment, said that it 'never provides information about possible or actual business relationships'.

2 Commerzbank stated, when asked to comment, that it could 'not comment on potential and actual client relationships', but that from 2008 Commerzbank International S.A. 'implemented a strict clean money strategy'.

3 DZ Bank stated on enquiry that it had 'never actively offered clients shell companies'. Recently the bank has 'been systematically dissociating itself from clients who have not displayed the requisite tax transparency'.

4 HypoVereinsbank said that it could not give 'any further information beyond that which is publicly available – in particular the annual reports of UniCredit Luxembourg S.A.'.

5 LBBW informed us that it was prompted by 'press reports on other institutions' dealings with so-called offshore companies' to 'take a closer look' at

the past business activities of the former Landesbank Rheinland-Pfalz International S.A. (LRI), which was a subsidiary of LBBW from 2008 to 2010. However, in view of its ongoing investigations, the bank could 'not comment further on this matter'.

6 BayernLB, responding to our enquiry, said it 'goes without saying' that it does not offer shell companies. It said it could 'not find out at the present time, due in part to Luxembourg banking secrecy' whether the subsidiary LBLux, which has since ceased trading, set up the individual offshore companies that we quoted by name. However, it had decided 'to review the matter'.

7 Deutsche Bank, when asked to comment, said that it 'never provides information about possible or actual business relationships'.

8 Deutsche Bank, when asked to comment, said that it 'never provides information about possible or actual business relationships'.

9 Deutsche Bank, when asked to comment, said that it 'never provides information about possible or actual business relationships'.

10 Deutsche Bank, when asked to comment, said the website had been redesigned in 2013 and can now be found at www.db-ci.com.

11 Deutsche Bank, when asked to comment, said that the US Justice Department had come to a non-prosecution agreement with Deutsche Bank (Switzerland) AG. The US Justice Department had agreed not pursue a criminal prosecution against Deutsche Bank (Switzerland) AG 'in connection with possible tax law violations by undeclared US accounts managed by Deutsche Bank (Switzerland) AG'. However, it had to pay 'a fine of around $31 million'.

12 Deutsche Bank, when asked to comment, said it 'never gives information' about possible or actual preliminary investigations.

13 Deutsche Bank, when asked to comment, said that it 'never provides information about possible or actual business relationships'.

14 Commerzbank said, when asked to comment, that 'from 2008, Commerzbank International S.A. systematically and proactively redirected the business without any external regulatory compulsion'. It said the public prosecutor's office had 'welcomed' this.

15 UBS's official statement reads: 'This business is integrated into UBS's local German business and is entirely subject to German regulation and German law.'

16 A UBS spokesperson said, when asked to comment, that 'for legal and regulatory reasons' she was unable 'to comment on individual persons,

companies or supposed customer relationships'. She said, however, that UBS had been 'explicitly telling its customers for a long time that they need to resolve their tax situation'.

17 BayernLB, responding to our enquiry, said it 'goes without saying' that it does not offer shell companies. It said it could 'not find out at the present time, due in part to Luxembourg banking secrecy' whether the subsidiary LBLux, which has since ceased trading, set up the individual offshore companies that we quoted by name. However, it had decided 'to review the matter'.

18 BHF Bank said, when asked to comment, that the information in our possession was 'largely incorrect', but that it was unable to discuss any details without breaching banking secrecy. DZ Bank informed us that the investment companies the bank currently has in its portfolio are 'demonstrably tax-compliant'. Commerzbank did not respond to an enquiry concerning the ship mortgage bank associated with it, other than to say that 'the business purpose of Deutsche Schiffsbank AG was to finance maritime shipping'. HSBC had not replied to our enquiry on this subject at the time of going to press.

19 Berenberg Bank said, when asked to comment, that it was trying 'insofar as we are able' to ensure 'that clients meet their tax obligations'. There had been 'a significant change', it said, in attitudes towards 'this issue' among citizens, lawmakers and banks in recent years.

20 Berenberg Bank stated, when asked to comment, that the 'creation and marketing of shell companies [...] was never part' of its business model. Berenberg and its subsidiaries had 'never actively offered or marketed shell companies'.

21 Berenberg Bank said, when asked to comment, that 'for reasons of banking secrecy and data protection' it was unable to comment on this matter. However, it said, Berenberg Bank (Switzerland) AG knows and documents 'the associated beneficial owners for all accounts that it manages'.

22 Deutsche Bank, when asked to comment, said that it 'never provides information about possible or actual business relationships'.

24 A raid by the Vikings of finance

1 For Bjarni Benediktsson and Ólöf Nordal's responses, see the second half of Chapter 24.

2 Shortly before the copy deadline for this book, the prime minister's wife said the bank had made a mistake when, in 2007, it entered her current husband's name as shareholder. It had always been her company, she said.

3 At the time of going to press, Sigmundur Gunnlaugsson had not responded to a request for comment on this subject.

4 The fact that the prime minister's wife said they no longer invested in Icelandic stocks after her husband became a politician, i.e. in early 2009, weighs in favour of this version of events.

5 At the time of going to press, Sigmundur Gunnlaugsson had not responded to a request for comment on this subject.

6 When asked, Benediktsson confirmed that he had been one of the owners of the company. It had held a property in Dubai, and he had declared both these facts, he said. Asked why he had claimed never to have held assets in offshore companies, he explained that he had 'not been aware' that the company was registered in the Seychelles.

7 Benediktsson said he had not been opposed to the purchase. He told our colleague Jóhannes Kristjánsson that he had not known that his company appeared in the data.

8 Asked about this, Ólöf Nordal's husband got in touch and explained that Landsbanki set up the company for him, but that it had not been used. Ólöf Nordal herself told us the company had been set up before she entered parliament, which is why she had not declared it.

25 Dead-end trails

1 Shortly before the copy deadline for this book, Argentina apparently reached an agreement with NML. This presumably makes the charges obsolete.

2 At the time of going to press, Ali Dabaiba had not responded to a request for comment.

3 At the time of going to press, Ali Dabaiba had not responded to a request for comment.

4 At the time of going to press, Ali Dabaiba had not responded to a request for comment.

5 At the time of going to press, Riad G. had not responded to a request for comment.

6 At the time of going to press, the two businessmen had not responded to a request for comment. Nor had the managers of the hotel in the Scottish Highlands.

7 At the time of going to press, neither Riad G. nor Ali Dabaiba had responded to a request for comment.

26 United by marriage, united by money

1 At the time of going to press, Jürgen Mossack had not responded to a request for comment.

2 At the time of going to press, Arkady and Boris Rotenberg had not responded to a request for comment.

3 A law firm engaged by Gennady Timchenko said – without mentioning specific companies prior to this book's copy deadline – that Timchenko was not aware of any circumstances that constituted a sanctions violation by a US person.

27 Star, star, Mega Star

1 The Messi family did give a public statement, reported in UK newspaper the *Mirror* on 4 April 2016, stating: 'the Panamanian company referred to in the reports is a completely inactive company, which never held open accounts nor funds and which comes from the former company structure put in place by Messi's previous financial advisers, the fiscal consequences of which have already been normalised, with all the income that comes from exploitation of his image rights, prior to and after the procedure carried out in the courts, having been declared before the Spanish Treasury.'

28 The fourth man and FIFA

1 Hugo and Mariano Jinkis were not available to respond to a joint enquiry by us and the ICIJ before the copy deadline for this book.

2 Hugo and Mariano Jinkis were not available to respond to a joint enquiry by us and the ICIJ before the copy deadline for this book.

3 At the time of going to press, Juan Pedro Damiani had not responded to a request for comment.

4 At the time of going to press, Juan Pedro Damiani had not responded to a request for comment.

5 At the time of going to press, Juan Pedro Damiani, Eugenio Figueredo and Mossack Fonseca had not responded to a request for comment.

29 The 99 per cent and the future of tax havens

1 Nicholas Shaxson, *Treasure Islands* (Vintage Books: London), 2012.

2 Michael G. Findley, Daniel L. Nielson, J.C. Sharman, *Global Shell Games* (Cambridge University Press: Cambridge), 2014.

30 The cold heart of the offshore world

1 Leticia Montoya did not respond to a subsequent written enquiry before the copy deadline for this book. Instead a Mossfon spokesman sent a general statement saying that a person can be the director of several companies. Our detailed questions went unanswered.

2 Responding to a written enquiry, Ramses Owens informed us several days after the interview that he had 'never' provided a 'nominee beneficial owner' service. Confronted with the content of a letter sent by him that talks about how Mossfon is providing the nominee beneficial owner for a company, Owens replied that it should have read 'nominee shareholder' or 'shareholder trusteeship', in other words it was a clerical error. Asked whether he was sure about this, considering there were several such documents, Owens did not reply before the copy deadline for this book.

INDEX